Palgrave Studies in the History of Finance

The study of the history of financial institutions, markets, instruments and concepts is vital if we are to understand the role played by finance today. At the same time, the methodologies developed by finance academics can provide a new perspective for historical studies. Palgrave Studies in the History of Finance is a multi-disciplinary effort to emphasise the role played by finance in the past, and what lessons historical experiences have for us. It presents original research, in both authored monographs and edited collections, from historians, finance academics and economists, as well as financial practitioners.

More information about this series at
http://www.palgrave.com/gp/series/14583

Joël Félix · Anne Dubet
Editors

The War Within

Private Interests and the Fiscal State in Early-Modern Europe

palgrave
macmillan

Editors
Joël Félix
University of Reading
Reading, UK

Anne Dubet
University of Auvergne
Clermont-Ferrand, France

Palgrave Studies in the History of Finance
ISBN 978-3-030-07443-2 ISBN 978-3-319-98050-8 (eBook)
https://doi.org/10.1007/978-3-319-98050-8

Cover illustration: Photo 12/Alamy Stock Photo
Cover design by Laura de Grasse

This Palgrave Macmillan imprint is published by the registered company Springer Nature Switzerland AG
The registered company address is: Gewerbestrasse 11, 6330 Cham, Switzerland

Contents

Notes on Contributors

Robert Bernsee is a lecturer at the Institut für Wirtschafts und Sozialgeschichte, at the Georg-August-Universität Göttingen, Germany, and researches the history of corruption and ethics in early-modern Germany.

Anne Dubet is professor of Early-Modern Spanish History at the University Clermont-Auvergne, France, specializing in the history of finances and politics in early-modern Spain. Her most recent book is *La Hacienda Real de la Nueva Planta (1713–1726), entre fraude y buen gobierno* (Fondo de Cultura Económica, Madrid, 2015) and she co-authored with S. Solbes Ferri, *El rey, el ministro y el tesorero. El gobierno de la Real Hacienda en el siglo XVIII español* (Madrid, Marcial Pons Historia, 2019).

Agustín González Enciso is a professor of Economic History at the University of Navarra, Spain. He was a Research Fellow at Harvard and Yale, and a visiting professor at the Universidad Católica Argentina. He specialises in the Spanish economy of the modern age, notably on questions of industrial and financial history of the seventeenth and eighteenth centuries.

Joël Félix is professor of European History at the University of Reading, UK. His specialism is in early-modern fiscal and political history, particularly in France. His main publications include *Finance et politique au siècle des Lumières* (CHEFF 1999) and *Louis XVI et*

Marie-Antoinette (Payot 2006). With J. Swann, he is the editor of *Crisis of the Absolute Monarchy* (British Academy/OUP 2013), and he has recently edited *Before Fiscal Transparency* (*Histoire & Mesure* 2015).

Aaron Graham is Leverhulme Early Career Fellow (2016–2019) at UCL. He received his D.Phil. from the University of Oxford in 2012 and was a British Academy Postdoctoral Fellow at Jesus College, Oxford between 2012 and 2015. His broad area of interest is the history of politics, finance, society and the state in the British Isles and Empire between 1660 and 1840.

Toon Kerkhoff is an assistant professor at the University of Leiden, in the Institute of Public Administration. His research and teaching are characterised by a continuous historical approach to core questions in public administration and politics; most notably on corruption, integrity, public values and civil service reform.

Marie-Laure Legay is professor of History at the University of Lille III (France) and specialist of early- modern political and fiscal history, particularly history of fiscal control, accounting and monetary policy.

Sébastien Malaprade holds a postdoctoral research fellowship at the EHESS, Paris. He received his Ph.D. from the EHESS (2015) which was devoted to the history of the Jurado family in seventeenth-century Spain.

François R. Velde is a senior economist and research advisor in the economic research department at the Federal Reserve Bank of Chicago. Velde's primary research on monetary history and monetary theory has been published in numerous journals.

Patrik Winton is a researcher at the Department of History, University of Uppsala, Sweden. He is currently involved in a research project that focuses on the relationships between the Swedish state and the international credit markets in the eighteenth and early nineteenth centuries.

List of Tables

CHAPTER 1

Introduction: Corruption and the Rise of the Fiscal State

Anne Dubet and Joël Félix

State-building is one of the most distinctive and enduring features of early-modern European history. To explain this phenomenon historians, sociologists, economists and political scientists have successively developed and refined analytical models of state formation. They have formulated a number of concepts, such as the confessional state (Oestreich) the tax state (Schumpeter 2012), the fiscal state (Bonney 1999; Yun-Casalilla et al. 2012), the fiscal-military (Brewer 1989) or fiscal-naval state (O'Brien 2005), the bureaucratic state (Weber 2013), the contractor state (Palmer, in Bowen 2013: 241) and so forth. These concepts do not merely serve to reflect specific methodologies, fields of interests or problems of empirical validation when put to the test in the study of specific polities (city-state, territorial state, composite state, empire), regimes (absolute or limited) and organising principles (dynastic, patrimonial, bureaucratic, etc.). To an extent the concepts on offer account

A. Dubet (✉)
University of Auvergne, Clermont-Ferrand, France
e-mail: Anne.dubet@uca.fr

J. Félix
University of Reading, Reading, UK

J. Félix and A. Dubet (eds.), *The War Within*,
Palgrave Studies in the History of Finance,
https://doi.org/10.1007/978-3-319-98050-8_1

for the radical nature of the transformations at work in a period which had to absorb the impact of the Reformation and long-term changes encapsulated in the scientific revolution, the military revolution, the financial revolution and, of course, the development of capitalism in a world economy. They also reveal the extent to which state development, in the era before the fully fledged nation state and modern parliamentary regimes, was a slow process, usually path-dependent and involving incremental change, the scope and intensity of which depended on a multiplicity of variables, most notably location, time and agency (Ertman 1997). If international competition and domestic conflict over access to the sources of power played a vital role in shaping different types of regimes, it seems now clear that their characteristics and resilience hinged upon a complex mix of social, economic, political, legal, religious and cultural components (Braddick 2000; Gorski 2003).

As a response to exogenous and indigenous challenges, state formation in general, and the rise of the fiscal state in particular, was a conflictual process at its heart, with short and long-term transformative effects. Most obviously, international warfare altered the balance of power in Europe, occasionally destroying and creating states, and remodelling social relations. Tilly's aphorism that 'states make war and wars make states' nicely sums up a seesaw model to describe what seems like the inevitable evolution from the end of the Middle Ages onwards. The argument, however, remains a relatively crude explanation and has been further explored to explain successes and failures, in particular to explain state's successes on the battlefield depended upon access and organisation of economic and capital markets (Tilly 1990). Still, the circularity of the initial aphorism tends to subsume social experience in the state, the end of history being either a situation of total war and potential annihilation of the enemy, or of unstable peace under hegemons and coalitions.

While scholarship remains broadly focused on the roots of state's successes and failures across time and space, with long-term political stability and economic growth as yardsticks, much of the new research is concerned with the institutional and cultural foundations rather than the material basis of the state's projection of power through sheer accumulation of military or naval forces (Acemoglu and Robinson 2012). Although mobilisation and end use of resources are two sides of the same coin, management of warfare was also about solving tensions between demand and supply, and of course legitimacy. In this respect, the extraordinary needs imposed by warfare did not only call for a fiscal-military state, capable of raising money and credit to fund war operations, but also a contractor state to organise procurement. In other words, the sources of power rest on the interplay between coercion, or use of the legitimate monopoly of violence by the ruler, and collaboration, or the relation between public and private interests, to protect society and promote the common good.

Many recent works concerned with state-building in early-modern Europe have highlighted the crucial role played by various private groups in helping rulers access larger pools of resources to display their personal glory and sustain their dynastic interests. However, as Parrott (2012) observed in the case of the business of war in the age of the military revolution, a humanist tradition sees the connection between private and public interests as essentially a fraught one, which prioritised individual profit over the ruler's authority and the quality of service. Recent research on corruption and anti-corruption in history have reinforced the complex nature of the relation between the two spheres by showing, on the one hand, that their separation was a relatively recent development, which built upon more precise definitions of corruption, but, on the other hand, that the long-term evolution was anything but linear (Kroeze et al. 2017). In medieval and early-modern Europe, for instance, introduction of venality, or the sale of offices by rulers, coincided with specific rules for appointment, transmission and accountability of offices. Various works also argue that criticisms of the patrimonial nature of public functions were not essentially meant to target venality as such but served political strategies aimed at regulating access to offices (Artola and Dedieu 2011). In addition, research on the techniques, objectives and impact of audits of officers who collected and spent tax revenue suggest that the procedures did not seek to prohibit profit in the management of public monies but to distinguish between lawful and unlawful benefits (Legay 2010; Dubet and Legay 2011) especially when set in the context of the bitter rivalries pitting financial interests and political factions (Graham 2015; Andujar Castillo et al. 2016; Kleer 2017).

In the wake of the financial crisis of 2007–2008, and the series of scandals relating to corporate sectors and private actors, it seemed appropriate to explore the role of institutions in maintaining trust and fighting corruption, as well as in promoting political stability, economic growth and equality of opportunities. To this effect, this volume, which proceeds from an international conference organised at the University of Reading on 4–5 December 2015, co-funded by ESRC and IUF, investigates the issues of trust and corruption in the management of tax revenue and expenditure in early-modern Europe. As mentioned, the subject of corruption has attracted renewed attention in a number of recent studies with emphasis on cultural, political and, lately, intellectual dimensions of corruption (Waquet 1992; Storrs 2009; Hoenderboom and Kerkhoff 2008; Kerkhoff et al. 2013; Buchan and Hill 2014). Yet on fiscal corruption specifically there is no specific study to match the important work done in particular on venality and officers in early-modern Europe (Andujar Castillo and Ponce Leiva 2016; Doyle 1996, 2004). This volume proposes to fill this gap by exploring the discourses and practices of the various actors involved in fraudulent activities and their denunciations, as well as the rulers' and the states' responses. From the outset, two common pitfalls have to be avoided. Firstly, assessing the action of early-modern agents on the basis of a modern definition of corruption risks promoting an inaccurate teleological model of the phenomenon, and discarding evidence of repression of corruption, for instance through trials and visitations, as historically meaningless or pointless attempts to engage with structural causes. Secondly, it risks fuelling the common fantasy about a conspiracy by early-modern elites accused of hiding their personal greed and moral remorse behind the ethos of noble and free service when consciously committing a crime, an early-modern crime which is none the less set against modern standards. This volume is more interested in examining when and why social actors started considering the ethos of service and the rewards of gifts as the intolerable expression of elite domination and exclusive access to money and honour.

To overcome such pitfalls, this volume pays special attention to early-modern fiscal actors through analysis of discourses and practices of fraud and corruption. Discourses are analysed in varied contexts, essentially on occasion of political conflicts, usually coinciding with attempts to instrumentalise anti-corruption within and outside institutions, and judicial procedures over accusations of fraud. Here, the work of theoreticians is supplemented with the views of various individuals, coming from diverse social and political groups, for the purpose of identifying whether there was an early-modern culture of corruption in general, and of corrupt actions in particular. Practices cannot be separated from discourses, particularly in the case of denunciations of others' malfeasance. For this reason, the chapters in the volume are essentially case studies. Their authors did not seek to establish a catalogue of repetitive notions about corruption which were often foreign to the political culture of early-modern agents. On the contrary, corruption and its repression are studied through primary sources: law and legal treatises, documents on fiscal decision-making and arbitration between private/public interests, judicial sources produced for trials, accounts, etc.

The volume spans the last two centuries of the *Ancien Régime* and maps onto a vast geographic area encompassing Southern Europe (Spain) and Scandinavia (Sweden), including Great Britain, France, the Southern Low Countries, the Dutch Provinces, Prussia and Bavaria. These territories include both Catholic and Reformed confessions, absolute monarchies (Spain, France, Prussia, Bavaria) and limited parliamentary regimes (England, Dutch Provinces, Sweden). The case studies examine different types of corruption pertaining to the collection of taxes and the payment of state expenditure, the issuing of debt and circulation of financial assets, coinage and counterfeiting, and accountability in general. They also examine different levels in the principal–agent relations: government and governed, government and fiscal agencies, fiscal agents and employees, governed and fiscal agents.

This volume does not claim to be an exhaustive history of fiscal corruption in early-modern Europe. Yet the variety of the approaches of its ten cases studies, combined with the results of recent literature, bring significant new knowledge which helps map out a number of key notions about the relations between the fiscal state, its agents and the public. The following table is an attempt at a typology of principal/agent relations and their long-term evolution, or, as it were, a model of fiscal ethics. A left-to-right reading of the table would certainly open to the accusation of a linear and teleological interpretation, which, as we will see, is not supported by the findings for this volume. Work on the Netherlands (De Vries and Van der Wroude 1997) and Britain (Hoppit 2012) cast doubt about the validity of an all-purpose of the Old Regime (Doyle 2012) throughout early-modern Europe prior to 1789, as a means to account for crises and modernisation of traditional structures (Table 1).

Despite its normative aspect, the table should be read with the assumption that definitions of corruption did exist in both the early-modern and modern periods, but that success at tackling it was a complex process, which could be stopped, reversed or pushed, and depended on the interplay of a number of variables.

In this respect, the chapters collected in this volume are testimony to the permanence of concerns about fiscal corruption, of its condemnation

Table 1 Mapping the war within: the ethics of public good and private interests

	Early-modern age			*Modern age*		
	Agent 1 Stage A *Subject*	Principal Stage 1 *Early-modern state*	Agent 2 Stage A *Fiscal agent*	Agent 2 Stage B *Fiscal agent*	Principal Stage 2 *Modern state*	Agent 1 Stage B *Citizen*
Society	Aristocratic	Dynastic	Plutocratic	Egalitarian	Republican	Individual
Governance	Elitist	Absolute	Patrimonial	Meritocratic	Limited	Democratic
Scope	Domanial	Territorial	Intermediary	Direct	National	Local
Ethos	Moral	Glory	Profit/gift	Salary	Virtue	Economic
Discipline	Family	Secrecy	Private	Public	Transparency	Self
Tensions	Inequality	Justice	Venality	Open access	Politic	Equality
Control	Petitions	Visitations	Account	Contract	Parliamentary Commissions	Elections
Organisation	Rank	Hierarchic	Associate	Bureaucratic	Collegial	Class
Character	Friendship	Despotism	Failure	Distrust	Instability	Distrust
Organisation	Patrimonial	Mercantile	Monopolistic	Competitive	Liberal	Opportunity

and the existence of tools to fight it. While the specific case studies confirm broad failure to remedy unlawful practices or inefficient institutional arrangements, they also show how tensions, at different level of analysis, paved the way for new perspectives on governance of finance, and a willingness to engage with the costs of corruption, especially at the end of the period under study. Altogether, they focus the spotlight on the ways in which cultural, economic, financial, military, monetary, religious and political institutions shaped common or specific attitudes towards fiscal corruption and government finances. In so doing, they address familiar questions about the timing, rhythm, geography and efficiency of change in early-modern Europe.

Although the frontier between public and private interests evolved in the period under examination, nonetheless the relations between these spheres differed substantially from those in our time. Then tax revenue was usually considered as a monopoly of the Prince or his dynasty, in some cases of provinces, but rarely as the money of a sovereign nation. For this reason, zeal in the service of the monarch did not prohibit personal or corporate profit from management of royal funds. This is illustrated by the rapid upward trajectory of the Spanish jurist analysed by Malaprade, the justifications provided by Swedish merchants studied by Winton, the words of cardinal Fleury and Lavoisier on tax farming cited by Félix, or the benefits allowed to businessmen as exemplified by Dubet, González Enciso and Bernsee in the Spanish and German monarchies. These examples imply convergence between the interests of private agents and the ruler's needs, but also between credit and honour (Malaprade, Graham, Winton). Yet the moral dilemmas identified in the English Pay Office (Graham) and the Talhouët scandal (Velde) remind us that the ethics of the private sphere, essentially personal and familial credit, and those of the public sphere, with the rise of the fiscal state and debt, could pave the way for deceptive or honest relations and fiscal policies.

The principle whereby services to the ruler should be rewarded by commensurate profits had important consequences. Firstly, relying upon private interests to fill in ruler's treasury was deemed desirable (González Enciso, Bernsee, Winton, Dubet). Secondly, venality, or the sale of public offices, was not considered reprehensible in principle but could be so considered in fact, when covering abuses, in particular when individuals sold public offices for their personal benefit (Knights 2017). The case study of counterfeit of French coinage evidences the existence of such nuances in the definitions of corruption. Thirdly, in absolute monarchies, finances being the preserve of the ruler circulation of accounts was limited to individuals of the highest calibre (Bernsee, Dubet, Graham, Legay), a secretive practice which political economy condemned in rather later times. Velde shows that the transparency and impartiality of the rules established by the Paris brothers to liquidate the System of John Law through a Visa of the debts was relative, the king secretly granting favours to creditors. Even in limited monarchies, like Sweden, where the *arcana imperii* had to be shared fiscal information remained the preserve of a small and collegial elite (Winton), the tools for fiscal transparency had yet to be invented and implemented (Félix 2015). Moreover, friendship and love, and their manifestation through gifts, presents and patrons/clients relations, were part and parcel of the various mechanisms which linked states and financiers as well as financiers and credit markets to fund expenditure. Corruption applied essentially to the cases of gifts made with dubious intention (subornation, bribery), extortion of money (concussion), lies (to the king or assemblies) and forgery of fiscal documents (Graham, Winton, Velde). In absolute monarchies, the king determined rewards to financiers and businessmen, and made these profits lawful (Bernsee, Dubet).

The benefits granted to agents for services on behalf of the king, in particular in collection of taxes, could be financially ruinous (González Enciso) and costly politically (Kerkhoff) for the king and the public. If the largest beneficiaries from the rise of the fiscal state were not necessarily those most widely condemned by public opinion, as in the case of French *traitants* and *tax farmers*, the ability to manoeuver and dispense with their services remained hazardous (Félix). Yet, against the background of the English financial revolution, credible commitment and the rise of markets, fiscal policy under Louis XIV and Louis XV raised new questions, both at home and abroad, about the compatibility of the ruler's and private interests, as shown in the cases of currency manipulation and restructuration of royal debts (Legay, Velde).

Early-modern attitudes towards corruption belonged to a world which was fundamentally rooted in inequality. Inasmuch as corruption was defined by the pursuit of private motives through personal actions, the likelihood of accusation of and condemnation for fraud usually depended on individuals' social backgrounds such as, of course, noble status, but also on patronage as well as notions of credit and honour (Malaprade, Winton, Kerkhoff). At this level, differences in the type of regimes and confessions does not seen to have applied, although the humanist concept of virtue, which appeared late in France, became synonym with equality and the cult of nation (Linton 2001; Bell 2009). Meanwhile corruption was not defined only in legal terms, alongside civil law, but also, and at times above all, through a variety of norms: in particular the concepts of justice and fairness, as defined by Christian morals, with their connotations of friendship and love, but also canon law and natural law. These conflicting norms could be more compelling than the ruler's law and, as such, justify infraction and escape repression (Velde, Legay).

Yet elites did not consider that all had equal access to these codes of conduct. This reality invites us to scrutiny of arbitration processes at stake in trials of corruption rather than bluntly condemn the inefficiency of judicial repression via measurement of fraud reduction. In general, analysis of the objectives of the parties involved in legal cases concerning corruption has emphasized their symbolic and political dimensions and, consequently, the importance of assessing the efficiency of repression along these objectives. This interpretation helps understand the rationale behind royal clemency (considered more efficient, politically, because linked to individuals, than pure repression). Also it forces historians to seriously consider the competing strategies put forward by rival agents rather than adopting a binary logic contrasting innocents with culprits. This is especially true given the lack of clearly defined rules when monitoring cases of corruption in the context of warfare which created extraordinary situations.

The chapters in this volume suggest that a broad consensus existed among various social groups regarding the definition of corruption in the management of tax revenue until the 1750s. This consensus is visible in the debates where those involved levelled at each other similar criticisms praising or blaming venal acts or altruistic services motivated by love of the king or the community. No substantial divergence can be detected between the definitions of fraud put forward by moral and legal theoreticians and agents on the ground, as revealed in letters, interrogations and indictments. There was no difference either between the discourses of merchants and bankers and members of the nobility, at least when they can be clearly identified (Bernsee, Félix, Legay, Malaprade, Velde, Winton).

An examination of how and why the common culture about corruption and its repression came to be contested and considered as the ideology of an archaic and aristocratic ethos detrimental to the both the interests of the ruler and the nation still remains to be undertaken. Before the French revolution, the relationship between lawful and unlawful access to the ruler's money, both in monarchic or republican states, had already initiated reforms of the fiscal state. Their chronology, however, varied from place to place. As a fiscal military state, England ranked among late starters, at least until the English civil war which, like the Dutch Revolt, initiated substantial transformations in taxation and tax collection, the organisation of credit and access to markets (Dickson 1967; Neal 2000; Coffman 2013; T'Hart 2014); and eventually the system of procurement (Buchet 2013; Knight and Wilcox 2010). Elsewhere, pragmatism was most often the rule where rulers faced the alternative between monopoly and competition and, in general, direct administration or private intermediation. When public temporarily won over private, such as in Spain and France, governments usually justified their choice with help of an anti-corruption discourse. By and large, however, fiscal policy was less concerned with rooting out fraud than with maximising of returns, through securing better terms in contractual arrangements, and the reduction of asymmetric information by access to data on specific sources of revenue and expenditure. The existence of hybrid forms combining direct administration (*régie*) and tax farms, or monopoly and competition, confirms the flexibility of the relations between the private and public spheres. In this respect, the chapters in this volume contribute current reassessment of the notions of decline or backwardness of certain polities (Spain, Sweden) or, as in the case of France, the rationalisation of social action.

The cases studied in this volume show that the fiscal pressure of warfare, the political impact of military victory or defeat, the circulation of credit instruments and the refinancing of war debts opened up avenues for personal enrichment and fraud, and triggered anxieties and anger at the corruption of society and values. Hume's famous warning in his *Essay on Money* (1751) as to whether the state would kill debt or debt kill the state is, perhaps, the most striking statement about the permanence of factional attitudes towards the rise of the tax state and the transition to the modern fiscal state (Bonney), both in Britain (Hoppit 1990) and in Europe at large (González Enciso 2016). The clash reveals a lot about the destructive impact of warfare but, even more, about is creative dimension, especially its effects on political stability and economic development (O'Brien 2018). In the period covered in this volume, however, the military revolution and its potential reward for rulers seemed to have petted out in long wars of attrition with slow or uncertain results on the balance of power and the European state system (Kennedy). Yet the short-term results of the ongoing competition pitting dynastic, mercantile and confessional interests against each other fostered reflections on the sources of power and the comparative costs and benefits of European various polities and types of fiscal governance (Montesquieu 1750; Bonney 1995; Félix 2013).

As a matter of fact, polities tried to learn from their allies and competitors. Under pressure, rulers felt compelled, often unsuccessfully or at least slowly, to graft on foreign models to tackle domestic problems. Several case studies in this volume confirm that Louis XIV's wars constituted a major turning point in the attitude towards public good and private interest, but also that resumption of international warfare in the 1740s suddenly acted as another crucial period on the route towards the modern discourse and response to corruption. The evolution of monetary sovereignty in the Low Countries (Legay), the call on French tax farmers to establish a *Regie* of taxes in Prussia (Bernsee), the suppression of tax farming in the Dutch Provinces (Kerkhoff) and Spain (González Enciso), the role of foreign alliances in fiscal policy in Sweden (Winton) show beyond doubt that institutional change cannot be understood in an hermetically sealed environment where change was impossible. As time went by, rulers and the public gained access to information about available resources and method of extracting and even increasing them. Under the pressure of war, polities were compelled to cherry-pick and adopt components of foreign models. After all, Edmund Burke's crusade against corruption in Britain consciously built upon Necker's policy of cuts on expenditure, or the so-called *economical* reform. Conversely, Necker made clear that the British political model inspired his policy to remedy the constraints of war finance by accessing international credit markets and the pillars implementing credible commitment, notably publicity of royal accounts (Félix 2013).

Necker's refusal to accept the traditional and substantial gift—or *pot-de-vin*—offered to the finance minister by the tax farmers when contracting the new lease for the collection of tax exemplifies the changes at work in the culture and the practice of corruption in the management of finances. Like many other eighteenth-century reformers across Europe, Necker could not modernise overnight the complex institutional canvass which framed early-modern relations between service to the ruler, personal profit and public good. The modern definition of corruption and the tools to fight it had yet to be formulated by polities, implemented by government and internalised by fiscal agents. From the 1750s, however, the transition was supported by new theories about private interest and the accumulation of wealth, notably by the likes of Mandeville with his *Fable of the Bees* (Hundert 2005), the *physiocrats* and their fight against private financiers and for the abolition of mercantile regulations, Adam Smith's division of labour and invisible hand (Hill 2006), and Jeremy Benthams' Panopticon (Foucault 1979). Still, the French Revolutionary and Napoleonic Wars and the Pax Britannica were to play a crucial role in activating the modern paradigm of corruption and implementing the relevant practices to fight it.

Needless to say, the chapters in this book act as spotlights on the wide-ranging question of private interest and the rise of the fiscal state. They do not intend to offer a comprehensive analysis of the various issues relating to corruption over time and across space in early-modern Europe, but to identify some key problems set in different contexts, and, hopefully, stimulate further research in the field. Some of the papers presented in 2015 have not been included in this volume, either because their authors discussed their published or unpublished findings (Martinez, Waddell) on-going research (Knights).[1] In the volume, European polities are unequally represented, partly because the organisers drew upon established networks of experts on private interest (Contractor State) and corruption (Anticorrp in Netherlands, VENACORRU and DINACOR in Spain), partly because of their inability to attract or identify other experts from elsewhere countries. Consequently, the many aspects of corruption in the management of early-modern finances could not be fully addressed. Two areas in particular have not been much explored here. One concerns the connections between the theories and practices of corruption. The other relates to the impact of the Reformation on individual and institutions in the age of the confessional state. However, the reader will find useful references to the most recent literature on these aspects in the various chapters.

As this book suggests, crises and institutional change proceed from agency and its impact on the correlation between discourses and practices concerning the definition of power, its distribution and access to it.

[1] See the conference programme at http://www.reading.ac.uk/fiscal-history/.

In the wake of the financial crisis of 2007–2008 it hard to assess whether new regulations, criminal convictions and fines imposed on corporate agencies and private actors will re-form or re-define relations between public good and private interest. It is even harder to forecast their future in the context of Brexit and Trumpism. At the very least the challenges ahead confirm the relevance of studying the ways in which early-modern polities dealt with their wars within.

References

Acemoglu, D., and J.A. Robinson. 2012. *Why Nations Fail: The Origins of Power, Prosperity, and Poverty*. New York: Crown Business.

Andújar Castillo, F., and P. Ponce Leiva (eds.). 2016. *Mérito, venalidad y corrupción en España y América, siglos XVII y XVIII*. Valencia: Albatros.

Artola Renedo, A., and J.P. Dedieu. 2011. Venalidad en contexto. Venalidad y convenciones políticas en la España moderna. In *El poder del dinero. Ventas de cargos y honores en el Antiguo Régimen*, ed. F. Andújar Castillo and M.M. Felices de la Fuente, 29–45. Madrid: Biblioteca Nueva.

Bell, D.A. 2009. *The Cult of the Nation in France: Inventing Nationalism, 1680–1800*. Cambridge: Harvard University Press.

Bonney, R. 1995. *Economic Systems and State Finance: The Origins of the Modern State in Europe 13th to 18th Centuries*. Oxford: Oxford University Press.

Bonney, R. (ed.). 1999. *The Rise of the Fiscal State in Europe c. 1200–1815*. Oxford: Clarendon Press.

Bowen, H.V. 2013. The Contractor State, c. 1650–1815. *International Journal of Maritime History* 25 (1): 239–274.

Braddick, M.J. 2000. *State Formation in Early Modern England, c. 1550–1700*. Cambridge: Cambridge University Press.

Brewer, J. 1989. *The Sinews of Power: War, Money and the English State 1688–1783*. London: Unwin Hyman.

Buchan, B., and L. Hill. 2014. *An Intellectual History of Political Corruption*. New York: Palgrave Macmillan.

Buchet, C. 2013. *The British Navy, Economy and Society in the Seven Years War*. Woodbridge: Boydell Press.

Coffman, D.M. 2013. *Excise Taxation and the Origins of Public Debt*. Basingstoke: Palgrave Macmillan.

De Vries, J., and A. Van der Woude. 1997. *The First Modern Economy: Success, Failure, and Perseverance of the Dutch Economy, 1500–1815*. Cambridge: Cambridge University Press.

Dickson, P.G.M. 1967. *The Financial Revolution in England. A Study in the Development of Public Credit, 1688–1756*. London: Macmillan.

Doyle, W. 1996. *Venality: The Sale of Offices in Eighteenth-Century France*. Oxford: Oxford University Press.

Doyle, W. 2004. Changing Notions of Public Corruption, c.1770 to c.1850. In *Corrupt Histories*, ed. E. Kreike and W. Chester Jordan, 83–95. New York: University of Rochester Press.

Doyle, W. (ed.). 2012. *The Oxford Handbook of the Ancien Régime*. Oxford: Oxford University Press.

Dubet, A., and M.L. Legay. 2011. *La comptabilité publique en Europe*. Rennes: Presses Universitaires de Rennes.

Ertman, T. 1997. *Birth of the Leviathan: Building States and Regimes in Medieval and Early Modern Europe*. Cambridge: Cambridge University Press.

Félix, J. 2012. Finances. In *The Oxford Handbook of the Ancien Régime*, ed. W. Doyle, 75–92. Oxford: Oxford University Press.

Félix, J. 2013. The Problem with Necker's Compte-rendu (1781). In *The Crisis of the Absolute Monarchy: From the Old Regime to the French Revolution*, ed. J. Swann and J. Félix, 107–125. Oxford: The British Academy/Oxford University Press.

Félix, J. 2015. Finances. Paths to Fiscal Transparency. *Histoire & mesure* 30 (2): 3–22.

Foucault, M. 1979. *Discipline and Punish*, trans. Alan Sheridan. New York: Vintage.

González Enciso, A. 2016. *War, Power and the Economy: Mercantilism and State Formation in 18th-Century Europe*. London: Routledge.

Gorski, P.S. 2003. *The Disciplinary Revolution: Calvinism and the Rise of the State in Early Modern Europe*. Chicago and London: University of Chicago Press.

Graham, A. 2015. *Corruption, Party, and Government in Britain, 1702–1713*. Oxford: Oxford Historical Monographs.

Hill, L. 2006. Adam Smith and the Theme of Corruption. *The Review of Politics* 68 (4): 636–662.

Hoenderboom, M.P., and A.D.N. Kerkhoff. 2008. Corruption and Capability in the Dutch Republic: The Case of Lodewijk Huygens (1676). *Public Voices* X (2): 7–24.

Hoppit, J. 1990. Attitudes to Credit in Britain, 1680–1790. *The Historical Journal* 33 (2): 305–322.

Hoppit, J. 2012. Reformed and Unreformed Britain, 1689–1801. *In Doyle* 2012: 506–521.

Hundert, E.J. 2005. *The Enlightenment's Fable: Bernard Mandeville and the Discovery of Society*, vol. 31. Cambridge: Cambridge University Press.

Kerkhoff, T., T. Kroeze, and P. Wagenaar (eds.). 2013. Corruption and the Rise of Modern Politics in Europe in the Eighteenth and Nineteenth Centuries: A Comparison Between France, the Netherlands, Germany and England. *Journal of Modern European History* 11 (1): 19 et sq.
Kleer, R.A. 2017. *Money, Politics and Power: Banking and Public Finance in Wartime England, 1694–96*. Oxford: Oxford Universoty Press.
Knight, R., and M.H. Wilcox. 2010. *Sustaining the Fleet, 1793–1815: War, the British Navy and the Contractor State*. Woodbridge: Boydell & Brewer.
Knights, M. 2017. *Anticorruption in Seventeenth- and Eighteenth-Century Britain*, ed. R. Kroeze, A. Vitória, and G. Geltner, 181–196.
Kroeze, R., A. Vitória, and G. Geltner (eds.). 2017. *Anti-Corruption in History: From Antiquity to the Modern Era*. Oxford: Oxford University Press.
Legay (Marie-Laure) dir. 2010. *Dictionnaire historique de la comptabilité publique, 1500–1850*. Rennes: Presses Universitaires de Rennes.
Linton, M.A. 2001. *The Politics of Virtue in Enlightenment France*. Basingstoke: Palgrave Macmillan.
Mandeville, B. 1924. *The Fable of the Bees: Or, Private Vices, Publick Benefits: By Bernard Mandeville. With a Commentary Critical, Historical, and Explanatory by FB Kaye*. Oxford: Clarendon Press.
Montesquieu, baron de. 1750. *The spirit of laws*. London: J. Nourse and P. Vaillant.
Neal, L. 2000. How It All Began: The Monetary and Financial Architecture of Europe During the First Global Capital Markets, 1648–1815. *Financial History Review* 7 (2): 117–140.
O'Brien, P. 2005. Fiscal and Financial Preconditions for the Rise of British Naval Hegemony, 1485–1815. Working Papers, 91/05. Department of Economic History, London School of Economics.
O'Brien, P.K. 2018. The Costs and Benefits of Mercantilist Warfare. *Financial History Review* 25 (1): 97–112.
Parrott, D. 2012. *The Business of War: Military Enterprise and Military Revolution in Early Modern Europe*. Cambridge: Cambridge University Press.
Schumpeter, J. 2012. The Economics and Sociology of Capitalism. The Crisis of the Tax State. In *Navies and State Formation. The Schumpeter Hypothesis Revisited and Reflected*, ed. J.G. Backhaus, 21–78. Berlin: Lit Verlag.
Storrs, C. (ed.). 2009. *The Fiscal-Military State in Eighteenth-Century Europe. Essays in Honour of P.G.M. Dickson*. Farnham: Ashgate.
T'Hart, M. 2014. *The Dutch Wars of Independence: Warfare and Commerce in the Netherlands 1570–1680*. London: Routledge.
Tilly, C. 1990. *Coercion, Capital and European States. AD 990–1992*. Cambridge: Wiley-Blackwell.

Waquet, J.C. 1992. *Corruption: Ethics and Power in Florence, 1600–1770*. University Park: Pennsylvania State University Press.
Weber, M. 2013. *From Max Weber: Essays in Sociology*. London: Routledge.
Yun-Casalilla, B., P.K. O'Brien, and F.C. Comín (eds.). 2012. *The Rise of Fiscal States: A Global History, 1500–1914*. Cambridge: Cambridge University Press.

CHAPTER 2

Credit and Discredit of Financiers in Wartime: Defrauding and Serving the Crown in Seventeenth-Century Spain

Sébastien Malaprade

In early-modern European monarchies, the reinforcement of the royal state apparatus, combined with the increasingly exorbitant costs of wars, routinely led to financial crises. Resorting to fiscal emergency procedures and issuing ever-growing amounts of sovereign debt became standard budgetary policy. Not only did this lead Europe's rulers to face difficult issues of fiscal compliance, but it also fostered the emergence of a new form of strategic thinking concerning budgetary matters, with the goal of minimising the risk of insolvency and default. And yet the eagerness to balance revenues and expenses often remained at odds with the requirements of the battlefield.

In the seventeenth century, Spanish economic observers (*arbitristas*) were quick to criticise the poor judgment of the Habsburgs and

I express my gratitude to Fabrice Langrognet, Isabel Perera and Romy Sánchez for helping me translating and revising this text.

S. Malaprade (✉)
École des Hautes Etudes en Sciences Sociales,
Centre de Recherches Historiques, TEPSIS, Paris, France

J. Félix and A. Dubet (eds.), *The War Within*,
Palgrave Studies in the History of Finance,
https://doi.org/10.1007/978-3-319-98050-8_2

their ministers: it was the cause, in their view, of Spain's financial turmoil. Unable to pass the reforms he had wished to, Gaspar de Guzmán, Count-Duke of Olivares long remained the ideal culprit in that regard, until his efforts were revived by Elliott (1989). It is true that, under Olivares' guidance (1621–1643), the Spanish monarchy went through one of the worst crises in its history (Ruiz Martin 1990; Gelabert 2001). In addition to the military defeats by the French during the Thirty Years War, a couple of uprisings erupted in Portugal and Catalonia in 1640 and 1643. Other factors also accounted for the sorry state of affairs documented by the historians: the flow of gold and silver from America was dangerously drying up; due to bad harvests and acute food shortages, the population was on the wane in a significant number of towns and villages; a lack of liquidities and rapid price increases not matched by an equivalent inflation of wages were seriously weakening the Iberian economy. The economic crisis was soon echoed by a political one.

Financial hardship had the effect of bringing businessmen to the fore. Over the past two decades, historians have sought to demystify the negative vision that had long prevailed—that of an unsustainable trend fueled by bankers' supposedly insatiable greed. Now, their contribution to the construction of the monarchical system is being reconsidered (Dubet and Luis 2011; Félix 2015, 2016). While critics denounced the immorality and cupidity they saw in private bankers, the Crown's financial officers were also blamed. In addition to their judicial roles, institutions such as the *Chambres de Justice*[1] in France and the 'visits' (*visitas*) of the Spanish financial officers offered catharsis. There were ways to manage and, at intervals, to satisfy the popular thirst for vengeance against public profiteers. Officers, ministers of the Treasury, treasurers, tax farmers, and military suppliers (*asentistas*) were all subject to deep resentment, on both sides of the Pyrenees. The public (and literary) pinion would routinely unmask infamous thieves under the guise of loyal servants of the king, 'demons' who were robbing the people and stealing the king's treasure (Moya Torres y Velasco 1730: 157).

Many a detractor cried foul over the immense fortunes that these men were thought to have amassed during their time in public office. On the one hand, the rapidity of any upward mobility was bound to raise issues of its legitimacy in societies where inertia was held in high regard, and where the ideal of stability was deemed to be in accordance

[1] See Chapter 9 by Joël Félix *supra*.

with the harmony of the cosmos itself. On the other hand, personal gains accumulated while the individual held office were almost certain to be SEEN AS a sign of suspicious dealings. In court, excessive enrichment could be viewed as the decisive proof of guilt. An anonymous pamphleteer in Louis XIII's France wrote that 'as soon as someone is given a position in the treasury services, however poor he might be, he immediately becomes a wealthy man, growing overnight like pumpkins and rotten mushrooms".[2] Far from being merely rhetorical, the metaphor underlines the double meaning of the word 'corruption' in the early-modern period. In addition to getting rich quickly, the term referred to the decomposition of a living organism (Dc Covarrubias 1611: 242–243; Furetière 1690). The comparison was also meant to be a warning, a reminder of the fate awaiting those fattened up by the fiscal-financial system (Dessert 1984).

The present chapter is about one of those finances' administrators, Rodrigo Jurado y Moya. A Grand officer of the Crown's treasury and eminent lawyer (*letrado*), he amassed an exceptional wealth between the 1620s and 1640s—the peak years of the crisis in Spain. But he eventually had to face trial during a judicial investigation (*visita*) and was sentenced with losing his offices and paying a heavy fine. The primary goal of this study is to examine the resources into which these individuals could tap, particularly because the mechanisms of asset accumulation by Castilian *letrados* is still largely unfamiliar to the historiography of public finances. To that end, the present work analyses the 1643s *visita* against the Council of Finance (*Consejo de Hacienda*). *Visitas* give historians a rare insight into officers' speculative strategies and their relationships to bankers. Combined with notarial and private records, these legal sources help better understand how Jurado made the most of economic troubles. The second objective is to examine the prevailing ideas about corruption at the time, in particular the extent to which the boundaries between what was considered fair and unfair, legal and illegal, honest and dishonest changed over time and between spaces. In 2013, an investigation into the treasurer of Spain's ruling party resulted in convictions of fraud and money laundering precisely at the moment when the country was facing a serious recession.[3] In a similar vein, the perception of corruption in

[2]Bibliothèque Historique de la Ville de Paris, 8-BRO-029674 (43), *Le pot aux roses descouvert par un financier réformé*, Paris (1624?).

[3]The Luis Bárcenas case, ex-treasurer of the Partido Popular.

early-modern Europe largely depended upon the sociopolitical and economic circumstances when a scandal broke.[4] In this respect, the severity of the ruling against Jurado partly reflected the discrepancy between his rising wealth and the contraction of the Crown's finances.

While the charges of fraud brought against officers are relevant to this chapter, one needs to take in consideration their defence strategy, and to see it neither as a collection of preposterous arguments that they did not believe themselves nor put forward to minimise the extent of their misdeeds (Waquet 1984). On the contrary, the historian must reconstruct the logic underlying their discourse, taking into account their ability to take advantage of a complex judicial system. Among the justifications put forward by both the accused and their accusers, the concept of 'credit' played a crucial role, the meaning of which need to be explored, and this concept is one whose economic meaning cannot be disassociated from its moral connotations.

By focusing on the bankers' role in the financial evolution of the Spanish monarchy, the existing literature has unintentionally marginalised the treasury officers, often portrayed as mere bureaucrats with limited room for action. By contrast, the micro-historical perspective offered by Rodrigo Jurado's case directly points to the manner in which these individuals constituted essential elements in the process of securing loans and ensuring the liquidity of the bond market in the early seventeenth century. If the task of this paper is to shed light on the fiscal and financial functions of Philip IV's government through the self-interested strategies of the officers and their families, it is imperative that their practices be connected to those of businessmen. And it is certainly in the case of accusations of fraud that the permeability between these two categories was most visible.

1 A Meteoric Rise Viewed from the Moment of the Fall

Since the end of the Middle Ages, the *visita* was the main instrument at the monarchy's disposal to chastise and prevent abuses by treasury officers. This procedure, run by a judge called the *visitador*, was

[4] About the legitimacy to use the word corruption in early-modern society, despite its potential anachronism, see Bertrand (2013) and Ponce Leiva (2016).

designed to investigate a tribunal and its agents (Herzog 2000; Peytavin 2004). Beyond the judicial aspect, the *visita* had also clear political purposes: at the end of the trials, a college of judges would recommend the appropriate reforms to be implemented in order to improve the institutions visited. Though it was intended as an exceptional occurrence, the visit of the Council of Finance started to be conceived as a regular process in the second half of the seventeenth century. The one opened in 1643 went on without uninterruption until the beginning of the eighteenth century, and was led by no less than six different visitors. Visits were feared by officers, mainly because of the means the visitors had at hand and the methods of inquisition they used. In contrast to ordinary procedures in criminal matters, in which the accused would be aware of the witnesses' identity and declarations, the visit would keep the accused in the dark about what was being held against him.

In the historiography, Rodrigo Jurado remains associated with the *visita* that took place against the Council of Finance from July 1643, seven months after Olivares's disgrace. The inquiry into Rodrigo Jurado's dealings is among the most extensive to ever have been conducted in the seventeenth century. Its publicity, despite the customary discretion prevailing in such matters, reached beyond the circle of treasury officers. The matter was commented upon at Court in Madrid and in Andalusia, and provided some chroniclers with the opportunity to deride the acquaintances of Jurado with the Portuguese business circles.[5] In the opinion of one of Diego de Riaño y Gamboa's own successors (the *visitador*), while the 1643 visit became stagnant and unambitious, the inquiry split into two individual trials: one against Pedro Valle de la Cerda, a council member, and one against Rodrigo Jurado. Recent studies over the judicial fate of these two main victims (Gómez González 2016; Malaprade 2016) have now dispelled the doubts cast over the reasons for their sentencing (Domínguez Ortiz 1960). The respective lists of the felonies they were charged with bear witness to the convergence of their financial practices. In particular, both of them were prosecuted for their collusion with the bankers and the king's tax farmers, for having illegally acquired treasury bonds (*juros*), for having speculated on those same instruments on the secondary market through a scheme of front men, and bought fiscal jurisdictions sold by the Crown (*alcabalas*).

[5] Memorial Histórico Español, *Cartas de algunos padres de la Compañía de Jesús*, t. XVII, Madrid: Imprenta Nacional, 1863, p. 231, Letter (15 September 1643).

More generally, the accusations pointed to the excessive private gains of both ministers, and to their lavish lifestyles. While Rodrigo Jurado rejected the allegations of any improper dealing, he did not contest the value of the bonds nor of the fortune attributed to him. He had come to possess, in fact, one of the most impressive fortunes in Castile, as a consequence of his spectacular upward mobility.

The son and the grandson of commoners in the Andalusian province of Jaén, Rodrigo Jurado was born in 1584 in Villanueva de Andújar, a farming village of 2000 inhabitants, and would die in Madrid in 1650. He was the eighth child of a family of nine, and soon lost his mother (1587) and father (1597). His family was one comprised of honest landlords who had benefited from the economic growth of the sixteenth century. The financial basis of his grandparents' and parents' income was rooted both in olive oil production and in sheep and goat breeding. And yet the increasing financial resources of these humble property owners had not translated into political power. In a society where holding municipal offices was simultaneously a clear marker of social status and carried a presumption of noble origin, none of the Jurados had been part of Villanueva's municipal council.

In 1597, the will of Rodrigo Jurado's father stipulated that each of the children would inherit 1680 ducats.[6] Such capital immediately made him a member of the economic elite. Having accessed his fortune at a young age, Rodrigo chose to invest his money in lengthy university studies, beginning them at the rather humble University of Baeza. He then moved to the much more prestigious faculty of Seville, which formed a part of the Empire's colonial administration. However, after his studies had earned him the title of doctor in civil law to avoid a career overseas, he decided instead to gain access to the central government at the Court in Madrid. His engagement with the daughter of the *Cortes*' chief tax collector[7] brought him a step closer to this. Seven years after marrying Isabel de Orozco in 1617, a period during which he made little progress as an attorney in Madrid, Jurado assumed his father-in-law's accounting responsibilities. Overseeing a treasury of 40,000 ducats—revenue from

[6] In the beginning of the seventeenth century, the average dowry in Pozuelo de Aracava, a village near Madrid, was less than 100 ducats (Barbazza 2000: 153–139).

[7] The *Cortes* are the political assemblies of the realm of Spain. In that case they refer to the representative assembly of Castile.

the *alcabalas*[8]—Rodrigo Jurado would now manage funds that financed the administration of the *Cortes*.

With the support of Olivares's network, Rodrigo Jurado was promoted to the charge of prosecutor of the *millones* in 1634. His new position made him privy to the very heart of fiscal services. In the seventeenth century, fiscal revenues were mostly composed of contributions granted from the *Cortes* to the Crown, like the *servicios* or the *millones*. The latter tax was levied for the first time in 1590 and periodically renewed in the first half of the seventeenth century. As military operations became more intense in the 1630s, this tax collected on the consumption of ordinary goods became Castile's main source of revenue: in 1634, its value exceeded that of the *alcabalas*. The chair of the *Comisión de millones*, the *Cortes'* organ which administered the tax, stated that he had more money under his control in 1638 than the Council of Finance.[9] Aside from these prerogatives, the *Comisión* also served as a special court for legal conflicts pertaining to tax. At the point Jurado became its prosecutor, 180 ongoing investigations targeted *millones'* farmers.[10] To efficiently manage the indirect tax system, the prosecutor had to assess the reliability of candidates to farming positions, and to prosecute them whenever they failed to comply with their contracts' provisions.

Having established a solid reputation as a magistrate, Jurado earned the king's trust. In 1635, Philip IV granted him a commission with the purpose of recovering the accumulated arrears of the *millones*. Finally, in 1638, his career reached its peak when he obtained the office of prosecuting attorney of the Council of Finance, which came in addition to the office he held at the *Comisión de millones*. Consulted in every matter where the Crown's rights and financial interests were at stake, his mission consisted in safeguarding and expanding the king's properties. His expertise was both legal and financial: when contracts were being negotiated with the king's lenders, he would assess their credit and make

[8]A sales tax, one of the most important ordinary resources.

[9]Archivo Histórico Nacional (henceforth AHN), CS, 51343, Consulta (13 July 1638). During the first half of the seventeenth century, the Council of Finance struggled against the Cortes to control the *Comisión de millones*. In 1658, the *Comisión* is finally incorporated within the Council of Finance.

[10]AHN, Estado, 6399 (3 July 1634).

sure the agreement would not violate the best interests of the parties involved.

Rodrigo Jurado's charges soon proved very profitable: in less than twenty years, the family's fortune was multiplied 150-fold. In the early 1640s, the cumulative assets of Rodrigo and his younger brother Eufrasio were valued at more than 320,000 ducats. The prosecutor's annual revenue alone amounted to more than 12,000 ducats.[11] So great a fortune was uncommon, and it did not fail to elicit rumours and envy. Those in his Andalusian homeland watched how Rodrigo, with the help of his brother, regularly enlarged his territorial property to increase the profits of the family's olive oil business. Those within the Council of Finance in Madrid commented covetously on the prosecutor's wealth, which was not commensurate with his social rank. Indeed, a large part of Jurado's earnings were spent on a long and costly procedure to bestow honours upon his family—an effort to solidify their fragile nobility that eventually reached fruition in 1636. But in spite of his best efforts to legitimise his social metamorphosis and erase all traces of his low origins, Jurado remained until his death the target of attacks impugning his family's honour and the origin of his wealth, both of which were derived from his connivance with the business world. In Andalusia no noble family would marry his children while one of his colleagues, the Count of Montalvo, stigmatised Jurado's fortune, arguing that it exceeded his social status.[12]

2 Techniques of Advancement

By virtue of his stable positions in the *Cortes*, at the *Comisión de millones*, and at the Council of Finance, Rodrigo Jurado built relationships across the kingdom's main financial institutions. He was particularly connected to the comptrollers, known for their fiscal competences, who were charged with reviewing the treasurers' accounts. Of this group, Gaspar Antolín de la Serna stands out as one of Jurado's most faithful supporters. De la Serna, chief comptroller of the *Comisión de millones*, was a central player in the fiscal system and one of the finest specialists in the

[11] AHN, CS, 51243-1, Rodrigo Jurado's judicial defence.

[12] Archivo General de Simancas (henceforth AGS), CJH, 806, Memorial to the king (4 October 1640).

management of *millones*. Sources also suggest Jurado's proximity with several *contadores de la razón*, officials in charge of bestowing privileges upon, and of reviewing the *juros*' and *alcabalas*' accounts respectively. This is hardly surprising, given Jurado's greed for public rents earned from long-term annuities (*juros*) and *alcabalas*. Indeed, the comptrollers could provide him with valuable information concerning the quality and reliability of the *juros*' revenues. *Juros*' reputation not only depended on their interest rate but also relied on their situation: they were assigned on different tax revenues whose reputations were unequal (Álvarez Nogal 2009). Consider how the nature of Jurado's investment portfolio evolved when he entered the *Comisión de millones* in 1634: previously attracted to real estate, he now began to accumulate high-yield assets, exactly like bankers (Sanz Ayán 2015: 130–136). Both his ability to obtain information from financial officials, and his capacity to collect rents, explain this accumulation.

His acknowledged as prosecutor, as well as the 1635 commission letter on the *millones*' arrears, gave Rodrigo Jurado invaluable financial and political power. To understand his financial opportunities, we should recall the organisation of the fiscal system (Dedieu and Ruiz Rodríguez 1994). One of its tenets is fragmentation: each funding stream has its own form of collection, its own form of regulation, and its own set of actors. In contrast with the later eighteenth-century efforts of the Spanish Bourbons, the Habsburgs of Jurado's time neither had the will nor the ability to centralise their incomes. The *millones* were no exception. The *Comisión de millones* headed their administration, but each municipality represented at the *Cortes* organised its own tax collection. Municipal treasuries obtained fiscal revenue from collectors within their jurisdiction. Collectors, in turn, were chosen by local alderman—and they made sure to choose them well. Indeed, the role of tax collectors went beyond mere tax collection. They were also responsible for overseeing expense payments from the accounts assigned to them. Of these payments, the most important were the *juros*. And these assets were bought and sold on independent markets: a *juro* sold on the *alcabalas* of Valladolid could not be counted as revenue to the *millones* of Madrid. The multiplication of funds led to the multiplication of participants involved. For the king and his favourite, such an organisation was ambivalent. It furthered the ongoing corruptibility of the *millones*. But in the meantime, it also allowed the monarchy to delay payments or to negotiate information with bankers about the best fiscal revenues for their reimbursements with short-term debt titles—or *consignaciones* (Cárceles de Gea 1995; Dubet 2000).

From 1635 until the beginning of the 1640s, Jurado's commission on the *millones* had one mission: tracking down fraudsters by examining treasurers' accounts as well as coercing municipalities to pay the millions of ducats they owed. Thanks to his coercive power, and also to the agents and clerks he recruited among friends and professional acquaintances, the magistrate could claim control of the *millones*' income for all of Castile. Although fiscal information was compartmentalised, his position afforded him a birds' eye view that transcended these barriers. Between 1635 and 1639, he granted about twenty powers of attorney to sub-delegate judges so that they could go to cities where abuses and delays had been reported (Malaprade 2018). However, this undertaking was inhibited by several conflicts between different courts. Municipalities saw in Jurado's commission as Olivares's attempt to deprive them of their fiscal authority.

Nevertheless, these powers enabled Jurado to enquire (and obtain information) about the reliability of the *millones*' treasurers—in the first instance, by directly accessing their accounts. In Madrid, for instance, the king allowed him to "quickly seize the city's accounts to learn of the state in which they find themselves."[13] This authority therefore allowed him to ascertain whether the portion of the fund attributed to the *juros* (the *situado*) exceeded the total value of the revenue collected. The monarchy was used to issuing more *juros* than the revenue earmarked. So, the investors were prompted to seek information about the funds before buying *juros*. Jurado was thus able to adjust his purchases of *juros* based on the yields of the treasury to which they were assigned. He was also authorised to verify the nature of the goods taxed as per the treasury's deposits.[14] As with the farmers, the prosecutor was required "to be informed of the state of [the treasurers'] credit and the security of their goods"[15] guaranteed to the Crown. Having the prerogative to estimate these financial deposits offered Jurado information about the value of both real estate and transferable securities, many of which were *juros*. Like a notary, he benefited from privileged knowledge of businessmen,

[13] AGS, CJH, 747, King's order (12 February 1636).

[14] AGS, CJH, 772, *Consulta* (15 November 1636).

[15] Real Academia de la Historia (henceforth RAH), 9-3621 (244), Juridical defence of Miguel Montero.

liquidities, and resources which were likely to appeal to his whetted appetite. This is a crucial point, and one that prompted several polemical exchanges during the trial of 1643. The prosecutor was indeed charged with collusion and corruption of the *millones*' treasurers and farmers—two specific groups that, very often, worked as one.

Indeed, a substantial number of financiers took on both roles. In Castile during the 1630s many of them were Portuguese. Rodrigo's ascent coincided precisely with the emergence of a group of Lusitanian bankers. Recent historiography has shed light on the role of Portuguese bankers in providing credit (Studnicki-Gizbert 2007; Sanz Ayán 2013), but fewer historical works have studied tax farmers and treasurers. In fact, these groups' activities were often intertwined (Ruiz Martín 1990). In 1626 and 1627, collaboration intensified between Portuguese bankers and the Spanish crown. At Olivares's request, the court of the Inquisition began to soften its prosecutions of the *neo-conversos*,[16] who were suspected of backsliding towards their old religion. This was a response to the Crown's financial asphyxia. In 1627, Philip IV was forced to suspend payments for his sponsors, mainly the Genoese. Italian bankers' requirements on debts' reimbursement were considered excessive, forcing the Crown to turn to the Portuguese financial market instead. Hoping to obtain the best borrowing rates, the monarchy exploited the *neo-conversos*' lack of experience, as well as their social vulnerability.

At the beginning of the 1630s, when Portuguese bankers began to enter the tax farm market and get their hands on the most prized treasuries, Rodrigo Jurado expanded his Portuguese network. As a *millones* prosecutor, he was responsible for evaluating how solid the companies competing for the leases were, as he did with treasurers. But before any auction, the commission of the *millones* systematically consulted the prosecutor and almost always followed his recommendations. It is thus normal that *millones*' farmers should seek his goodwill, as he was a key figure in the attribution of leases. Whether it was through the power he exerted over Portuguese bankers, or through the friendship he had developed with them, Jurado urged the bankers to respond to his solicitations.

[16]The term refers to the Jews and the Muslims who had been converted at the end of the fifteenth century and the beginning of the sixteenth century.

Thus, when financial transactions required great discretion, Jurado would call upon on a group of confidants chosen from among his family, servants, friends, comptrollers, and a few trusted financiers, and gather them at his notary's office. In total, a dozen treasurers and farmers formed his regular core of collaborators. These insiders, essentially figureheads, helped to make Jurado's involvement more opaque. Thanks to assignments, donations and financial transfers to third parties, it becomes more and more difficult to get "up to speed" on the officer's patrimony, as a judge charged with sentencing Jurado once put it.[17] Thanks to the accounting, financial and administrative knowledge drawn from his activities, but also thanks to his network of informants and front men, Jurado could construct speculative strategies between 1635 and 1644. His attention now turned to finding currency, at a time when cash was running low.

In the seventeenth century, liquidity shortages were quite frequent. Two monetary systems coexisted in Spain at that time. In addition to a copper currency, the *vellón*, silver and gold currencies were also in use: the *escudo* and the *real de plata* (García Guerra 2006). The value of the latter varied very little until 1686. This strong and respected currency was the one used on international markets. It was also the one used to pay back the king's lenders, for military loans. *Vellón*, on the other hand, was for common exchanges within the domestic market. But over the course of the past century, the Crown had manipulated the *vellón*, maintaining its face value, but depreciating its real value by the coin debasement method. Popular distrust regarding the *vellón* sharpened the division between the two currencies. To compensate for *vellón*'s depreciation, a premium was set up to promote silver. This premium, in turn, was added to the legal conversion rate, and continued to increase through the beginning of the seventeenth century.

While the poor were the first affected by cash shortages, their grievances soon gained the attention of elites, who heard complaints of delayed wage payments and backlogs in public rents. The archives of the Council of Finance are full of requests from officers and soldiers worried about their unpaid wages and payments.[18] Even aristocrats fell victim to these shortages. Consider the experience of the Count of Montalvo,

[17]AHN, CS, 51243-1, Letter to Martín de Larreategui (3 May 1650).

[18]See for example AGS, CJH, 747.

already mentioned, who was jealous of Jurado's incomes. In 1640, the councilman deplored how difficult it was to recover his salaries: "I have only the salary of a counsellor of the Council of Finance, along with some indemnities given by a few other courts but I barely recover them and when it does happen it is with years of delay".[19] His remark suggests that membership of the financial elite was not sufficient to free oneself from financial difficulties.

In times of crisis, the extent of profits and wealth had more to do with the capacity and speed with which one recovers salaries and pensions than with their actual value. Merely possessing a good salary, a payment contract, or a pension title did not guarantee the receiving of their financial benefits. Thus, the circulation of orders (*libranzas*)—and their subsequent exchanges, transfers and discounted sales—reveal the existence of a debt market. The faculty to recover one's assets was more connected to the proximity of the relationship between creditors and debtors than one's social position. To that end, treasurers and cashiers became more and more important over this period. Sanz Ayán (2013) has noted how, in 1640, the monarchy's bankers negotiated which funds were to be assigned in exchange for their *asientos*. At that time, nearly 70% of total Castilian income was used to reimburse *asientos* or to pay *juros*' annuities. For those whose financial health depended on the quick recovery of their debts, it was critical to identify and obtain information about low-risk revenues. Bankers thus become masters in securing their reimbursement (*consignaciones*) from the most powerful treasurers, who often formed part of their financial entourage. For instance, in 1649, the visitor from the Council of Finance warned that tax collectors were controlling the funds and placing at their heads close collaborators who distributed *juros*' arrears unequally depending on the closeness of their relationship to the beneficiary.[20] Rodrigo Jurado, permeated with this financial culture, imitated their attitude. He thus demonstrated his ability to recover salaries, debts and *juros*' annuities.

With his accumulation of responsibilities as prosecutor, and the indemnities acquired by his commission from the *millones*, Jurado managed to pocket 5600 ducats, one of the kingdom's highest salaries. Given that the wages of public officers were usually paid from various funds,

[19]AGS, CJH, 806, Memorial to the king (4 October 1640).

[20]AHN, CS, 51272.

Jurado was able to reduce the number of his payees. Most importantly, his fees were held by treasurers of the *millones*, who were faithful and prompt in remuneration.[21] By virtue of the knowledge and the authority he exerted over these men, but also thanks to the benefits they gained by collaborating with him, the magistrate guarded himself against unfulfilled, incomplete, and delayed payments.

A similar logic affected his ability to access liquidity from loans with *millones*' financiers. Most of those loans seemed to depart from Christian and moral principles requiring the lender's consent and prohibiting any lucrative intentions (Clavero 1996). In the *visita*, several Portuguese businessmen claimed to be victims of these manipulations (a far cry from what was otherwise painted as a friendly donation for pecuniary services). According to them, the magistrate did not hesitate in tying the adjudication of *millones*' farm to a loan that he would never pay back.[22] Such allegations were indeed biased, but nonetheless, several notarial documenters did acknowledge the provision of distinct and diverse credit lines.

Jurado's sphere of influence was not limited to Castile. The prosecutor knew how to mobilise international monetary circuits in order to collect a large volume of capital. He would turn to intermediaries, who in turn looked for different lenders, such as traders, brokers or bankers. Thus, several sums were transferred to Rodrigo and his brother Eufrasio on the Sevillian market: 402,500 *maravedis* in 1642; and 2,399,642 *maravedis* the following year.[23] Such sums were bought from the stronger traders in town. Besides the indispensable Portuguese, such as Francisco Baéz, there was also the Genoese Bartolomé Dongo, as well as Juan Jacome Spinola, the correspondent of the Genoa banker Alessandro Pallavicino and the Flemish merchant Simon Canis.[24]

At a local level, providing credit and smaller transactions were often made with the help of the network of *millones*' administrators. Money transfers generated high costs; so Jurado used treasurers as provincial moneylenders. The territorial fragmentation of the funds, along with the influence of the Portuguese in municipal finance, enabled him to dispose

[21] AHN, CS, 51243-1, Rodrigo Jurado's juridical defence (1644).

[22] AHN, CS, 52670, Examination of witnesses (1643–1644).

[23] AHN, CS, 51243-2, Charges against Rodrigo Jurado (1644).

[24] AHN, CS, 51242-2, Enquiry of Juan de Lara, f. 160.

of cash in the various cities where his interests lay. Treasurers could thus provide money to his children, in the localities where they lived, as in San Clemente where his daughter and son-in-law resided.[25]

However, the terms of exchange were not always respected and Jurado's petitions were often considered to be usurious transactions. The Portuguese were not the only ones who were duped. Indeed, the magistrate also bought back low-priced debts from owners who could not recover them. Jurado then used his political and judicial influence to coerce debtors to pay. With his frontmen as his intermediaries (a practice forbidden to public officials), he was able to cash the assignments at their nominal value. This was the method he used against one of the heirs of Philip III's butler: the silver *reales*' debt was purchased in *vellón*. The speculative operation earned him 60,000 *reales* in benefits.[26]

The prosecutor's profits were then massively invested in *juros*. The logic of this was far from obvious as royal orders forbade ministers and public officers to possess such assets, except with a licence from the king. The prosecutor bypassed the law by using frontmen. Seven out of nine *juros* bought before the 1643 *visita* were obtained this way. On 13 November 1640, for example, Melchor de Cabrera, a close acquaintance of Jurado, bought a particular title assigned to the *millones* of Toledo. The comptroller, Manuel López de Salceda, granted the privilege and registered it under de Cabrera's name. A year later, in November 1641, Melchor de Cabrera recognised that the "*juro* was bought with the funds of Dr. Rodrigo Jurado [...] and thus both the principal and the interests to come belonged to him".[27]

But it is especially surprising to see that those bonds represented more than a third of Jurado's total fortune at a time when they had started to lose their attractiveness. The emission of a funded debt was an important resource for European monarchies (Toboso Sánchez 1987). In pursuit of their belligerent politics, Philip II and his son used this type of loan abundantly. The system provided investors with bonds, perpetual or lifelong, assigned to a particular revenue, in exchange for capital. In 1626, the *Cortes* granted Philip IV the right to use the *millones* to pay interests

[25] AHN, CS, 51243-1, Rodrigo Jurado's juridical defence (1644).

[26] AHN, CS, 51243-2, Charges against Rodrigo Jurado (1644).

[27] Archivo Histórico de los Protocolos de Madrid, 7039, fol. 77, Déclaration au profit de Rodrigo Jurado par Melchor de Cabrera (10 November 1641).

on new *juros*.[28] The Assembly would regularly concede these services in the years to come (1626, 1629, 1634, 1635, 1637, and 1639), and each time, the Crown issued *juros*, in which the owners of the oldest titles were given priority concerning the collection of their annuities. But as in seventeenth-century France, the context became worse for amateur public bond holders in Spain (Béguin 2012: 34–51). As discounts, ordered by the king to obtain greater surpluses, progressed, the *juros* depreciated. In 1605 and 1621, their interests (previously at more than 7%) were capped at 5%; but by 1635, all *juros* were affected by the *media anata*, a tax amounting to half of the annual interests. Here again, the dysfunctional system often forced the owners of the *juros* to accept unprofitable conditions. In Sevilla in 1643, they owned only 11% of the projected real value of the interests (Marcos Martín 2013).

For experts of finance, as for the Crown's bankers who saw part of the floating debt becoming a consolidated debt, these difficulties were eased by their knowledge of which the best funds were and who administered them. This is why, in spite of the *juros*' devaluation, acquiring them was still a good investment. Rodrigo Jurado thus combined three strategies. The first one followed a purely speculative logic: buying assets under par from disappointed owners. The second advantage was linked to the ease of transferring stocks. As we have seen, the ability to give away bonds enabled Jurado to hide behind his frontmen. Finally, the last strategy made use of his position within the fiscal system. Among all the assets in his portfolio, 87% were *juros* assigned to the *millones*. Between 1636 and 1642, 82% of the interests on those bonds were paid by five of his closest collaborators (Malaprade 2018). Moreover, 62% of his titles were based on the revenue of his province, especially in Andújar, where he assumed the public office of the comptroller of the *millones*. Jurado's actions gave priority to investments in his native region, where he knew their recovery would be assured, and on the *millones*, administrated by the faithful Portuguese.

A consequence of the extraordinary situation imposed by war was that fiscal structures and the servicing of the debt became more interdependent. In fact, the increase in short- and long-term debt demanded the making permanent of the fiscal system upon which the Crown's commitments rested (Béguin 2015: 16). On a social and economic level, the

[28] What induced, consequently, the *millones*' extension.

monarchy's crisis signalled a whole new distinction between privileged and non-privileged people. It is true that being exempted from taxes was a real advantage. But the most important gains were made by those who understood how to indirectly exploit the indebtedness of the monarchy and the indirect tax system. Socially, the accumulation of wealth led to the spectacular social advancements of some commoners and *conversos*, who tried their best to imitate noblemen and to erase their origins, albeit with great difficulty, given the hostility they faced. By contrast, those who made decisions based on poorly calculated risk faced social downgrading. The power of this elite (public officers, merchants, and financiers) was measured by its capacity to amass reliable information about the fiscal system and to mobilise intermediaries at all four corners of the Iberian Peninsula. The fragmented tax system stimulated information asymmetry. Combining service to a monarchy that was perpetually in need of money with the resources of finance, law and social networks was the key to power in times of crisis.

Thus, for some, success was built on financial injustices. In such conditions, everything seems to prove that a government willing to ignore the abuses of financial elites supported such inequalities. But this "functionalist" reading, which explains the leniency of the monarchy by pointing to its incapacity to punish, has two dangers (Bertrand 2013). First, it leads one to ignore the role of the *visitas* and the accusations of fraud. Second, it leads one to caricature financiers as those who only follow their private interests, neglecting their role in the maintenance of an efficient fiscal system. In fact, the means leading Jurado to progress in the socio-economic hierarchy are comparable to those that made him the King's prosecutor, and this was implicitly the claim of his defence. Thus, in order to better understand the fraud, one has to listen carefully both to the accused and his opponents.

3 Interpreting Corruption

The transformation of a *visita* of the Council of Finance into a personal investigation bears witness of its political spin. Traditionally, historians have linked the 1643 inquiry to Olivares' dismissal. The common wisdom had it that supporters of a purge within the administrative body of the disgraced *valido* in January, would have received satisfaction with the visit to be initiated in July (Gelabert 1997: 277; Sanz Ayán 2013: 153). The aim would then have been to oust from the Council of Finance the former faithful of the fallen minister. Yet a fine analysis of the relationships between the visit's victims and the judicial personnel shows that the prosecution was, in fact, a score settling act within the Olivarist faction itself. For one thing, the judges in charge of the inquiry were former followers of the Count. The relentless judicial harassment of Rodrigo Jurado would reveal the intention of those people to seize these strategic functions for themselves (Malaprade 2018). In this case, a political interpretation—laying the emphasis on circumstances and power games—would be more accurate. Such conclusions, however, do not preclude another, more generic one, according to which visits were means to periodically reaffirm the monarch's authority. The spectacular nature of certain trials corresponded to the royal desire to show off an infallible judicial authority. Members of *junta de la visita* recalled this in 1651: the visit permits the "restoration of the fair laws of His Majesty in their full force and vigor".[29]

But while political issues could be at stake in the trials, plans to get rid of an enemy needed to be converted into acceptable legal terms. To only view such a transposition—from the political order to the legal one—as a manoeuvre is legitimate solely if the historian replays the investigator's part and manages to prove beyond doubt the innocence of the indicted official. In all of the other cases, suspects tended to justify themselves based on notions which they thought were commonly agreed upon as to what constituted a condemnable action. Whether they lied or took pains to demonstrate the lawfulness of their behaviour, the accused believed in the criminal nature of the actions they had been charged with (Dubet 2016).

At once legal specialist, former attorney and magistrate, Rodrigo Jurado used all legal resources at his disposal to counter the visitor's arguments. His first strategy—a common one among indicted officers—consisted in a claim of procedural error. In his two handwritten defence briefs (written in 1644 and 1649), he alleged that the judge irregularly extended the scope of the investigation. Whereas Diego de Riaño y Gamboa commission letter granted him the right to investigate the Council of Finances, the visitor had abused his power by looking into the *Comisión of the Millones* as well. When it comes to the substance, however, the twenty-five levelled against Jurado comply with the commission

[29] AHN, CS, 50509.

letter's original directions.[30] First, the visitor was mandated to uncover "secret collusions" existing between members of the Council and business people. The term collusion should be here understood as synonymous with a relationship based on bribery, that is the abuse of power by a king's official who unlawfully requests monies from a third party. The second injunction the visitor had received dealt with verifying illegal purchases of *juros* and *alcabalas* by treasury officers while in office.

On that score, Jurado's defence strategy mixed several types of legitimisation. He stated that the ban on the acquisition of *juros* and *alcabalas* only applied to the officers of the Grand Chamber of Accounts, hence not to prosecutors like himself. To this legalistic rhetoric, he also added casuistical references. Certain ordinances, he explained, had become obsolete, such as the law prohibiting the selling out of goods by officials to a third party, which was "not followed nor applied since the court adopted it".[31] Furthermore, in order to sugarcoat his investments in *juros*, the prosecutor put forward their continuous decrease in value since the passing of a 1568 law that prevented officers from buying them. While the fraud accusation had been legitimate at times when the bonds paid good returns, he said, the law was now clearly obsolete since this form of investment had become financially precarious. Moreover, when he levied forced subscriptions, the king himself constrained his officers to purchase *juros*. This point, raised by Jurado, shows how the economic circumstances could blur the boundaries between the lawful and the unlawful. The assessment of fraud by no means followed an intangible set of criteria. Its recognition did not result only from the interpretation of positive law, but also from exogenous factors, which could modify the perception of the phenomenon. This is what Jurado suggested by asserting that "accidents and circumstances specific to our era render lawful and allowed what could cause difficulties or be liable to a prohibition".[32] His explanation matched the moralists' principles: as *juros* were not profitable, his intentions could not be considered as immoral.

As had been the case in the famous 1607 trial against Pedro Franqueza, a companion of the Duke of Lerma, the relationships between Rodrigo Jurado and businessmen played a pivotal role in the

[30] AHN, CS, 13200, *decreto* 83 (16 July 1643).

[31] AHN, CS, 51243-1, Rodrigo Jurado's juridical defence (1644).

[32] AHN, CS, 51243-1, Rodrigo Jurado's juridical defence (1644).

inquiry. Such complicities tainted a lot of the practices alleged by the judge against Jurado: purchases and sales of *juros* from and to Portuguese financiers, concealment of assets thanks to figureheads recruited in that very pool of people, calling on those same men to receive forced credits or gifts, etc. The list of charges referred to the crime by the ambiguous term of "correspondence". Its most common meaning is reported as positive: the correspondence implied a relation of confidence between two individuals (*Diccionario* 1729). Although the judge meant to refer by this term to the profits made by Jurado through the power he had wielded over treasury officers, he did not use the word "collusion", nor *cohecho* and *baratería*—i.e. the manipulation of justice in pursuit of an economic benefit. Jurado recalled, in that respect, that he had never been accused of those crimes. But under the guise of bonds of "friendship", Jurado was seen as having abused his power to obtain financial gains. Far from denying his acquaintances in the Portuguese circles, the prosecutor confirmed the visitor's allegations:

> ...to this day, all tax farmers have been coming to my house for their business; as for me, I have many times visited them to request credits of great value and services they have been willing to do for His Majesty. All of this I did for the sake of His Majesty.[33]

In an era of crisis, collaborating with Portuguese bankers and offering favour to wealthy lenders was critical in order to negotiate the best credit deals for the Crown. Since the kingdom's political system rested upon an amalgam of interpersonal and friendship relations (Dedieu 2005), denouncing the intimate connections between Jurado and the King's creditors could seem surprising. That was the implicit reasoning underlying the lawyer's argument. Secret exchanges within individual homes, and credit operations between private entrepreneurs and government officials, were just a manner forging or reinforcing a relationship of trust that was indispensable. In that vein, the gifts that would be offered after a tax farm had been adjudicated or a public contract had been signed were branded as the mere expression of gratitude by farmers towards considerate treasury officers.[34] What looked like bribery schemes and fraudulous cronyism were in fact part of brokering processes. Those were

[33] AHN, CS, 51243-1, Rodrigo Jurado's juridical defence (1644).

[34] AHN, CS, 51227, Francisco de Arevalo's juridical defence.

useful to the Crown, for they resulted in lower credit rates and donations, easier money transfers thanks to the Portuguese intermediation, exchange of information over the location of financial resources or the reliability of the various sources of revenue. Affinities between officers and businesspeople could not possibly be considered as blameworthy in themselves. They conditioned the efficiency of an entire political system in which the Crown's interests and those of private subjects had to be preserved. Philip III's favourite, the Duke of Lerma, emphasised how important it was to build friendships with Genoese bankers. This helped to restore the monarchy's credit.

Pleas from treasury officers often alluded to two distinct, insuperable measures of justice: the Christian ideal and the King's service. On the one hand, the intention was to prove that the aims of the suspicious deeds were honourable and, on the other hand, that they were serving the Crown's interests. In order to restore the horizontality, as it were, that the judges viewed as missing in his relationship with the financiers, Rodrigo Jurado insisted on the generous advances issued to the Portuguese, like the one received by Francisco Rodríguez Peñamacor.[35] According to the prosecutor, this individual had borrowed in 1642 the sum of 30,000 *reales* from the king's chief *asentista*, Jorge de Paz Silveira. Unable to repay the amount in time, the farmer was jeopardising the payments of the Flanders army. "Thinking (as is the case) that [he] was serving the interests of his Majesty", Jurado explained to the judge that he had elected to generously rescue Peñamacor from the predicament he found himself in. Yet in that case, references to the Christian principle forbidding usury and the indirect contribution to the military defence of the monarchy was not enough to convince the judge of his sincerity.

The fact that the notion of corruption is not limited to its legal component is well known. It also relies on a moral element which, in early-modern minds, would manifest itself in the notion of credit. The evaluation of a treasury officer's credit was a critical, and difficult operation during trials, for the criteria that led to its assessment were often implicit. That being said, we may affirm that credit resulted from the association of four sorts of individual capacities[36]: (1) the individual's

[35] AHN, CS, 51243-1, Rodrigo Jurado's juridical defence (1644).

[36] A synthesis of the different meanings given by old Dictionaries is set up in Fontaine (2008) and Lilti (2015).

professional aptitude and integrity; (2) his ability to provide the king with financial resources and guarantees of solvency; (3) his moral reputation, assessed by looking at the degree to which he abided by Christian values; and (4) the man's skills in persuading the world of the trustworthiness of the image he and his people projected, in other words his credibility. The difficulty of appraising credit, and hence its corollary, corruption, lies in the variability of each of those parameters.

The word "credit" and its derivatives are widely spread in judicial records pertaining to treasury visits. Apart from their financial meaning, they could be used to discredit a witness seen as unfit to be given a hearing, like that officer whose detractor declares that this man's "credit [equal] to that of the Devil".[37] But the notion served most of all in rebuilding a reputation that had been tarnished by infamous accusations. Such was the case in the efforts made by the wife of a comptroller of the Council of Finance to defend her husband, arraigned for unlawfully receiving monies while in office. After listening to her arguments, the judges acknowledged "services performed by Gerónimo de Canencia in the fulfillment of his duties, and the good credit he [had] maintained in that position".[38] As they ultimately reduced the officer's punishment—the indefinite removal from his office was commuted into a one-year suspension—the judges underlined the "piousness with which the legal provision [had been] attenuated". Here it is clearly apparent how the fraud determination did not only follow a legal reasoning. It supposed a holistic appreciation of the person's value, through the evaluation of that individual's moral, economic and professional credit. For that matter, some people presumed guilty would invoke their "fear of God"[39] to defend themselves, which was totally unsurprising in a world where human justice was subordinated to the divine order.

In the prosecutor's mind, a treasury officer's credit had to depend partially on his ability to procure the funds needed for safeguarding the monarchy. The operation by which the King's moneylenders would reap the symbolic benefits, through ennoblement, of their investments clearly points to the entanglement between the material and the immaterial. Indeed, in his last plea, Jurado claimed that his actions had not caused

[37] AHN, CS, 50505, Letter to García de Porras (9 June 1654).

[38] AHN, CS, 50509, Answer to the memorandum of Juana Trueque (1651).

[39] AHN, CS, 51227, Francisco de Arevalo's juridical defence.

any loss to the Crown, but instead that he had, thanks to his skills and connections, contributed to securing thousands of ducats that were badly needed for the kingdom's preservation.[40] The association of a putatively sound money management within the treasury offices to the military fortunes of the kingdom were a leitmotif in the great officers and ministers' defences. This argument was meant to counter the attacks by judges who would not hesitate blame military defeats on their financial wrongdoings. This was, for instance, what happened to José González, president of the Council of Finance between 1647 and 1651, whose wrongful management of public funds had, according to the judge, jeopardised the resources of the "soldiers of the *presidios*, and of the armies".[41] Acting like a banker, the former chair of the Council of the Finance fired back by precisely evaluating the sums collected by the Crown: during his tenure, the surplus he credited to himself amounted to 35,008,002 *escudos*. In addition, he listed about fifteen victories that the Spanish soldiers had won over the same years. Both José González and Rodrigo Jurado were financial experts with similar trajectories. As commoners who had amassed spectacular fortunes, they were subject to the same moral disparagement (Fayard 1981).

Whereas the political power González had accumulated eventually allowed him to avoid the fall, the fragile reputation of Jurado, by contrast, was not compensated by a political force of the same magnitude. When the visitor dwelled on his intimacy with the Portuguese circles, suspected of being closet Jews, he meant to dishonour Jurado. What was intended there was to alter the credit of someone who had become so close to a group that he could be assimilated with it. Those insinuations were given extra weight by considering the prosecutor's relationship to money. The most telling clue of his immorality lay in his ostentatious wealth and in the excesses of his pride. Relying on testimonies that had singled out Rodrigo Jurado's enrichment as far too meteoric, the visitor suggested that the prosecutor had been perverting the social order by refusing to "comply to his condition".[42] To no avail did the Andalucian try to paint, in his pleas, the image of an honest, parsimonious officer:

[40] RAH, 14-11584-15, f. 383, Rodrigo Jurado's memorandum (1649).

[41] Biblioteca Nacional de España, Porcones, 100-16, José González's juridical defence.

[42] AHN, CS, 51243-2, Charges against Rodrigo Jurado (1644).

"the decency with which I have lived is notorious, with no surfeit whatsoever in clothing, servants and gifts".[43]

As a new man, whose nobility was called into question, Jurado had to bear the full social consequences of his trial. For officers, individual visits entailed tremendous repercussions. The broadcasting of the news was bound to increase the infamy. Jurado had good reasons to fear the symbolic impact of searches that were targeting his family in Andalusia. "This caused a great scandal in that city [Andújar] and all the villages of its district; this cast discredit on myself and my brother".[44] For all his attempts at cementing his credibility through the printing of *porcones* (trial briefs), social shame did sully his family, as if in his own words "his entire lineage had committed a crime in the service of His Majesty".[45] In a retroactive, implacable logic, the discredit tainting Jurado and his relatives would become the irrefutable proof of his guilt.

4 Conclusion

For the past two decades, the historiography of the Iberian Peninsula has tried to add some nuance to the idea of a generalised crisis in seventeenth-century Hispanic monarchy. To underline its "resilience" (Storrs 2006), various studies have emphasised the Crown's audacious financial experiments (Álvarez Nogal 2008; Grafe and Irigoin 2006), its flexible fiscal negotiations with elites and municipalities (Ruiz Ibañez 1997; Fortea Pérez 1990), its military tenacity (Andújar Castillo 2004; Torres Sánchez 2016), and its ability to challenge the administration of a "polycentric" empire (Cardim et al. 2014). In an effort to underline the monarchy's need to sustain the expenses of its international political activities and inspire confidence in markets, several scholars have focused on the bankers of the Hapsburgs. By doing so, they neglected role of financial intermediaries—ministers, public officers, as well as their subordinates, such as clerks—in obtaining credit. Examining the role of the king's servant in the functioning of the fiscal and financial system enriches the history of the ways in which the monarchy financed itself.

[43] AHN, CS, 51243-1, Rodrigo Jurado's juridical defence (1644).

[44] AHN, CS, 51243-1, Rodrigo Jurado's juridical defence (1644).

[45] RAH, 14-11584-15, f. 383, Rodrigo Jurado's memorandum (1649).

In this sense, studying Rodrigo Jurado's trajectory and the strategies he elaborated within the *millones*' administration framework seeks at least to add nuance to, if not abolish, the boundaries between officers and financiers. Relationships between the prosecutor and the businessmen reveal not only an intense collaboration, but also the emergence of hybrid phenomena. Despite their efforts to differentiate one from the other, a common culture, values and interests linked the men who gravitated to financial administration. Whether they were of noble or common extraction, these elites obtained their power through their service to the Crown and had anchors both in court and on the ground. They used the same speculative practices, the same financial intermediaries and the same networks for credit and information. Their interest in maintaining a fiscal system mainly controlled by municipalities explains the success of fiscal negotiation between the king and the municipalities. Far from being an anomaly, this situation resulted from the administrative organisation of the crown's finances: the system's rationality relied upon the entanglement between monarchical, private, and corporatist interests.

Comparing the social advancement of officers and financiers, caricatured by the existing literature, is also valid. While some were able to reach the top without attracting negative attention, a great majority of the others faced criticism for their thirst for wealth and for the speed of their ascension. By looking at how the wheel of Fortune turned for them, the importance of the notion of credit in corruption as a social phenomenon comes into plain sight. Understanding this notion of credit, which has not been analysed very much by scholars of corruption, is important and deserves more attention. While credit is an analytical tool that explains the ductility of fraudulent practices that legal norms themselves are not enough to account for, one must also define what constitutes a good financial administration built largely upon the mutual confidence of its protagonists.

References

Álvarez Nogal, C. 2008. L'argent du roi et les hommes d'argent. In *Les finances royales dans la monarchie espagnole (XVIe–XIXe siècles)*, ed. A. Dubet, 187–188. Rennes: Presses Universitaires de Rennes.

Álvarez Nogal, C. 2009. Oferta y demanda de deuda pública en Castilla. Juros de alcabalas (1540–1740), Estudios de historia económica, n°55, Madrid: Banco de España.

Andújar Castillo, F. 2004. *El sonido del dinero. Monarquía, ejército y venalidad en la España del siglo XVIII.* Madrid: Marcial Pons Historia.

Barbazza, M.M. 2000. *La société paysanne en Nouvelle-Castille, Famille, mariage et transmission des biens à Pozuelo de Aravaca (1580–1640)*. Madrid: Casa de Velázquez.
Béguin, K. 2012. *Financer la guerre au XVIIe siècle, la dette publique et les rentiers de l'absolutisme*. Paris: Champ Vallon.
Béguin, K. (ed.). 2015. *Ressources publiques et construction étatique en Europe (XIIIe–XVIIIe siècles)*. Paris: Comité pour l'Histoire économique et financière de la France.
Bertrand, M. 2013. Penser la corruption. *e-Spania* 16.
Cárceles de Gea, B. 1995. Del juez de comisión al comisario real (1632–1643): El fraude fiscal como agente del 'gobierno económico'. *Stvdia historica. Historia moderna* XIII: 155–175.
Cardim, P., T. Herzog, J.J. Ruíz Ibañez, and G. Sabatini (eds.). 2014. *Polycentric Monarchies*. Eastbourne: Sussex Academic Press.
Clavero, B. 1996. *La grâce du don. Anthropologie catholique de l'économie moderne*. Paris: Albin Michel.
De Covarrubias, S. 1611. *Tesoro de la lengua castellana o española*. Madrid: Luis Sánchez.
Dedieu, J.-P. 2005. Amistad, familia, patria... y rey. Las bases de la vida política en la Monarquía española de los siglos XVII y XVIII. *Mélanges de la Casa de Velázquez* 35 (1): 27–50.
Dedieu, J.-P., and J.I. Ruiz Rodríguez. 1994. Tres momentos en la historia de la Real Hacienda. *Cuadernos de Historia Moderna* 15: 77–98.
Dessert, D. 1984. *Argent, pouvoir et société au Grand Siècle*. Paris: Fayard.
Diccionario de la lengua castellana.... 1729. t. II. Madrid: Francisco de Hierro.
Domínguez Ortiz, A. 1960. *Política y Hacienda*. Madrid: Editorial de derecho financiero.
Dubet, A. 2000. *Réformer les finances espagnoles au siècle d'or, le projet Valle de la Cerda*. Clermont-Ferrand: Presses Universitaires Blaise Pascal.
Dubet, A. 2016. La moralidad de los mentirosos: por un estudio comprensivo de la corrupción. In *Mérito, venalidad y corrupción en España y América, siglos XVII y XVIII*, ed. F. Andújar Castillo and L. Ponce Leiva, 213–234. Valencia: Albatros.
Dubet, A., and J.-P. Luis (eds.). 2011. *Les financiers et la construction de l'État en France et en Espagne (milieu du XVIIe siècle-milieu du XIXe siècle)*. Rennes: Presses Universitaires de Rennes.
Elliott, J.H. 1989. *The Count-Duke of Olivares: The Statesman in an Age of Decline*. New Haven and London: Yale University Press.
Fayard, J. 1981. José González (1583–1668) 'créature' du comte-duc d'Olivares et conseiller de Philippe IV. In *Hommage à Roland Mousnier: clientèles et fidélités en Europe à l'Epoque moderne*, ed. Y. Durand, 351–358. Paris: Presses Universitaires de France.

Félix, J. 2015. La monarquía francesa y los financieros en el Antiguo Régimen. El ejemplo de los traitants durante la Guerra de los Nueve Años, 1689–1697. *Tiempos Modernos* 8 (30).

Félix, J. 2016. Los historiadores y los financieros de la Francia del Antiguo Régimen. *Mélanges de la Casa de Velázquez* 46 (1): 21–31.

Fontaine, L. 2008. *L'économie morale, Pauvreté, crédit et confiance dans l'Europe préindustrielle*. Paris: Gallimard.

Fortea Pérez, J.I. 1990. *Monarquía y Cortes en la Corona de Castilla, las ciudades ante la política fiscal de Felipe II*. Salamanca: Cortes de Castilla and León.

Furetière, A. 1690. *Dictionnaire Universel*. La Haye and Rotterdam: Arnoud et Reinier Leers.

García Guerra, E. 2006. Moneda en España en los siglos XVI–XVIII. In *La economía en la España moderna*, ed. A. Alvar Ezquerra, et al., 201–240. Madrid: Istmo.

Gelabert, J.E. 1997. *La bolsa del rey. Rey, reino y fisco en Castilla (1598–1648)*. Barcelona: Crítica.

Gelabert, J.E. 2001. *Castilla convulsa, la crisis de la monarquía, 1631–1652*. Madrid: Marcial Pons.

Gómez González, I. 2016. Entre la corrupción y la venalidad: Don Pedro Valle de la Cerda y la visita al Consejo de Hacienda de 1643. In *Mérito, venalidad y corrupción en España y América, siglos XVII y XVIII*, ed. F. Andújar Castillo and L. Ponce Leiva. 231–250. Valencia: Albatros.

Grafe, R., and A. Irigoin. 2006. The Spanish Empire and Its Legacy: Fiscal Redistribution and Political Conflict in Colonial and Post-Colonial Spanish America. *Journal of Global History* 1 (2): 241–267.

Herzog, T. 2000. Ritos de control, prácticas de negociación: pesquisas, visitas y residencias y las relaciones entre Quito y Madrid (1650–1750). In *Nuevas Aportaciones a la historia jurídica de Iberoamérica*. Madrid: Fundación Hernando de Larramendi-Mapfre.

Lilti, A. 2015. Le pouvoir du crédit au XVIIIe siècle. *Annales. Histoire, sciences sociales* 4: 957–978.

Malaprade, S. 2016. Enriquecerse en tiempos de crisis: el control de los tesoreros y de los arrendadores de millones por un fiscal bajo Felipe IV. In *Mérito, venalidad y corrupción en España y América, siglos XVII y XVIII*, ed. F. Andújar Castillo and L. Ponce Leiva, 235–266. Valence: Albatros.

Malaprade, S. 2018. *Des châteaux en Espagne, mobilité sociale et gouvernement des finances au XVIIe siècle*. Toulouse: PULIM.

Marcos Martín, A. 2013. Deuda pública, mercado crediticio y actividades económicas en la Castilla del siglo XVII. *Hispania* LXXIII (243): 133–160.

Moya Torres y Velasco, F.M. 1730. *Manifiesto universal de los males envejecidos que España padece*. Madrid: Francisco Laso.

Peytavin, M. 2004. *Visite et gouvernement dans le royaume de Naples (XVIe–XVIIe siècles)*. Madrid: Casa de Velázquez.

Ponce Leiva, P. (ed.). 2016. *Mérito, venalidad y corrupción en España y América, siglos XVII y XVIII*. Valence: Albatros.

Ruiz Ibañez, J.J. 1997. *Las dos caras de jano. Monarquía, ciudad e individuo. Murcia, 1588–1648*. Murcia: Universidad de Murcia.

Ruiz Martín, F. 1990. *Las finanzas de la Monarquía hispánica en tiempos de Felipe IV (1621–1655)*. Madrid: Real Academia de la Historia.

Sanz Ayán, C. 2013. *Los banqueros y la crisis de la Monarquía Hispánica de 1640*. Madrid: Marcial Pons.

Sanz Ayán, C. 2015. *Un banquero en el Siglo de Oro*. Madrid: La Esfera de los libros.

Storrs, C. 2006. *The Resilience of the Spanish Monarchy, 1665–1700*. Oxford: Oxford University Press.

Studnicki-Gizbert, D. 2007. *A Nation Upon the Ocean Sea. Portugal's Atlantic Diaspora and the Crisis of the Spanish Empire, 1492–1640*. Oxford: Oxford University Press.

Toboso Sánchez, P. 1987. *La deuda pública castellana durante el Antiguo Régimen (juros)*. Madrid: Instituto de Estudios Fiscales.

Torres Sánchez, R. 2016. *Military Entrepreneurs and the Spanish Contractor State in the Eighteenth Century*. New York: Oxford University Press.

Waquet, J.-C. 1984. *De la corruption, Morale et pouvoir à Florence aux XVIIe et XVIIIe siècles*. Paris: Fayard.

CHAPTER 3

"I Carry a Serpent in My Bosom, Which Devours Me": Finance, Morality and the Public Service in the Nine Years War, 1688–1697

Aaron Graham

In July 1696 the deputy-paymaster of the British army in Flanders, Richard Hill, was in the throes of a moral reckoning. "I walk about as impudently as other men", he told his friend William Blathwayt, the secretary at war, "but God knows I carry a serpent in my bosom which devours me". He had been forced to lie to public creditors across the region to find the money that the army required, selling them bills of exchange on the Pay Office in London in the full knowledge that the office did not received enough money from the Treasury to answer even a tenth of these bills. His sense of the public interest, and the need to keep the British army in the field during the Nine Years War (1688–1697) against Louis XIV and French tyranny, was therefore not enough to dilute his anguish at the moral betrayal this involved. His experience, and that of the Pay Office in London during this period, therefore

A. Graham (✉)
University College London, London, UK

J. Félix and A. Dubet (eds.), *The War Within*,
Palgrave Studies in the History of Finance,
https://doi.org/10.1007/978-3-319-98050-8_3

offers the opportunity to examine not only the depth of the connections between finance and morality in the early-modern world, but also what it took to drive them apart. Although morality was the bedrock of finance in this period, underpinning the shared trust that made commerce possible, it could clash with the moral duties that public officials dealing in finance owed to their king and country. Officials such as Hill found themselves caught between the rising sense of impartial public duty and the continuing importance of personal commercial morality that uniquely characterised the early-modern period.

1 Financial Moralities and Mentalities

Finance and morality were inextricably intertwined because financial networks in the early-modern period, like almost all other commercial networks, were almost entirely dependent on shared trust.[1] Although political and legal structures existed to police and punish breaches of contract, these were unwieldy and unreliable, especially when it came to managing complex networks operating across many legal jurisdictions and borders. Trust allowed merchants to short circuit this process and devolve agency to their contacts overseas, secure in the knowledge that they could rely on them to serve their interests faithfully. Because trust was therefore the lynchpin of long-distance trade and commerce, merchants sought to embed it into some of the most basic and fundamental elements of society. At one level trust embodied a strong expectation of shared economic interests; the agent had an incentive to serve his principal honestly and effectively, not only because he generally received a commission or share of the profits on each transaction but also because this might provide the basis for further transactions. Trust could also be created and maintained through existing social networks based on family, regional identity or religion, which not only provided a means to police behaviour by circulating information and imposing sanctions for breaches of trust, but also provided a further sense of shared identity and interests which strengthened these mutual obligations (Trivellato 2009: 21–41, 132–176, 194–233; Grassby 2001: 217–251, 290–296, 300–311). These elements underlay the notable strength of Jewish, Huguenot and other religious networks in this period. Finally, trust

[1] For a survey of this literature see Graham (2013a).

could be created or strengthened through cultural factors, such as friendship, mutual gifting and the maintenance of a "good correspondence" (Trivellato 2009: 177–193, 225–249; Smail 2005: 449). All of these factors converged to make trust a personal or moral quality, built on a sense of faith and shared interests between the actors or parties in any commercial transaction.

It was not until the mid-nineteenth century that commerce and morality began to be thoroughly disentangled, and until then fraud and other financial malfeasance were therefore both criminal offences and moral crimes, since they betrayed the trust that both sides had invested in the relationship (Taylor 2013; Searle 1998; Robb 2012).[2] They undermined, in other words, the culture of credit, trust and moral obligations that Muldrew (1998) and Finn (2003) have shown supported finance across this period. The collapse of the South Sea Bubble in August 1720, for example, was marked by an outpouring of literature that condemned its directors as sinks of moral depravity who were guilty of criminal acts and a wider betrayal of the public trust (Paul 2011: 88–111; Hoppitt 2002; Banner 1998: 41–87; Dickson 1993: 24–34). The directors were therefore placed on trial before a parliamentary committee of secrecy in 1721 and fined large sums for their betrayal of trust as a warning to others (Sperling 1962: 34–36). Commentators such as Archibald Hutcheson drew a direct link between these crimes and other symptoms of social disorder that emerged during the crisis, such as the actions of women, Jews and Catholics, to argue that the nation therefore required wholesale moral regeneration in order to restore its social and moral virtue. He was only the loudest voice in a rich vein of polemic that had been growing in scale since the explosion in financial trading and speculation in the 1690s, which many felt had isolated commerce and finance from its moral and social anchors. Stock-jobbing in particular was seen as a form of unproductive speculation that served no useful economic purpose and aimed only at quick profits, without any real morality or sense of the public good, and Daniel Defoe condemned the entire practice as "a trade founded in fraud, born of deceit, and nourished by trick, cheat, wheedle, forgeries, falsehoods, and all sorts of delusions" (Defoe 1719: 3).

[2]For example, the usury laws restricting levels of interest to 'fair' or morally appropriate rates were only repealed in Britain in 1854.

However, while popular perceptions of finance and morality have been studied in some depth, much less has been written on the mentalities of commercial and financial criminals, and their own sense of morality. Undoubtedly many were irredeemably criminal in nature, but studies of coiners, forgers, poachers and smugglers by Hay and Linbaugh (2011), Frykman (2013), Gaskill (2000) and others has shown that some could isolate themselves from this moral calculus, especially in "social" or victimless crimes. The connection between commerce and morality could also be prised apart by a sense of the public interest, as shown by Yamamoto's groundbreaking study of the tory entrepreneur Sir Humphry Mackworth. Having sunk many thousands of pounds into a mining venture in Wales between 1697 and 1704 that would provide metals for the national economy and livelihoods for local workers, Mackworth saw the venture as a patriotic and philanthropic enterprise as well as a commercial one, and this gave him some degree of comfort as he stole the shareholders' funds to keep it afloat. "Mackworth's religious perception of his own dishonesty therefore exonerates him from the worst charges of rank hypocrisy, and reveals the complex interworking of piety, sin and repentance in a commercial setting", notes Yamamoto, adding that the company was therefore "not simply a vehicle by which Mackworth aspired to do good in the world ... [but also] a place of agony and atonement where he had to acknowledge Satan's temptation and the near impossibility of eradicating sins" (Yamamoto 2011: 824, 829).

This suggests that early-modern financiers lived, like Mackworth, in a complex moral world, in which they were forced to weigh up competing moral impulses and bring them into some acceptable sort of equilibrium. This chapter seeks to push this further by examining the further moral demands made by patriotism and the public service in its most direct form. Whereas Mackworth perhaps only felt this in a diffuse way, this period saw the emergence of a growing class of public officials on whom the moral demands of the public service weighed far more heavily. Building on Brewer (1989) and his study of the British excise as a "Weberian" institution in which officials were isolated from society and subordinated to impartial bureaucratic and patriotic norms, Braddick (2000), Ogborn (1998), Ashworth (2003), and others have argued that this imposed on officials a new moral framework intended to supersede all others. Only by the application of impersonal standards of behaviour and the cultivation of an official mindset or mentality that cut across loyalties to family or patrons could the public be served. Other work by Beckett (1986), Brooks (1987), and Farrell (2016) has argued that this was never wholly achieved, even in the excise, but it nevertheless created a set of expectations that clashed with the realities of public service, in particular the continued reliance of the British fiscal-military state on private contractors. Both the army and the navy used merchants and manufacturers to supply everything from food and fuel to transports and ships, creating what Knight and Wilcox (2010) have described as a "contractor state".[3] How could finance and morality operate in a system that supported impartial and impersonal public conduct but in reality relied on commercial partnerships that were rooted in honour, reputation and personal trust?

My previous work on the Pay Office and its officials in the early-eighteenth century has identified at least two responses among the Paymasters of the Forces and their staff. Charles Fox, who occupied the office between 1702 and 1705 and the start of the War of the Spanish Succession, denied that any tension existed and insisted on a rigid conformity with rules and procedures. This made for accurate accounts but at the expense of the allied army in Flanders, which was starved of funds by this rigid attitude and had to rely on public officials and military officers to bridge the gap with their own credit (Graham 2013??: 80–87). His successor James Brydges likewise saw no contradiction at all between morality and finance, but only because he felt that the public was served best when he acted as a financial entrepreneur. The private cash he advanced to regiments was a "civility" he owed them as a gentlemen, and the "gratifications" that he received from them were merely the marks of civility they in turn owed him (Graham 2015: 126, 214). "Brydges was conscious of the legal and moral objections to his conduct", I have suggested, "but appealed to higher values of friendship and civility, and ... to the benefits that the public service had, from his perspective, received". The diary of Samuel Pepys shows that he was of much the same mind, gratefully accepting the gifts offered to him as secretary of the Navy Board in the 1660s and 1670s but denying that they had clouded his judgement as a public servant (Pool 1966: 37–43; Noonan 1984: 375–380; Knights 2014: 21–27, 32–35). Neither Brydges nor Fox therefore saw any real contradiction between morality,

[3] See also Graham and Walsh (2016).

finance and the public service in the early-eighteenth century, and therefore they had no problems reconciling them all with each other.

These two mentalities though are probably best seen as the two extremes of a very wide continuum of financial morality, and others emerge from a study of their predecessors during the Nine Years War, when financial pressures on the army in the Low Countries eventually became so great that it sometimes came close to collapse. As has already been noted, Richard Hill, increasingly worried continually about his obligations to his country, to his financial contacts and also to God, as the demands of warfare forced to him lie, cheat and deceive in order to raise funds for the army. His spotless reputation was only maintained at the expense of lenders across Flanders whom he tricked into lending him money on unreliable securities. The Pay Office in London faced equally acute dilemmas. To keep up Hill's credit in Flanders and support the public service, it was necessary to maintain the illusion of credit within the Pay Office, even if this meant appearing to sacrifice both morality and the public service to the insatiable personal demands of Richard Jones, first earl of Ranelagh, as Paymaster-General of the Forces. The demands of the public service therefore broke apart the neat overlap between finance and morality, and required public officials to choose between their private and public moral obligations.

2 The Last Temptation of Richard Hill

Between 1692 and 1698 the deputy-paymaster in the Low Countries, responsible for managing the flow of money from Britain to the army, was Richard Hill. Born in 1656, until 1692 he seemed destined for a career in the Church of England, and although he was then side-tracked into the public service he seems to have brought this strong sense of religious calling into his office life. As a diplomat, for example, he risked the precarious alliance against Louis XIV in 1703 and 1704 by pressing the Duke of Savoy to protect the Protestant Vaudois living in Piedmont.[4] The fortune he enjoyed after his retirement from public affairs in 1705 "was all acquired by himself from his employments and his own improvements of it", Arthur Onslow later wrote, "and without any reproach as

[4] Randolph Vigne, 'Hill, Richard (1655/6–1727)', *Oxford Dictionary of National Biography* (Oxford, 2004) (http://www.oxforddnb.com/view/article/13289, accessed 16 March 2017).

to the manner of it that I ever heard of" (Burnett, IV, 310–311). In his survey of the court in 1710, the Jacobite writer John Macky noted that Hill had "a genius for business and ...[was] a gentleman of very clear parts, and affects plainness and simplicity in his dress and conversation ... beloved for his easy access and affable way by those he has business to do with" (Scott 1902: X, 284). Hill therefore maintained his reputation for honour and integrity in the midst of perhaps the most serious financial crisis that the country had faced for several decades, but at great personal cost, since the needs of the public forced him to betray the trust that he owed to his contacts in Flanders.

The unprecedented financial demands of the Nine Years War exhausted established fiscal precedents and demanded a range of expedients to carry the British fiscal-military state up to the Treaty of Ryswick in 1697. The Bank of England was floated in 1694 to help raise funds, and the Land Bank in 1696, and Exchequer Bills were set up to provide further credit (Dickson, 46–59). D. W. Jones (1988) has argued that this coincided with a prolonged commercial downturn and coinage crisis that made it hugely expensive to raise money at home and remit it abroad, since a large part of the silver and gold currency was already disappearing overseas to buy imports. This successively narrowed the options open to Hill, who had brought his strong moral convictions to the post. "His Majesty can hang me when he will if there wants one farthing of his money", he informed the king's military secretary William Blathwayt in November 1692, for example, "and he shall hang me too if ever I make a farthing advantage of it by lending or advancing it to anybody".[5] However, as the supply of cash began to falter in 1693 and 1694 this resolution came under increasing strain, and Hill had to bend or break the rules of the office in order to do what he felt best for the army. The Hanoverian troops in English pay demanded subsidy payments in March 1694, for example, and Hill reluctantly agreed to pay them, "for I have given my word, which I have not yet been poor enough to break".[6] They also demanded about £2000 for arrears from May 1693, and although

[5]Bodleian Library [hereafter BOL], MS Eng Hist d.146 f. 25r–27r, Hill to Blathwayt, 17 November 1692. All dates are 'new style' (i.e. Gregorian calendar) as used in Europe, unless noted.

[6]BOL, MS Eng Hist d.146, f. 193r, 197r, Hill to Blathwayt, 11 March 1694, 1 April 1694.

he had not received any orders Hill paid it to them, "to sweeten the dose ... [and] in ready money, God help me".

His extensive correspondence with Blathwayt, which lasted into 1697 and is currently scattered between the British Library and Bodleian Library, shows that as the supply of cash dried up, Hill was forced into more desperate expedients that put his own sense of morality under further pressure. Despite the successful flotation of the Bank of England in July 1694 it was some time before the effects were felt in Flanders, and Hill complained to Blathwayt that it was becoming impossible to raise the 900,000 fl or £90,000 per month that the army required. (Dickson 1993: 54–56; Jones 1988: 12–15). "I believe there is not so much money unemployed in all these towns here", he wrote in October, "[and] if there were, no man will lend but upon *caution b[o]urg[e]oise* [sic], and such sums as bear no manner of proportion to our necessities".[7] Hill meant that the merchants and bankers in commercial towns such as Amsterdam, Antwerp, Rotterdam, Ghent and Anvers would only lend to him on good security, shaped ultimately by the personal trust that existed between them. Since this did not yet exist, Hill despaired for the army, as he had only about 100,000 fl to hand. "[It] has almost broke my heart or my brain", Hill noted, "[and] I have not the courage to think that 14 days hence we shall have almost 50,000 men in a starving [condition] here, in a country where we have not credit for a turnip". By holding back cash until it was urgently needed and forcing the provisions and forage contractors to use their own credit, Hill was able to eke out his funds, but he complained in November that his money was now totally exhausted. "Half a loaf is better than no bread", he told Blathwayt, "... [but] all my Lord Ranelagh's credit is quite out, and since yesterday morning we begin to live upon providence".[8]

By the winter of 1694 the British army in Flanders was therefore in the midst of a severe financial crisis that risked its entire effectiveness, and Hill experienced moral anguish at the thought that he might be deficient in his duty as a public servant. The situation eased somewhat in 1695 as

[7]British Library [hereafter BL], Additional Manuscripts [hereafter Add. MS] 56241 f. 14r, Blathwayt to Hill, 11 June, 1694; BOL, MS Eng Hist d.146 f. 209r, Hill to Blathwayt, 23 October 1694.

[8]BOL, MS Eng Hist d.146 f. 13r–15r, 17r–19r, 149r–51r, 205r–207r, Hill to Blathwayt, 15 November 1694, 22 November 1694, 11 December 1694, 18 December 1694.

the Bank of England injected a degree of credit and liquidity into the money markets in London and Flanders (Dickson 1993). Unfortunately Hill's letters to Blathwayt for this period do not survive, but Blathwayt's replies throughout the year make it clear that Hill was reaching the limits of his resources. Whereas in the past he had been able to rely on Ranelagh sending out bills of exchange from the remittance contractors in that could be encashed by their correspondents, it was now necessary for Hill to draw his own bills on the Pay Office in London and sell them to merchants or bankers in Flanders who wanted cash in London. "[It is] not to be made use of, except [if] by the delay or disappointment of the intended negotiation it shall become absolutely necessary for the support of the troops", Blathwayt told him in October 1695, "... [but] you have another string to your bow ... and little enough for such a numerous family".[9] The only other option open to Hill was to ration his cash further, which led to accusations of corruption and favouritism from certain officers in the army. "He would have us believe here ... that you make an advantage yourself by your payments", Hill was told in November 1695, for example, "but I well know how scantily we supply you, and am satisfied you don't distribute your payment scantily ... and if there be any distinction made, you that are upon the place can best judge of the necessity of it".[10] The needs of the public therefore required Hill to sacrifice his reputation for impartiality among some parts of the army, but as the financial situation collapsed in 1696 and 1697 his dilemmas became even more troubling.

By the beginning of 1696 the good effects of the Bank of England were dissipating and the credit of the British state began to plunge. Measures were put in hand to raise more money by floating the Land Bank, and by embarking on a contentious reform of the coinage, but meanwhile there were grave difficulties scraping together sufficient money for the army in Flanders. (Dickson 1993: 56–57; Jones 1988: 23, 25). "My credit is broke everywhere", Hill complained to Blathwayt in successive letters, adding that he was some £200,000 in arrears and that the rate of exchange had fallen precipitately against the pound sterling,

[9] BL, Add. MS 56241, Blathwayt to Hill, 18 October 1695

[10] Shropshire Archives [hereafter SA], Hill MS, 112/1/503, Abbott to Hill, 15 November 1695.

and that he would therefore have to draw bills on Ranelagh under protest, "since I have such positive orders and such great necessities, though it goes against my soul to lose so much money of the nation".[11] Even this was not sufficient. He reported in late March that three regiments were on the verge of mutiny, despite his efforts to pay them all equally, and by April he was almost three months in arrears.[12] By July he was in a state approach panic. The exchange had fallen so far that the pound sterling was now worth over twenty percent less than its intrinsic value, and since the contractors in Britain were being paid with tallies or paper instruments at a discount of twenty five percent, "the money I get here costs 47 percent to the King and the kingdom. Is it not time to shut up this issue anyway!"[13] Hill therefore found himself in anguish that the nation was therefore losing almost half the value of whatever money it was able to remit overseas, but he could see no alternative if the army was to be kept in the field.

Hill's main moral dilemma came, however, from the expedients he adopted. Not only was Ranelagh unable to remit him any money, he was also unable to pay the bills for more than £100,000 that he had sold to local bankers to raise cash for the army since 1695. "The bills I have drawn on him all lie protested", Hill told Blathwayt, "...and the only reason why they do not come back is because the person interested knows I am not able to reimburse them".[14] He had nevertheless continued to sell bills to the bankers and merchants, exploiting their trust and deceiving them by offering bills that he knew might never be paid. The anguish created by this contradiction between his patriotic duty and personal morality was almost unbearable. "This breaks my sleep, and I fear a great many more honest men sleep as ill, and that afflicts me to death", he confided to Blathwayt, adding that he might be able to get hold of some money in a few days, "[but then] I shut my doors till I receive some assistance, and will do penance the rest of my days for my own sins and the folly of those who have trusted me so much".[15] As noted above,

[11] BL, Add. MS 9730 f. 11r–19v, Hill to Blathwayt, 1 January 1696, 2 January 1696, 5 January 1696, 12 January 1696, 16 January 1696.

[12] BL, Add. MS 9730 f. 43r-v, 45r-v, 47r, 51r, Hill to Blathwayt, 26 March 1696, 2 April 1696, 6 April 1696, 12 April 1696.

[13] BL, Add. MS 9730 f. 63r–64r, Hill to Blathwayt, 22 July 1696.

[14] Ibid.

[15] Ibid.

he was particularly distraught at the contradiction between his public image as a man of honour and his private deceit, concluding that "I walk about as impudently as other men, but God knows I carry a serpent in my bosom which devours me". Despite this betrayal, his funds were already exhausted—"unless I am assisted from Heaven or from Earth or from Hell I cannot get a schelling more"—and he was only finally bailed out by Ranelagh and the Pay Office in August, who sent him bills for 100,000 fl. Together with some 330,000 fl he borrowed from the paymaster of the Dutch forces, this allowed him to hold out for a few weeks.[16]

By the end of August though his moral anguish returned, since bills for about £50,000 had been returned from London protested for non-payment, and he could not spare the cash to reimburse the holders. "How to repay "em I know not", he told Blathwayt in September, "[and] how to ruin poor men who gave me credit I know less".[17] Neither was he hopeful that enough cash would arrive in time, which would force him to use the same practice again and further deceive the lenders he had already misled. "I am the boldest Britain alive, since I can think of staying here in the condition I am in", he wrote, "... [and] I suspect myself [?capable] of more folly and knavery than I did believe I was." He had to maintain this outward persona as well in order to give the lenders no grounds for suspecting him further, or else avoid them entirely, and this gave him further grounds for embarrassment. "I am going to Anvers, where a hundred people are enquiring for me upon the Exchange", he told Blathwayt the following week, "and from thence I shall have a mind to go to Loo, if I durst".[18] From Anvers he complained that he had been forced to pay out some of his limited remaining cash to keep his reputation afloat, including 20,000 fl to the bread contractors "for a peace offering".[19] By 29 October he was in Brussels waiting for 100,000 fl to arrive from Britain, "without which I dare not return to Anvers or Flanders", but none had come by 1 November and so he was forced to return, projecting confidence once more in order

[16] BL, Add. MS 9730 f. 67r, 69r, Hill to Blathwayt, 8 August 1696, 12 August 1696.

[17] BL, Add. MS 9730 f. 73r, Hill to Blathwayt, 17 September 1696.

[18] BL, Add. MS 9730 f. 73r, Hill to Blathwayt, 17 September 1696.

[19] BL, Add. MS 9730 f. 75–75r, Hill to Blathwayt, 22 October 1696.

to conceal his anguish. "I will venture again to Anvers and thence to Gant [*i.e.* Ghent]", he told Blathwayt, "with a sanguine face, as if I have received a land tax".[20]

The pressures on Hill's resources and reputation only eased in mid-November, when Ranelagh was able to send him some 450,000 fl, but this still left the army about five months in arrears and even in December he was still reluctant to face the creditors he had deceived. "I dare not go back to Anvers, where I owe so much", and he warned Blathwayt on 10 December that, "I have held out to the last extremity longer than I did believe I could".[21] He continued to remain downbeat, complaining two weeks later that British credit remained low because the parliament had not yet taken measures to restore any confidence among bankers in Flanders.[22] "All their bustle to restore credit does just destroy the little which was left", he complained, adding coarsely that "…if I see an act of parliament to restore credit, I shall [also] expect to see one to restore maidenheads". This comment played on existing tropes which linked the capricious and fickle nature of credit with stereotypical female qualities, such as Daniel Defoe's "Lady Credit" in *The Compleat English Tradesman*, in this case conflating credit and virginity and demonstrating the importance of reputation in maintaining both (Backsheider 1981; Sherman 1996: 41–64). There are no further letters between Blathwayt and Hill that demonstrate how Hill dealt with the further financial problems of 1697, as the war wound down, but enough has been presented to demonstrate that the competing and contradictory demands of public finance in this period caused acute moral problems for Hill, since the demands of the public required him to betray the obligations he owed to merchants in Flanders and the personal trust, honour and reputation that had been invested in these relationships.

[20]BL, Add. MS 9730 f. 77r–78r, 79r, Hill to Blathwayt, 29 October 1696, 1 November 1696.

[21]BL, Add. MS 9730 f. 85–86r, 97r–98r, 99r, 104v, Hill to Blathwayt, 15 November 1696, 22 November 1696, 6 December 1696, 10 December 1696.

[22]BL, Add. MS 9730 108r, Hill to Blathwayt, 24 December 1696.

3 Ranelagh and Financial Immorality

Hill's counterpart in London was the deputy-paymaster Mordecai Abbott, who served in the Pay Office between 1694 and 1700 without a single blemish. As a Protestant Nonconformist from Ireland he was technically in breach of the penal laws, but was lauded—even flaunted—after his death in 1700 as one of the few moral exemplars who had "discharged their places with ... integrity, and with unwearied diligence, and a spotless honesty, [and] carried an untainted reputation to their graves" (Wilson 1830: ii, 251). Funeral sermons commended him as "a true Nathanael, who ... might be said to keep himself unspotted from the world, ...for he acted like Joseph in the court of Pharaoh" (Piggott 1700: 76; Harrison 1700: 43–48). How far Abbott in fact faced the same problems as Hill and was forced into similar moral compromises cannot now be seen, since none of his private letters survive. He has in any case largely been overshadowed by Ranelagh, who was dismissed from his post at the Pay Office for corruption and malfeasance in 1703, and has in general been treated as an embodiment of these vices, and accused of sacrificing the public service, his financial responsibilities and his personal standing for his own selfish ends (Sperling 1955: 137; McGrath 2004). Using for the first time Ranelagh's letters to Blathwayt and Hill, which have likewise been scattered among several archives in Britain and America, this section will argue that he actually brought a strong sense of public duty to his post, even if this required him to sacrifice his own reputation to uphold the ultimate interests of the public.

Among the most damning evidence against Ranelagh has been the evidence of the parliamentary commission convened in 1702 to examine his accounts (Cruickshanks et al. 2002: iv, 521–527; Sperling 1962: 136–137; Graham 2013?). One of the commissioners was James Brydges. Their report to parliament in November 1702 charged Ranelagh with a number of crimes. His accounts for the period between 1687 and 1692 were inadequate, and the commissioners complained that he had failed to submit to them the proper ledgers, vouchers and accounts. "Notwithstanding all these difficulties", they had concluded that Ranelagh had illegally taken credit for interest on monies sitting in his account; had accepted paper instruments or tallies from the Exchequer without proper accounting controls; had paid warrants for regiments dated several years after they had been disbanded; had paid them as complete despite the lack of muster rolls confirming this; had discharged himself with vouchers that failed to conform to proper procedure; and had paid over money to officials in the Pay Office acting as agents for himself, or on warrants that he knew were forged (Cobbett, iv, 98–102). The accounts for the period between 1692 and 1702 defied proper auditing, and appeared to have been deliberately confused in order to prevent examination (Cobbett, iv, 125–126). Even a basic examination though seemed to show that Ranelagh had broken the law by failing to keep the proper accounts, and had paid out at least £150,000 "to several persons for several circumstances, and on several occasions without specifying the services or occasions". On 7 December the House of Commons resolved that he was guilty of misappropriation, and on 2 February 1703 he was expelled in disgrace (Cobbett, iv, 125–126).

Ranelagh's correspondence suggests by contrast that his zeal for the public service was genuine, and his rewards far less than the opportunities open to him. He noted to Blathwayt in August 1692, for instance, that his current salary of £10,000 per year "is too great a sum for me to think of, though it may be … I want it sufficiently", and so he proposed to place it in the hands of the king, "to avoid all objection which either the commission of accounts or my brethren of the House of Commons may make against so large a donative".[23] By May 1693 he was on the verge of bankruptcy, and pressed Blathwayt to secure some grants or warrants from the king that would enable him to answer his creditors. "If I miscarry in it I must think of retiring to some sanctuary or other, for the decree against me will certainly be executed as soon as my privilege of parliament [for exemption from arrest for debt] ceases", he noted to Blathwayt, adding that even if the warrant could not immediately be paid to him by the Treasury it would at least keep his creditors quiet and persuade them to accept interest on his debts.[24] The reason for this financial pressure was that whatever cash or credit he could spare was immediately ploughed into the army in order to bridge the gap that was opening up between the army's demands and the Treasury's supply.

As early as June 1692 he had written to Blathwayt that the Lords of the Treasury were falling behind in their payments, adding that he was ready to obey the king's orders "when enabled so to do by the Treasury,

[23] BL, Add. MS 9735 f. 89r-v, Ranelagh to Blathwayt, 5 August 1692 o.s.

[24] BL, Add. MS 56242 f. 19r, 21r, Ranelagh to Blathwayt, 9 May 1693 o.s., 23 May 1693 o.s.

for sure I am till then I cannot pay one farthing, it being well known that I have no money lying idle in my office".[25] Like his predecessor Sir Stephen Fox and successor James Brydges, Ranelagh tried therefore to keep up the flow of cash to the army by feeding his own private credit into the system, advancing money for weeks and then months until the Treasury could find the cash to repay him. For example, in September 1692 he noted that the large consortium of remittance contractors under Sir Joseph Herne had refused to send over some 35,000 rixdollars or £7900 for the Hanoverian troops in Flanders without some guarantee or security for repayment. "I have been forced to engage my own security to Sir Joseph", he told Blathwayt, "... so I am still at stake for the remain[der]", adding that the Treasury had also refused to pay another tranche of funds, "[but] the worst come to the worst, I will use my own credit to pay it, within a month at furthest".[26] In May 1693 he explained to Blathwayt that in order to secure £6000 for the forage contractors he had "pawned my credit to Sir Joseph Herne, the Lords [of the Treasury] having not as yet supplied me with one farthing of that money".[27] As I have argued elsewhere, his counterparts such as Brydges saw this as an important aspect of their public duties, for which they might expect the same reasonable reimbursement as any private contractor risking their own money for the sake of the public (Graham 2015: 95–96, 105, 184–187, 214–215). Ranelagh's actions in 1692 and 1693 suggest that he was desperately trying to balance his duty to the public against his reputation and credit, and the duties he owed to the contractors.

As in Flanders, the Pay Office in London was therefore already under strain as the English financial system began to contract in 1694, though once again not enough correspondence has survived to offer much detail. Ranelagh warned Blathwayt in May and June, for instance, that the arrears owed to Herne and the other contractors had already reached £45,000, making it impossible to supply the troops already on campaign or to clear their outstanding arrears.[28] It was only through the application of direct personal pressure by Ranelagh that Herne had even

[25] BL, Add. MS 56242 f. 9r, 11r, Ranelagh to Blathwayt, 8 April 1692 o.s., 26 April 1692 o.s.; BL, Add. MS 9735 f. 85v, Ranelagh to Blathwayt, 24 June 1692 o.s.

[26] BL, Add. MS 56242 f. 15r-v, Ranelagh to Blathwayt, 16 September 1692 o.s.

[27] BL, Add. MS 56242 f. 21r, Ranelagh to Blathwayt, 23 May 1693 o.s.

[28] BL, Add. MS 56242 f. 27r, 29r, 33r-v, 35r, Ranelagh to Blathwayt, 12 October 1693 o.s., 29 May 1694 o.s., 19 June 1694 o.s., 14 July 1694 o.s.

agreed to remit the last tranche of subsistence, and Ranelagh began to worry that the bills of exchange which Hill had drawn from Flanders would have to be sent back protested for lack of payment, blasting Hill's credit. "The giving you this melancholy account is very uneasy to me", he told Blathwayt, "… [for] I cannot see any present comfort … [and] I am more than a little afflicted to send you so mortifying a prospect".[29] In July he managed to raise a further £5000 for Hill, "and this bill I procured without the assistance of the Lords [of the Treasury]", he told Blathwayt, "but I believe they will enable me to comply with my engagement to them from whom I borrowed it".[30] His own credit and reputation was therefore pledged on behalf of the army but were also reaching their limits, and he warned Hill in October 1694 that "we are at the bottom of all our funds, and should you draw bills and that I shall not be able to pay them here, it will only be a prejudice to the credit of my office … my hands are tied".[31]

Hill's attempts to raise money for the army in 1694 by selling bills to local lenders in Flanders were therefore mirrored in London by frantic efforts to exploit whatever trust was still remaining between Ranelagh and his contacts. He "prevailed" with Herne to supply bills on credit in May and June, for example, by putting off paying the bills that Hill had drawn on him from Flanders.[32] Abbott's letters to Hill in 1695 suggest that by this point the Pay Office was even more reliant on Ranelagh's personal credit and Abbott's reputation as a man of honour to persuade parties in London that their obligations would ultimately be honoured. "Our distress continues upon us", Abbott noted in July 1695, for instance, "… [and] I am labouring hard to pay your small bills, which have run through many hands and would be very prejudicial to go back protested, but at the same time I do what I can in the greater bills".[33] Two months later he warned Hill that it was impossible to find cash, "[and] I believe to gain time you must [?concert] the old trade

[29] BL, Add. MS 562424 f. 31r, Ranelagh to Blathwayt, 15 June 1694 o.s.

[30] BL, Add. MS 56242 f. 39r, Ranelagh to Blathwayt, 27 July 1694 o.s.

[31] BOL, MS Eng Hist d.146, f. 211r, Ranelagh to Hill, 23 October 1694 o.s.

[32] BL, Add. MS 56242 f. 27r, 29r, 31r, 33r, Ranelagh to Blathwayt, 12 October 1693 o.s., 29 May 1694 o.s., 15 June 1694 o.s., 19 June 1694 o.s.

[33] SA, Hill MS, 112/1/486, Abbott to Hill, 17 July 1695 o.s.

of drawing [bills], and how that can afford such a supply ... I cannot see".[34] As in Flanders, the financial pressures on the Pay Office in 1694 and 1695 therefore began to prise apart the links between morality, finance and public service, forcing Ranelagh and Abbott to make hard moral choices about the personal obligations they owed to themselves and others. Was it better, in particular, for Ranelagh to be seen as corrupt and unscrupulous if it reassured his creditors that money could always be found to answer their needs, from his own purse if necessary?

By May 1696, Ranelagh was forced to admit to Blathwayt that "my concerns are in a very distracted condition and are like to continue ere [sic] except His Majesty in his wonted goodness be graciously pleased to assist me". The Treasury had failed to release the necessary money and Ranelagh's own credit was exhausted, "so that I have not only spent the little ready money I had but I have also run myself into a considerable debt".[35] He did not need to mention that for the Paymaster-General of the Forces to be declared bankrupt, pursued by creditors and bailiffs, and eventually arrested and imprisoned like a common debtor, would irretrievably blast the entire credit of the country at a point when the entire financial system seemed on the verge of collapse. He therefore asked Blathwayt to ask the king to grant him some £3000, and his letters appear almost apologetic, in stark contrast to the brazen confidence of his public persona. "Since begging for myself is a very uneasy tack to me, you will I hope forgive me if I employ so good a friend as Mr Blathwayt to move His Majesty on my behalf", he wrote, adding that the sum he proposed would only have a minor impact on the revenue, "[and] I humbly hoped I shall not be looked upon as a bold beggar, especially [?since] I have seldom used the trade, and, if now relieved, am resolved to [?foreswear] it".[36] Blathwayt replied that "His Majesty seemed not a little surprised, believing Your Lordship had been more easy in his

[34] SA, Hill MS, 112/1/492, Abbott to Hill, 14 September 1695 o.s. Abbott added 'we have some hopes that since you have had a successful campaign we shall be able to borrow somewhat considerable upon the credit of the Exchequer in general, and that so we may be helped out till our new Parliament gives us some further credit'.

[35] Baker Library [hereafter BAL], Kress MS, Ranelagh to Blathwayt, 30 June 1696 o.s., 10 July 1696 o.s.

[36] BAL, Kress MS, Ranelagh to Blathwayt, 26 May 1696 o.s.

affairs", pointing to the success of this deception. Ranelagh was almost pathetically grateful for the grant that Blathwayt secured, replying with "my hearty thanks for your kind and obliging solicitation of my private concern" and offering his further humble thanks to the king, "assuring him that if a true and loyal heart and faithful service can deserve his favour I shall never want it".[37]

In the meantime, however, Ranelagh's financial position continued to decline. "I am under very ill circumstances", he repeated at the end of June 1696, "for to support the King's service (which to the utmost of my power I always shall do, as in duty bound) I have accepted all the bills drawn upon me to the value aforementioned, and by my acceptance I am liable to pay every farthing of those bills, or to be arrested and my goods seized for not doing it".[38] He claimed once again that only his parliamentary privilege kept him from arrest for debt. "This melancholy narrative … you will please to lay before the King, with my humble request to him that he will not think any of the misfortunes which now attend his service have proceeded from any neglect of mine", he continued, "for I can neither pay bills drawn upon me nor make remittances thither except [when] enabled by the Lords of the Treasury", adding that "I have engaged my own credit and furnished all that possibly I could get together to support Mr Hill's credit abroad". Hill likewise told Blathwayt that Abbott was doing everything he could to prevent the bills being sent back, by stringing along the agents in London until money could be found.[39] Abbott admitted in May that they were accepting all the bills that Hill could draw, even though they had no cash, and on 11 July he wrote that "we are miserably distressed for money … I have this day been hunting out the several persons in whose hands your bills are and using the best rhetoric I could to prevent their return … but if I cannot be supplied before next post I dread the consequence".[40] The needs of the public service therefore left Ranelagh and Abbott with no option but to mislead the agents in London about the credit of the Pay

[37] BAL, Kress MS, Ranelagh to Blathwayt [undated but circa. July 1696 o.s.] and 10 July 1696 o.s.

[38] BAL, Kress MS, Ranelagh to Blathwayt, 30 June 1696 o.s.

[39] BL, Add. MS 9730 f. 63r–64r, Hill to Blathwayt, 22 July 1696.

[40] SA, Hill MS, 112/1/526, 527, 528, 529, 532, Abbott to Hill, 15 May 1696 o.s., 22 May 1696 o.s., 5 June 1696 o.s., 12 June 1696 o.s., 23 June 1696 o.s. and (for the quotation) Hill MS, 112/1/534, Abbott to Hill, 11 July 1696 o.s.

Office, in the hopes that money would arrive just in time to allow their bills to be paid off.

About £45,000 was finally released in September 1696, but the bulk of it was sent over to Flanders to help Hill pay the current costs of the army, which still left bills worth about £80,000 in circulation and no prospect of further funds. "That which afflicts me most", wrote Abbott, "is that though I send you nothing, yet I cannot get money to pay your bills here, which must inevitably destroy your credit, for if you have not money to pay 'em when they return it cannot be expected you should draw again".[41] Two weeks later he managed to send another £30,000, but admitted that he had been unable to get any more money for the bills "and I do all I can to persuade the people to keep them on this side", adding that the Treasury was trying to find ways to pay off a few bills at a time.[42] By May 1697, this had brought the total down by some £13,000, but Ranelagh was forced to confess that he had only £17,500 to answer the £67,000 that continued in circulation, "[which] are very pressing, and I fear will all go back protested, to the ruin of Mr Hill's credit".[43] Having kept these bills circulating for over a year, by stringing their owners along with vague and unreliable promises of payment, the Pay Office was therefore only rescued by the conclusion of the Treaty of Rijswick in September 1697, which immediately revived public credit and enabled the Treasury to raise enough money to answer the bills.[44] Ranelagh was already able to report to Blathwayt on 27 August that "our credit recovers to a miracle", and at the end of September he promised to send over £200,000 shortly, noting that he had pressed the affair firmly "because I think it is the duty of every good subject to contribute to his utmost to make that great King easy who conduct and courage have so apparently, by God's blessing, given quiet and safety to all Christendom, that he may long and happily live, to enjoy the honour and benefits of it".[45] He also took the opportunity to press for warrant promised in 1693, and long since left in abeyance, to be paid.[46]

[41] SA, Hill MS, 112/1/536, Abbott to Hill, 1 September 1696 o.s.

[42] SA, Hill MS, 112/1/538, Abbott to Hill, 18 September 1696 o.s.

[43] BAL, Kress MS, Ranelagh to Blathwayt, 'On this day sevennight' [undated but c. May 1697 o.s.] and 'Your two warrants' [undated but c. mid-1697 o.s.].

[44] See above n. 22.

[45] BAL, Kress MS, Ranelagh to Blathwayt, 31 August 1697 o.s., 28 September 1697 o.s.

[46] BAL, Kress MS, Ranelagh to Blathwayt, 26 October 1697 o.s.

Ranelagh therefore seems to have accepted or even cultivated his reputation as a man of questionable morals, preferring to be considered solvent than saintly. Having spent much of his own money in order to support the public service, it was important that his own credit remain untarnished, and he therefore systematically misled the public creditors about the state of his own finances as well as those of the Pay Office. His answers to the commissioners of accounts in 1702 were wholly consistent with this reading of his conduct. Despite their best efforts the commissioners were unable to point to very few concrete examples of malfeasance, and Ranelagh pointed out that in many cases he had done more than follow the directions of William III given under the royal warrant and privy seal (Cobbett, iv, 103–126). "He has no power to issue the same but according to establishments, regulations or subsistence and the warrants signed by the Crown or according to the directions of the Lord High Treasurer", he noted to parliament, and had to obey them even if they overrode established practices. The only issue he did not address fully was the claim that he had deliberately confused the accounts in order to conceal his malfeasance, but this was probably because the real reason did not admit of an explanation. By paying sums on account and without proper paperwork, Ranelagh not only concealed the real level of indebtedness within the office from the public but could also borrow money within the office, drawing down the "clearings" used to pay for regimental clothing and using it to keep them fed while they were in the field. As Paymaster of the Forces in 1702 he used much the same behaviour, mingling separate balances in order to keep up the public credit until the money from taxes and loans began to come into the Exchequer (Graham 2015: 70–74).

4 Conclusion

Finance and morality in the early-modern period were therefore highly entangled and interdependent, but existed in an unstable equilibrium that could be prised apart by other factors. The cultivation of personal virtue and integrity was an effective way to build trust between financial parties, but officials in the Pay Office found that, under pressure, this could clash with their duties to the public. Whereas Charles Fox and James Brydges addressed this problem in the early-eighteenth century by embracing mentalities of public service and private conduct that denied that there was any real tension between them, their predecessors in the late seventeenth century agonised far more over these contradictions. As the first part of this chapter showed, Richard Hill found highly distasteful the deceit necessary for his role as a public official, and although he eventually decided that the needs of the public and the war took priority over the fortunes of men who had trusted him, this tension was never fully resolved. His reputation as a public servant of honour and integrity was gained at the expense of others. Ranelagh displayed a different mentality. In public a typical Restoration wit who embraced the moral ambiguities and profitable opportunities offered by his role, in private he emerges as a man of intense loyalty and patriotism, who was ultimately prepared to sacrifice his own wealth and reputation in order to serve the interests of the public, by misleading the world about the credit and solvency of the Pay Office.

Why did the problems of finance, morality and public service generate such varied reactions and mentalities within the Pay Office at the turn of the eighteenth century? Partly this seems down to individual character. Both Charles Fox and Richard Hill were men of very considerable religious conviction which spilled over into the public life, but whereas Fox was relatively rigid and unimaginative, and took office in the wake of Ranelagh's public trial for corruption, Hill perhaps had a stronger sense of the public interest, and by virtue of his position in Flanders was more aware of what would happen to the army if it were not paid. Fox therefore saw no contradiction at all between personal morality, public service and finance, because he was insulated from them, whereas Hill recognised their incompatibility and had to decide which were to be sacrificed in order to support the others. By contrast, both Ranelagh and Brydges felt their religion no less deeply but wore it much more lightly, like Pepys, and were more closely embedded in a Restoration culture where trust and credit were based in honour, obligation, gentility and civility.[47] It was thus easier for Brydges to treat his "gratifications" as mere tokens of appreciation, especially because he also served the interests of Marlborough as the embodiment of the national interest, or for Ranelagh to cultivate the reputation of an extravagant and corrupt spendthrift who was always flush with cash. Underlying this though was a loyalty to the interests of king and country, best exemplified by his touching letter to Blathwayt in May 1695 that "I will solicit here to the best of my skill; and so much pray let His Majesty know, with my humble duty, which shall never fail him whilst old Ranelagh live".[48]

[47] For Brydges, see Graham (2015: 95–96, 105, 184–187, 214–215).

[48] BL, Add MS 56242 f. 50r, Ranelagh to Blathwayt, 24 May 1695 o.s.

Examining the mindsets or mentalities of officials in the Pay Office in this period can therefore show that public service imposed its own moral demands that might either reinforce, or clash with, the moral demands created by early modern finance. The result was a spectrum of individual responses, which varied depending on the weight that these officials gave to particular demands. It was also something specific to the early-modern period, an era falling roughly between the 1550s and 1850s. Although there had always been an expectation that public officials would carry out their duties impartially and impersonally, without regard for personal considerations of honour and reputation, this expectation arguably increased in England during this period as successive waves of political reform strengthened the sense of national interest (Brooks 1987; Beckett 1986; Farrell 2016). At the same time, although expectations of morality are still not absent from finance and commerce even in the present day, it was only by the 1850s that the two began to be uncoupled, in a large part through the depersonalisation created by the proliferation of the joint-stock company (Trivellato 2009; Grassby 2001). In the 1690s, early-modern England was therefore in the midst of a long process of transformation in which the tensions between the private moralities of finance and public moralities of patriotism were particularly marked, forcing public officials such as Hill and Ranelagh to confront their own war within.

Acknowledgements I am indebted to Hannah Smith, Stephen Conway, David Parrott, Guy Rowlands and others for their comments on this chapter, and the original research on which it was based. I am grateful to the Bodleian Library, Oxford, and the Baker Library, Harvard, MA, for permission to cite material. The research for this chapter was funded by a Doctoral Scheme Award from the Arts and Humanities Research Council, and it was written up during an Early Career Fellowship supported by the Leverhulme Trust and University College London.

References

Ashworth, W.J. 2003. *Customs and Excise: Trade, Production and Consumption in England 1640–1845*. Oxford: Oxford University Press.

Backscheider, P. 1981. Defoe's Lady Credit. *Huntington Library Quarterly* 44: 89–100.

Banner, S. 1998. *Anglo-American Securities Regulation: Cultural and Political Roots, 1690–1860*. Cambridge: Cambridge University Press.

Beckett, J.V. 1986. Land Tax Administration at the Local Level 1693–1798. In *Land and Property: The English Land Tax 1692–1832*, ed. Michael Turner and Dennis Richard Mills, 161–179. New York: St. Martins Press.

Braddick, M.J. 2000. *State Formation in Early Modern England, c. 1500–1700.* Cambridge: Cambridge University Press.

Brewer, J. 1989. *The Sinews of Power: War, Money and the English State, 1688–1783.* London: Routledge.

Brooks, C. 1987. Interest, Patronage and Professionalism: John, 1st Baron Ashburnham, Hastings, and the Revenue Service. *Southern History* 9: 51–66.

Burnet, G. 1724–1734. *Bishop Burnet's History of His Own Time.* London: Thomas Ward.

Cobbett, W. (ed.). 1806–1820. *Parliamentary History of England*, vol. 36. London: T. Curzon Hansard.

Cruickshanks, E., S. Handley, and D. Hayton (eds.). 2002. *House of Commons, 1690–1715.* Cambridge: Cambridge University Press.

Defoe, D. 1719. *An Anatomy of Exchange-Alley; Or, a System of Stock-Jobbing Proving That Scandalous Trade, as It Is Now Carried On, to Be Knavish in Its Private Practice and Treason in Its Public.* London: E. Smith.

Dickson, P.G.M. 1993. *The Financial Revolution in England: A Study in the Development of Public Credit, 1688–1756.* 2nd ed. Aldershot: Gregg Revivals.

Farrell, W. 2016. The Silk Interest and the Fiscal-Military States. In *The British Fiscal-Military States, 1660–c. 1783*, ed. A. Graham and P. Walsh, 113–130. Routledge: Abingdon.

Finn, M. 2003. *The Character of Credit: Personal Debt in English Culture, 1740–1914.* Cambridge: Cambridge University Press.

Frykman, N. 2013. Pirates and Smugglers: Political Economy in the Red Atlantic. In *Mercantilism Reimagined: Political Economy in Early Modern Britain and Its Empire*, ed. Philip J. Stern and C. Wennerlind, 218–234. Oxford: Oxford University Press.

Gaskill, M. 2000. *Crime and Mentalities in Early Modern England.* Cambridge: Cambridge University Press.

Graham, A. 2013a. Review Article: Mercantile Networks in the Early Modern World. *Historical Journal* 56: 279–295.

Graham, A. 2013b. Auditing Leviathan: Corruption and State Formation in Early Eighteenth-Century Britain. *English Historical Review* 528: 806–838.

Graham, A. 2015. *Corruption, Party, and Government in Britain, 1702–1713.* Oxford: Oxford University Press.

Graham, A., and P. Walsh (eds.). 2016. Introduction. In *The British Fiscal-Military States, 1660–c.1783*, ed. A. Graham and P. Walsh, 1–21. Routledge: Abingdon.

Grassby, R. 2001. *Kinship and Capitalism: Marriage, Family, and Business in the English Speaking World, 1580–1740.* Cambridge: Cambridge University Press.

Harrison, T. 1700. *A Funeral Sermon on Mordecai Abbott Esq*. London: D. Brown & A. Bell.
Hay, D., and P. Linbaugh. 2011. *Albion's Fatal Tree: Crime and Society in Eighteenth-Century England*, 2nd ed. London: Verso.
Hoppit, J. 2002. The Myths of the South Sea Bubble. *Transactions of the Royal Historical Society* 12: 159–165.
Jones, D.W. 1988. *War and Economy in the Age of William III and Marlborough*. Oxford and New York: B. Blackwell.
Knight, R., and M. Wilcox. 2010. *Sustaining the Fleet, 1793–1815: War, the British Navy and the Contractor State*. Woodbridge: Boydell Press.
Knights, M. 2014. Samuel Pepys and Corruption. *Parliamentary History* 33: 21–35.
McGrath, C.I. 2004. Jones, Richard, Earl of Ranelagh (1641–1712). In *Oxford Dictionary of National Biography*. Oxford: Oxford University Press.
Muldrew, C. 1998. *The Economy of Obligation: The Culture of Credit and Social Relations in Early Modern England*. London: Palgrave Macmillan.
Noonan, J.T. 1984. *Bribes: The Intellectual History of a Moral Idea*. New York: Macmillan.
Ogborn, M. 1998. *Spaces of Modernity: London's Geographies, 1680–1780*. New York and London: The Guilford Press.
Paul, H. 2011. *The South Sea Bubble: An Economic History of Its Origins and Consequences*. London: Routledge.
Piggott, J. 1700. *A Funeral Sermon Upon the Said Occasion of the Death of Mordecai Abbott Esq*. London: Dan Brown, A. Bell, E. Tracy, and M. Fabian.
Pool, B. 1966. *Navy Board Contracts, 1660–1832: Contract Administration Under the Navy Board*. London: Archon Books.
Robb, G. 2012. *White-Collar Crime in Modern England: Financial Fraud and Business Morality, 1845–1929*. Cambridge: Cambridge University Press.
Scott, T. (ed.). 1902. *The Prose Works of Jonathan Swift, D.D.* London: G. Bell & Sons.
Searle, G.R. 1998. *Morality and the Market in Victorian Britain*. Oxford: Oxford University Press.
Sherman, S. 1996. *Finance and Fictionality in the Early Eighteenth Century: Accounting for Defoe*. Cambridge: Cambridge University Press.
Smail, J. 2005. Credit, Risk, and Honor in Eighteenth-Century Commerce. *Journal of British Studies* 44 (3): 439–456.
Sperling, J. 1955. Godolphin and the Organization of Public Credit, 1702 to 1710. Unpublished PhD thesis, University of Cambridge.
Sperling, J. 1962. *The South Sea Company: An Historical Essay and Bibliographical Finding List*. Boston: Kress Library of Business and Economica.

Taylor, J. 2013. *Boardroom Scandal: The Criminalisation of Company Fraud in Nineteenth-Century Britain*. Oxford: Oxford University Press.
Trivellato, F. 2009. *The Familiarity of Strangers: The Sephardic Diaspora, Livorno, and Cross-Cultural Trade in the Early Modern Period*. New Haven: Yale University Press.
Wilson, W. 1830. *Memoirs of the Life and Times of Daniel De Foe*. 3 vols. London: Hurst, Chance, and Co.
Yamamoto, K. 2011. Piety, Profit and Public Service in the Financial Revolution. *English Historical Review* 521: 806–834.

CHAPTER 4

The Spanish Monarchy and Financier Fraud During the Early Eighteenth Century: A Morality of Favours and Negotiation

Anne Dubet

Historians of fraud under the Old Regime often come up against this apparent contradiction: the coexistence between rigorous norms, a judicial apparatus seemingly created for their application, and corrupt practices. The contradiction can be partly resolved by adopting an approach to fraud mindful of the reasons why, according to the policymakers of the Old Regime, fraudulent acts were reprehensible, and of the objectives in persecuting those guilty of fraud. An examination of the policies put in place during the reign of the eighteenth-century Spanish Bourbon King, Philip V, to limit fraud associated with the handling of his monies provides an example. The affirmation of the king's authority is expressed in the changing relations that he forged with his agents and creditors. However, these relations remained regulated by the reciprocal gift,

A. Dubet (✉)
University of Auvergne, Clermont-Ferrand, France
e-mail: Anne.dubet@uca.fr

J. Félix and A. Dubet (eds.), *The War Within*,
Palgrave Studies in the History of Finance,
https://doi.org/10.1007/978-3-319-98050-8_4

whereby those who handled the king's money competently were entitled to expect legitimate rewards from the sovereign and his creditors.

1 Good and Bad Intentions: A Casuistry of Corruption

The morality of fraud barely changed between the seventeenth Century and the reign of Philip V. Historians of law specialising in modern Iberian monarchies have taught us much about its content, offering us keys to the interpretation of judicial procedures at the time. Clavero (1991, 1996), Hespanha (1993), Vallejo (1998), and Garriga (2006) have highlighted the pre-eminence of right over positive law. This right rests on a conception of equity compatible with privilege and inequality amongst groups or individuals. Respect for right must be the prime objective of judges: their mission is less to apply written norms literally than to re-establish social harmony as confirmed by the study of judicial practices (Garnot 1996; Mantecón 1998). In these circumstances, the non-application of a sanction designed for the fraudulent act is not necessarily synonymous with the inefficiency of the judicial apparatus. Political history specialists confirm this. For instance, Herzog (2004) analyses the investigations undergone by the magistrates of certain American tribunals of the King of Spain in eighteenth century at the end of their remit and the ceremonial accompanying these: the objective is not so much to sanction corrupt judges as to demonstrate royal justice in action. Peytavin (2003), in a study of 'general visits' of the Italian territories of the monarchy in sixteenth and seventeenth century, comes to similar conclusions.

The second contribution of the historians of law concerns the criteria for distinguishing corruption from virtue. The analysis is based on a study of the doctrinal texts of Spanish jurists and theologians, sometimes widely disseminated in Europe, as well as on compilations of laws, essentially those of the sixteenth and seventeenth centuries. These historians show that the obligations of the men of the Old Regime were governed not only by the entitlement to justice but also, and above all, by love or its visible manifestations, friendship and charity. Clavero demonstrates this through usury, one of the criteria of fraud in the domain of finances. Lending money is an act of charity or friendship. The loan cannot be venal if lender and borrower wish to remain virtuous. Commutative justice (that which relates to contracts) does not therefore authorise the excess paid at the time of reimbursement unless it is a question of an indemnity designed to restore equality between the value received and that which is reimbursed, an indemnity known as *interesse*. This happens if there is a difference of 'estimation' between the cash received and that which is reimbursed, legal expenses, a loss of profit or a cost emerge clearly. The restriction is entirely relative: the skill with which the sixteenth-century Spanish theologians thus justify the exchanges between merchants involved in the American trade is well known (Cavillac 1983). In the other cases, to pay (and make others pay) for the act of lending is as blameworthy as paying (and making others pay) for love, the churchmen equating usury with prostitution. However, in the case of a money loan, since love creates obligations, it is legitimate, indeed desirable, to reward the service rendered with another act showing gratitude—a gift made voluntarily by the borrower and received by the creditor as such, not as the price of the loan. This gift may be a monetary one. Thus, in cases where the sum given back is greater than that which was received, if it is not a question of an indemnity, the legitimate or illegitimate nature of the excess price paid depends solely on the intentions of lender and borrower. The one may sin (if his intentions are mercenary) whereas the other would be sinless (Clavero 1991).

Garriga describes the same logic in the magistrates' way of thinking. The judge must be impartial, but a present given to a judge without any intention of buying his sentence and received as such, as a gratuitous gift, is legitimate. The only reason which ought to prompt honest judges to refuse it is that witnesses and those on trial might mistake the judges' intentions (Garriga 2006). This explains the reasoning of moralists, jurists and officials accused of corruption, concerning the distinctions to be laid down on the basis of the value of the gift and its timing (before or after the judge's verdict): it is not the criteria of fraud that are being put forward here, but indications which provide a clue to the intentions of the magistrates and those on trial, in the absence of a confessor or an inquisitor to scrutinise those intentions. Researchers' interest in the culture of the participants here demands a reinterpretation of the regulations and of positive law. In my opinion, it enables one to understand why exacting norms go hand in hand with law courts dispensing few penalties. One and the same practice may be reprehensible or not, according to the intentions of the participants, and these intentions, deep-seated, are difficult to detect.

This grid of interpretation can readily be applied to the domain of finances. As is already known, in Spain, it was commonplace from sixteenth century onwards to remunerate the loans made by large-scale creditors (the *asentistas*) by offering them *adehalas*, gratuitous gifts carefully separated from the price of the exchange and from the *interesse* in their contracts (Ruiz Martín 1975; Sanz Ayán 2013). Certain government officials highlighted these non-juridical obligations necessary to regulate the association between the King and the monied men to improve the state of finances. Thus, the Duke of Lerme, the favourite of Philip III, openly cultivated the friendship of the most influential Genoese (García García 1996). In the event of embezzlement, existing criteria for dealing with corrupt judges applied to the office holders of the monarchy. Malaprade demonstrates this in the case of the public prosecutor Jurado, who in 1643 defended himself against a charge of having forced Portuguese bankers to give him presents: the latter were allegedly given voluntarily and according to the custom of the commission of which he was a member; apart from which, living in modest circumstances, he would not, he said, be motivated by greed (Malaprade 2018). At the end of the day, accounting officials were not automatically guilty if they used the money entrusted to them by the king for their own affairs or these of their guarantors. Here also, good and bad intentions in the part of the participants enable a line to be drawn between misappropriation of public funds and then mere retention. This is demonstrated in the appraisal drawn up by Waquet of the opinions of seventeenth- and eighteenth-century European theologians and jurists concerning the issue. For these authors, often Spanish, there is not a shadow of doubt that the treasurer who takes money from the funds entrusted to him by the king, with the intention of not giving it back, lays himself open to the most serious penalties, for theft or embezzlement. The case of the official who withdraws money while manifestly intending to give it back the instant the king needs is different. The fault is slight, nothing at all in the view of the most indulgent. Some add that the practice is inevitable when treasurers and depositors are accountable to royal funds with their own goods and those of their guarantors (Waquet 1984). That is the argument put forward by a late seventeenth-century Genoese financier in order to refute a project aimed at confiding the monarchy's loan funds to remunerated administrators: Philip II, he observed, would subject his money to a huge risk because, in the present situation, 'if the receivers provide guarantors, it is in proportion to the usefulness of the money that they derive from delaying payments. And it is well known that with this gain they help their guarantors, and sometimes even pay the latter's guarantees' (Dubet 2000). For sure, the author of the argument is serving his own interests here, but he presents these arguments unvarnished to the king as if it were a legitimate reason. Although, according to Waquet, the agents lie to others or to themselves, it is noteworthy that they all state the same reasons. Thus, the most rigorous theorists are those who, considering the actions of judges or financiers, attribute to them dishonest intentions. But all the theologians and jurists studied admits that the agents, if their intentions were pure (neither mercenary no greedy), would have nothing with which to reproach themselves before God on account of these same actions.

Things hardly changed at the beginning of the eighteenth century. Embezzlement still depended on the intentions of the perpetrators. In Florence, the *provveditore* Gondi kept a register of gifts received, marks of the gratitude of those he governed and of his prestige (Waquet 1984). During the War of the Spanish Succession, in order to avoid the accusation of embezzlement, the paymaster of the British forces on the Continent endeavoured to make believe that the commissions he received to pay the expenses assigned to his fund were the gifts of friends (Graham 2013). In Spain, Alejandro de Vega, knowledgeable about financial institutions—he was employed at the General Treasury then at the Secretariat of Finances—bears witness that, up to 1713, the tax farmers dealing with Castilian contributions received assignations on their funds. By exacting commissions from the king's creditors in order to pay them their due, the tax farmers were obliging them to pay for what ought to have been free (Dubet 2015a). The regulations of the General War Treasury which was created in 1703 forbade army treasurers from exacting gifts from soldiers or deceiving them by buying up on the cheap their *certificaciones de alcances*, i.e. certificates of debt. The inspectors of those same treasurers were not allowed to extort from bearers of assignations fees for which no provision had been made, which would have meant associating deceit with an abuse of power. Forbidding spontaneous gifts seems to have been less urgent. It is really the extortion of a gift or deceit that constituted the fault. That is why the abuse seemed more conspicuous when the victims were defenceless: those on low incomes, soldiers, widows. That said, when it was the king (or, with the king's agreement, his minister) negotiating a discount with a creditor, the context straightaway became that of gratuitous subsidies for a monarch who could not possibly be greedy. The confessor of the queen

Isabelle Farnese, second wife of Philip V, described the rules of the game in 1726. Verdes Montenegro, former Finance Minister (*Ministro de Hacienda*), was suspected of having granted the payment of a longstanding debt to the Elector of Bavaria in return for a discount. According to the confessor, the transaction would have been lawful if the king had been responsible for it (Dubet 2015b). Thus, the king can lay claim to the (gratuitous) reward for his bounty. As for his agents, it is acceptable for them to strike up frequently unequal relations of reciprocity—those of friendship and clientage—with the rest of his subjects, starting with his creditors.

Stealing the king's money was just as blameworthy as in the previous century. The financiers were still suspected of being usurers—'bloodsuckers of the poor'—and indeed, thieves. Thus Vega believed that the suppliers of provisions for the army and navy and the other contractors overestimated the prices of their supplies, thereby exceeding the fair price permitted by scholasticism. Certain tax farmers did likewise when, in order to make a local payment in the king's name, they claimed excessive transport costs (*conducción*); the same persons or others provided bills of exchange at inflated rates. That said, if some gains were forbidden, others were authorised. The *adehalas* mentioned above—gratuitous rewards given to businessmen—continued to figure in contracts arranged with the king. All of the skills of a good minister of finances, according to Vega, consisted in reserving them for deserving businessmen by proportioning them to their merit (Dubet 2015a). As for retention of money, it seemed hardly culpable in itself when unaccompanied by aggravating circumstances. According to the *Dictionnaire des Finances* (1727), an accounting official retains when he withholds money 'to the detriment of the king or of the person to whom it belongs'. The definition given for France seems to have been applicable in Spain. This criterion was thus at work in the case brought in 1724–1727 against Fernando Verdes Montenegro, General Treasurer of the king (1721–1724) then Minister of Finances (1724). He was accused of an omission in registering receipts that would have allowed him to make personal use of the funds. It was the deceit (the voluntary omission) which rendered the practice blameworthy: the prosecutor spelt out aggravating circumstances in order to rend enough substance to the charge—the delay in payments to troops, employees of the royal court, and chief army suppliers. There was also the misappropriation of funds: as treasurer, Verdes Montenegro had allegedly reversed the order of priority of payments that he was required to make, instead of implementing the Minister's (index: Minister of Finances) decision (Dubet 2015b). A more serious suspicion hung over those responsible for royal funds: they loaned to the King, at interest, the money withdrawn (by retention) from their funds. This preoccupation is well described by Legay (2011) in the case of eighteenth-century French finances. In Spain, Vega, shares it. It is less the retention pure and simple than the added deceit which is at stake here. It is well known that one of the chief meanings of the word 'fraud' is, precisely, deceit.

According to the elements of doctrine already described, accounting officials, royal inspectors, tax farmers, suppliers of the armed forces and contractors defraud when they deceive (which is almost a pleonasm), when they abuse their power in a way perceived as such by their victims and when they are greedy or usurious(index: usury). However, the handling of royal funds is compatible with the benefactions from royal creditors and the monarch, in so far as the financial interests are legitimate ('interesse') and the gifts are not extorted by threat or deceit. The question which arises at this point is to know whether the moral imperative of the unsolicited gift was universally shared by Catholic society at the time, as Clavero thinks, and until when, or whether it is an aristocratic ethic, as Waquet suggests in his study of eighteenth-century Florentine corruption. It would also be useful to examine what the situation is in the modern protestant world. Whatever the case, the variety of potential scenarios outlined in early-eighteenth century Spain theoretically limit the possibilities of corruption but do not go against the lies of the guilty or the false accusation of their enemies. That variety also obliges us to question above all the real objectives of the would-be reformers of corruption, so as not to mistake the meaning and effectiveness of their policy.

2 Fresh Compromises with the 'gens d'affaires', or Monied Men

In what ways did Philip V, the first Bourbon King of Spain (1700–1746), inaugurate a new policy regarding fraud? The syntheses which have focused on his reign since the fifth centenary of his accession, in 2000, have ceased to contrast the order established by the Bourbons with the disorder and corruption of the Hapsburgs who ruled Spain until 1700. Nevertheless, a positive definition is wanted of political and financial strategy in the monarch's entourage, especially since it was perhaps multifaceted. As has been demonstrated for taxation and trade, the views of his most trusted ministers were varied, and even contradictory. Thus, the decisions successively implemented under Philip V's reign do not obey a clear and progressive programme (Delgado Barrado 2007; Dubet 2018). That said, his trusted ministers, when they rose above their differences, were in agreement that the king and those closest to him (ministers, queen, courtiers) be given a personal role in the direction of affairs that under Charles II, his predecessor suspected of allowing his prerogatives to be usurped by Councils and influential ministers (Dedieu 2010; Vázquez Gestal 2013).

The change concerned decision-making in the first place. The businessmen were not the only men capable of fraud. One of the characteristics of this reign was the effect made to correct what were regarded as abuses by officials deemed too autonomous, to the point where they were usurping a royal prerogative. Those are the terms of Jean Orry, an unofficial financial advisor to Philip V up to 1706 and from 1713–1714. He focused on the royal Councils which organised venality of offices and had their own treasuries. As for the commanding officers of the army, they chose the lower ranking officers. The heads of royal households and stables were, de facto, independent as regards expenditure and the choice of the employees. The decisions of one and another of these persons, ratified too automatically by the king, led to expenditure which he could not control. On top of all this, there was collusion in the army between officers and suppliers. To boot, lack of coordination between those responsible for the different kinds of expenditure resulted in a large number of accounting officials receiving contradictory orders. According to Orry, the remedies were chiefly political. It was a question of reinforcing the private channel (*vía reservada*) which consisted in obliging local officials to address themselves to the king via a new Secretary of War Dispatches (*Secretario del Despacho de la Guerra* created in September 1703), and then of Finances and War (*Secretario del despacho de Guerra y Hacienda,* July 1705), in order to circumvent the Councils. The Secretary, who dispatched affairs arriving by this channel privately with the king, gave orders in the latter's name, a solution which supposedly provided against usurpation of the king's powers by the Councils and the high-ranking military officers. He was additionally responsible for the financial affairs within his remit, such as the contracts for army supplies, thus assuring both the king and the latter's creditors that decisions taken would be put into effect. The new General Treasurer for War was placed under the king's exclusive orders. The Secretary implemented the sale of titles of nobility, the robes of knights of the military orders and other honours, as well as the military and civil offices, with the collaboration of trusted financiers like Juan de Goyeneche. In the army there came about an extra indirect form of control, perhaps suggested by the businessmen, to prevent extortionate demands from officers to suppliers (de Castro 2004; Andújar Castillo 2000, 2004, 2008; Teijeiro de la Rosa 2002; Dubet 2009). As for the Councils, parts of their governmental domain was entrusted to the new Secretary and, in 1717–1718, some were relieved of their individual treasuries. The discontent of the military and the Councils served to those wielding power to be a good indication of the success of the reform. They made do with it, uncertain as they were in 1705 about estimated war expenditures for 1704. In contrast, the reform of the royal households ran into resistance from their heads, members of the upper nobility who in the 1730s were still reticent about the idea of adopting 'regulations' which stipulated in advance the details of their annual expenditure (Gómez Centurión and Sánchez Belén 1998; Dubet 2009, 2017).

This reforming process which, in Orry's terms, was aimed at bolstering some effective substance to the king's authority where financial matters were concerned was not unambiguous. Since the reform of the 'Nueva Planta' in 1713–1714, which created several Secretaries of Dispatches in charge of separate departments, the advocates of collegial management of finances by the Secretaries opposed those who, like the Ministers of Finances Campoflorido (1717–1726), Patiño (1726–1736), Torrenueva (1736–1739), Iturralde (1739), Campillo (1741–1743) or Ensenada (1743–1754), wanted the Secretary of Finances to be solely responsible for the distribution of funds. Others, who were particularly vocal during the reign of Louis I in 1724,[1] accused the Secretaries of Dispatches of despotism and wished to restore the administration of finances to the various royal Councils, especially that of Castile. However, like the supporters of the Secretaries of Dispatches, they wanted this administration placed in the hands of the Councils to be more 'executive' than in the seventeenth century: which meant that the decisions taken had to be effectively implemented, with the king

[1] Following the abdication of Philip V on 10 January 1724, his son Louis reigned until his death at the end of August. Philippe was then best rated by his entry return to the throne.

no longer willing to accept the mere 'obedience' of his subjects. The conflict over spheres of power which pitted the head Secretary of War and Finances Dispatches instituted in 1703–1705 against the Councils gave way, once several Secretaries had being created in 1714, to tension between the Secretary of Finances and the most spendthrift of his colleagues, those of the Navy and War departments, when those posts were given to different persons.[2] The argument of Campoflorido, Torrenueva and Iturralde is that their colleagues embarked on excessive and sometimes illegitimate expenditure, acting in collusion with fraud on the part of their subordinates or incapable of comprehending the machinations of the latter. The argument is reversible: in 1724, at the time when a novel form of multiple Councils was trialled, the promoters of collegiality were thinking in terms of reciprocal control of the Councils and of the Secretaries of Dispatches who would be subordinated to these Councils; in 1740, a *junta* of finances was formed in which the Secretaries for Finances and for War, the heads of royal households and the lieutenants-general of the Navy were supposed to negotiate their respective budgets (Andújar Castillo 2005; Dubet 2015b, 2017).

In fact, if the struggle against fraud was a recurrent justification for projects discussed or implemented, it was not the greater or lesser effectiveness of rival projects to prevent fraud—which no one quantified—that determined the monarch's choices. The figure of the Minister of Finances responsible for almost all the distribution of finances prevailed for political reasons, not without conflicts. In October 1726, Patiño managed to become the only minister allowed to give orders to the General Treasurer, in its capacity as Secretary of Finances, and he also occupied the Secretariats for the Navy and Indies (1726) and War (1733). Royal support is explicable by his ability to put an end to several months of intense tension at court by his emerging as leader of the dominant faction, as well as by his determination to serve the queen's interests in Italy (Guerrero Elecalde 2012; Vázquez Gestal 2013). The solution adopted was held from stable, doubtless because of the support of several business establishments, which allowed Patiño to increase expenditure without discrediting the General Treasury (Dubet 2017), and perhaps also because of Patiño's ability to quell his opponents

[2] In 1726, Jose Patiño received the two departments of Finances, both the Indies and the Navy, plus, in 1733, War. There was thus no conflict between these different ministers until his death in 1736.

(Teofanes Egido 2002; Téllez Alarcía 2015). It was nevertheless called into question after his death (November 1736), when his three successors (Torrenueva, Iturralde and, once again, Verdes Montenegro) came up against Ministers for the Navy and War and heads of royal households eager to regain financial independence. In February 1741, Campillo obtained the same ministries as Patiño, on the grounds that the *junta* of finances of 1740, far from forcing the extravagant Ministers to compromise with the Minister of Finances, was so divided that no decision on expenditure was taken. He also won over the queen, by presenting himself as an expert in the Italian domain at the moment of financing fresh campaigns.[3] From his ministry onwards, the Finance Minister's control over the entire 'distribution' of royal funds was hardly ever questioned again (Torres Sánchez 2012).

The other aspect of reform concerned tax collection operations and the uses to which expenditure was put. The potential for fraud on the part of the businessmen in this area disturbed those in power. We have seen that the latter were inclined to suspect the former of usury, abuse of power, omission in registering receipts and duplication that could mask embezzlement. But for all that, the solutions adopted during the first half of this century were not aimed at ousting them from the administration of royal finances, but in settling with the best of them on compromises to guarantee them benefits likely to make them reliable, provided they renounced other benefits. Such was Orry's intention in his 1702 discourse on the customs tax farms. In his opinion, the reason for fraud was that the tax farming contracts were short in duration and caused rivalry between tax farmers, driven to lower tax rates without royal backing, and indeed to traffic with the *methedores*, smugglers who introduced merchandise clandestinely into the country. The solution that Orry commended was not state management but a single large tax farm incorporating all the customs duties and ensuring a steady income for the person in charge of it (Dubet 2009). His arguments were repeated to justify the reform that he adopted in 1714: these taxes were combined into a single unit, the 'Rentas Generales' (general revenues), confided to the administration 'by a single hand' of a junta partly composed of businessmen. At the same time all the funds were placed in the hands of a General Treasurer of the 'Rentas Generales'. According to Campoflorido, a party

[3]This was how Astraudi, who had formerly been indebted to Campillo, construed the situation in 1776. Rodríguez Villa 1882, Chapters 8 and 9.

to the *Nueva Planta* reforms, the choice of state management was not attributable to the conviction that leasing of tax farms was more open to fraud or yielded less—he observed the opposite in 1716. It had been dictated by the nature of most of the customs duties, easy to levy on a daily basis and with a high overall yield. The most difficult to collect, on the contrary, had to be left to the skill of the tax farmers (Dubet 2015b). The other great innovation of 1713–1714, the creation of provincial revenues ('Rentas Provinciales'), consisted in regrouping the different contributions of the Castilian provinces in a singular tax farming contract per province. This initiative came from the businessmen who had won the king's favour, Navarrians Juan de Goyeneche, Juan Bautista de Iturralde and their customary associates. In the short-term, the aim was to reimburse them for the provision of army supplies that they had undertaken at the end of the war (Aquerreta 2001). Several justifications were given for the operation, such as the better yield of taxes (evaluated by Orry) and the fact that the tax farmers accorded credit to the King, as Campoflorido records. But it is the third reason that concerns us. According to Campoflorido, the big tax farmers established in 1714 did less harm to the poorest taxpayers that the local oligarchies to whom recourse had to be to collect provincial revenues by the state management method. The tax farmers were easier to control—by means of the Finances Council, of which Campoflorido was then Governor—than the local potentates whose intrigues were concealed by the Council of Castile (Delgado Barrado 2007; Dubet 2015b). In other words, they ought to have been less abuse and fraud in this quarter.

As regards the army suppliers, the choices made in the matter were of the same order. Orry was keen on concentration right from the War of Succession. This is the policy followed in general for the contracts to supply provisions to the land and sea forces—one single contract in each case for the whole 'continent' of Spain. The monarchy therefore always reserves the possibility of arousing competition between the businessman, modifying the nature of the privileges granted to the suppliers, and even returning temporarily to state management system. It thus preserved control over the 'rules of the game' (Torres Sánchez 2002, 2013). State management was, however, a flawed solution: Campoflorido and Vega believed that it lent itself to fraud just as much as contracts with supply enterprises. In short, the businessmen were mistrusted for their inclination towards fraud, but their services, especially their credit, had to be secured. That is why for the two men quoted but also for Orry, Patiño, Iturralde, Campillo or Ensenada, the perfect Minister of Finances had to be above all 'intelligent in financial matters', able to enter into discussions with the businessmen so as to inspire confidence in them but also to detect their possible fraud (Dubet 2015c).

This policy of compromise with trusted businessmen emerged particularly clearly in the domain of keeping control over royal funds. The most significant reform here was the creation of a General Treasury for War (*Tesorero Mayor de Guerra*) in 1703, then 1705. It consisted of a network of army treasurers selected by the General Treasurer and functioning like one sole repository of funds, as did the *Trésorier général de l'extraordinaire des guerres* in France.[4] The General Treasurer exercised daily control over 'his' treasurers, aimed at forestalling omissions in registering receipts by a simple procedure: the army treasurers would not give a receipt to farmers and receivers of taxes who paid them funds, obliging the latter to claim it from the office of the General Treasurer in Madrid. In return for their expenditures, they got a simple receipt from sergeant majors or suppliers which they had to present to the General Treasurer in order to see the sums of money registered on their expenditure account. The method, designed by Orry in 1703, might have been inspired by the practices of the French big tax farmers or the general companies of suppliers of provisions, which this Frenchman knew by experience (Ozanam 1989; Hanotin 2009). The General Treasurer of the *Rentas Generales*, from 1714 onwards, and his equivalent for the tobacco revenue, in the 1720s, functioned on an identical manner. Added to this type of control based on the contradictory interests of army treasurers, receivers and farmers of taxes, suppliers and troops desirous of being paid, was the more classic one of the visual of the inspector per army treasurer.[5] The plan was fine-tuned by means of successive instructions from the Treasury, particularly at the time when, alongside army quartermasters deployed in the course of the war in the Aragonese territories recaptured by force, as well as in Castile, Andalusia, Galicia and Extremadura, each of the provinces without an army had assigned to it, in 1714 then in 1718, a provincial intendant, a treasurer (called a paymaster in 1718) and an inspector. The system was maintained only in those provinces accommodating troops and their quartermasters in 1721 (Kamen 1964; Dubet 2011).

[4] For which see Rowlands (2002).

[5] On seventeenth century practices, see Esteban Estríngana (2003).

It can be clearly observed in this instance how the General Treasurer controlled his treasurers. The control bearing upon him relied on other mechanisms. Apart from his rendering of accounts to the the Major Chamber of Accounts (*Tribunal Mayor de Cuentas*), a long time after his period in office, the mainspring was the confidence that he inspired in the person(s) in charge of finances, as indicated by the stated criteria for choosing new General Treasurers. Correspondence with the Secretary of Finances and War Dispatches, José Grimaldo, and with Orry, then with the ambassador Amelot, was on a daily basis during the war, and the same applied from the 1720s onwards. After 1714, the Secretary for War and the Navy appears to have taken over. Beginning in 1717, the creation of the two new *contadurías de valores y distribución* (chambers of accounts of values and distribution) implied extra control: their task was to regularly compare the General Treasurer's statements of expenditures and receipts with the statements issued by those in charge of revenues (in order to establish the values—*valores*—derived from the revenue) and by treasurers, paymasters, and army suppliers (in order to establish details of distribution– *distribución*—i.e. the total expenditure and its apportionment). In the end, after 1724, the General Treasurer no longer chose his own inspectors, in order to prevent collusion. However, the requirement for sound moral standards remained paramount. The mechanisms described above turned out to be insufficient, so Campoflorido and Patiño added to them the propensity to behave as a good subaltern of the Minister, a model taken up later by Campillo and his successors in finances. The question was nevertheless debated in the 1720s: thus the Treasurer Nicolás de Hinojosa regarded himself as a collaborator on an equal footing with the Minister and thought that fraud stemmed largely from provincial 'subalterns' (Dubet 2015b).

My own opinion is that the preservation of this General Treasury during the reign of Philip V is the result of a compromise with the businessmen. It is noticeable, in fact, that the nature of the General Treasury for War changed at the time of the *Nueva Planta*. Up to June 1713, the General Treasurer of War received only part of the revenues earmarked for war; the rest of the income from fiscal contributions was disbursed by the tax farmers and receivers who had collected it under the supervision of the Finances Council and other bodies responsible for it; when anything was left over, it was confided to the former General Treasurer created in sixteenth century and controlled by the Finances Council. From 1713, almost all of the king's revenue in the Peninsula was entrusted to the General Treasurer of War created in 1703–1705. This had been seen as a simple quantitative increase (Kamen 1974). But the reform was more ambitious than that: from 1713, the General Treasurer was the only one authorised to make disbursements on behalf of the King in the Peninsula.[6] He therefore ceased to hold the title 'for war', while the former General Treasurer instituted in sixteenth century disappeared. Above all, the farmers of provincial revenues, the general treasurers of provincial, general and tobacco revenues, and the treasurers of mints, were no longer allowed to make payments except in the king's name, instead of receiving assignations on their own funds. This subjected them to control by the General Treasurer during their term of office, a situation unacceptable to some—their inspectors instanced it at the time of the Verdes Montenegro trial—but one which was maintained. They made the payments 'out of their' funds (specifying which monthly payment of taxes was to be used) on presentation of a provisional receipt from the General Treasurer, or indeed to a demand note issued by the cashier of the General Treasurer in Madrid. They were not empowered to accept a definitive receipt from the General Treasurer until after they had transmitted to him the receipts of the beneficiaries of the payments. According to Vega, this arrangement was designed to put a stop to embezzlement by the tax farmers. Everything therefore took place as if a compromise had been found with the financiers who had won the king's confidence in 1713–1714. The possibility of their profiteering on the distribution of funds was suppressed but, on the other hand, they saw the big provincial revenue farms and the treasuries of the most important revenues granted to them and continued to handle the supplies contracts, which also were centralised.[7] In fact, as Campoflorido, Patiño and Iturralde saw it, effective functioning of the General Treasury was dependent on the goodwill of the tax farmers of the 'Rentas Provinciales', the treasurer of the 'Rentas Generales' and that of the tobacco revenue. They regarded the transport tariffs claimed by the former for the payment of provincial receipts from

[6] An exception must be made for the Treasurer of the Navy, who remained autonomous to the great displeasure of Campoflorido (Solbes Ferri 2014) and of privileged revenues like the three papal gifts.

[7] In the 1720s, the general treasurer of the *Rentas Generales* was one of the Navarrians financiers (see *infra*) and the directors and treasurers of the tobacco revenue were financiers friends of Patiño from 1716 onwards.

the General Treasurer as being more honest that those of the merchant bankers who provided bills of exchange, and their promptness as a credit to the institution. Alternative solutions had been envisaged by the General Treasurer Nicolás de Hinojosa (1718–1720, 1726) and by the Duke of Ripperda, chief Minister of the King in 1726. According to Campoflorido, the former went to exchange companies to make his payments; the latter, who nominated Hinojosa perpetual Treasurer, received projects to create banks and had them archived in his offices. Patiño cut short the experiment and consolidated relations with the Navarrian businessmen who had supported Philip V during the War of Succession, like Goyeneche and Iturralde, and continued to lease out the majority of the 'Rentas Provinciales'. The solidarity between these tax farmers and the General Treasury became particularly explicit when Tomás de Iriberri, Goyeneche's nephew, initially treasurer of the 'Rentas Generales', twice became General Treasurer under the administration of this Minister (Dubet 2015b).

Campoflorido would have liked to go further in controlling the collection and distribution of funds carried out via the General Treasury. The 1718 reform, which extended the intendants and the Treasury to all the Spanish provinces, made provision for the replacement of tax repositories in the major town of every district by treasurers appertaining to the General Treasury. Likewise, the venal posts of inspector of each tax, at the municipal or provincial level, were to be eliminated, to the benefit of the new provincial inspector who flanked each provincial treasurer. His argument was that the posts to be suppressed were in the hands of local potentates who indulged in all sorts of abuses. The resistance of these groups, added to the fact that the king did not have the wherewithal to reimburse the posts in question, put an end to the project: in 1721, the posts of treasurers of the General Treasury and of provincial inspectors were abolished in the provinces without a permanent army (Dubet 2011). I believe that Campoflorido accepted this measure all the more readily in that maintaining the tax farmers of the *Rentas Provinciales*, whose fidelity seemed to him to be assured, allowed the General Treasurer, and the authority of the Minister to employ funds freely, even in the provinces where the Treasurer no longer had agents. From the point of view of Campoflorido, the 1721 compromise might have signified that the monarchy closed its eyes to possible fraud committed, during the early stages of tax collection, by the local potentates who continued to organise the collection at the local level on the king's behalf. On the other hand, once the money had been delivered to the repositories of the army treasurers in the provinces which had a treasurer or to those of the tax farmers of the *Rentas Provinciales*, or been registered on the books of the General treasurer of the *Rentas Generales*, of the treasurer of tobacco revenue and other officials obliged to make expenditures only in the name of the General Treasurer and under his control, the local potentates no longer had any command over it. Campoflorido and the Finance Ministers who succeeded him counted then on the General Treasurer to ensure that they controlled the distribution of funds by limiting, thanks to the procedures described above, the possibility of fraud on the part of the Treasurer's agents and those who disbursed money in his name. That does not, however, mean that all possibility of fraud was removed to, or even brushed aside by the Ministers.

3 The Minister, the Treasurer, and the Traffic in Promissory Notes

The fact is that the choices implemented remained ambivalent, between repression of the usurers and compromises with the suppliers of credit. The solutions brought to bear on the traffic in promissory notes illustrate this ambivalence. The question seems to have obsessed the governing body. During the War of Succession, according to Orry then Vega, the holders of assignations sold them at a reduced price to individuals sufficiently robust financially to wait for their payment. The latter were sometimes courtiers with enough know-how to get these securities recognised at their nominal price in the royal bureaus (Dedieu 2012). But usually they were tax farmers, army suppliers, treasurers. After the 1713 reform, the instrument changed. The talk was of little other than papers issued by the General Treasurer (these provisional receipts on the repositories of taxes and the bills—*boletines*—addressed to his chief cashier at Madrid) and of the documentary evidence produced by his subalterns. The General Treasurer's chief cashier handed over slips indicating remaining payment to be made when he could not make the total payments and he made out to treasurers and tax farmers promises to credit them with expenditure made in the name of the General Treasurer. The army treasurers gave soldiers certificates attesting to the pay still owing to them.

This apparent predominance of papers issued by the General Treasurer and his agents may be taken as an indication of the reform's success, since only the vouchers of the General Treasurer of the tobacco revenue seemed to be circulating likewise—some creditors of the king possessed them (Dubet 2015b). But these sales on the cheap of the General Treasurer's promissory notes were also the result of his delays in payment. In 1743, a young Treasury clerk, Gregorio de Estan, was prosecuted for having organised trafficking of this kind. He had sought out creditors wanting to sell the Treasurer's slips, his cashier's vouchers and other 'credits', and prepared to accept a 'loss' or discount of 35–40%, in order to put them in contact with buyers prepared to acquire them (*beneficiarios*) and to pay him a *gratification*. The sellers were identified: employees of royal courts of justice and royal households, and, in smaller numbers, minor army suppliers.[8] In 1725, far more important financiers were negotiating with the king the reimbursement of their promissory notes. Juan Bautista de Iturralde, who became Finance Minister in 1739, signed two contracts simultaneously with the king: one of these was a loan with which to reimburse businessmen listed (some of the principal creditors of the monarchy figured on the list) by paying them 'credits' received in the form of the Treasurer General's promissory notes in order to reimburse them for military supplies or bills of exchange.[9]

Why and to what extent was this trafficking culpable? The Estan affair provides the answer in terms of doctrine. Estan had encouraged usury, according to the experts of the subject, because any purchase of debts on the cheap is a disguised form of it. But another reason was voiced at this trial: trafficking is reprehensible because of its consequences. Estan did harm to the 'honour and reputation of the General Treasury and its employees'. Apart from that, he 'wronged royal finances'.[10] Some, however, were more guilty than others. In the Estan affair, the promissory note sellers at bay were not harassed, nor was any poor victim of usury (the borrower). The buyers could not be found, perhaps because they were powerful or generous enough to keep witnesses quiet? Because what was most embarrassing about the question of trafficking in promissory notes was the participation of individuals in business affairs with

[8] AHN (Archivo Histórico Nacional, Madrid), Consejos, leg. 38452.

[9] 'Demanda fiscal', on March 9, 1741, AHN, Estado, libro 802.

[10] 'Confesión' with the prosecutor Julián de Cañaveras, September 3, 1743. AHN, Consejos, leg. 38452.

the king. According to Vega, it was common practice for army suppliers and treasurers to purchase such promissory notes at a discount and exploit them afterwards at their nominal price in accounts with the king. On these occasions they added to usury the aggravating circumstance of a feigned service. In September 1740, in the aftermath of the fall of Iturralde, his enemies stirred up legal proceedings against him. According to the prosecutor Blas Jover Alcáraz, the poor quality credits restored to the king under the terms of the 1725 agreement had been replaced by good quality promissory notes delivered by the General Treasurer which the cashier of Iturralde's firm had reused for his loan to the king! Minister Campillo, in 1741, went further: Iturralde performed this operation and many others 'with what we call old papers [...] which he had not perhaps paid for at 1% of their value'.[11] However, not everyone assessed in that way the degree of guilt on the parts of the monied man in this matter. Jover Alcáraz spoke of 'feign service' and a 'usurious'operation. On the other hand, according to Campillo, there was 'no motive for proceeding against the Marquis and is representatives, because they had carried out this business with the greatest formality; it was negotiated, confirmed on and agreed with the most authorized royal ministers of the time'. The affaire was legitimate because the king had passed it in 1725 in full knowledge of the facts. The opinion of the legal solicitors of the Finances Council, given shortly after that of Campillo, helps to explain the Minister's argument. According to them, Iturralde and the other lenders had documents entitling their possessors to payments whose priority was 'recommendable', i.e. the payment was regarding as having a higher priority than that of other such papers. Apart from that, once the arrangement had gone through, they would be in a position to grant other loans to the king.[12] The profit derived from their purchasing promissory notes on the terms of the 1725 agreement was therefore a gracious reward designed to win their loyalty: which made it legitimate—and detriment to third parties who had sold these notes on the cheap was not mentioned. It goes without saying that in other cases, when the king was shamelessly deceived, as most often happened according to Vega, the argument proved untenable.

[11]'Demanda fiscal' on March 9, 1741. AHN, E, libro 802. Campillo to the king, on August 8, 1741. AGS, SSH, leg. 399–391.

[12]Sohiter's solicitors' advice, summed up at the king's *cédula* of 27 May 1742. AHN, Consejos, leg. 11542.

But there were even more guilty persons than the businessmen who entered into contracts with the king. The dominant position of the General Treasurer fuelled to fears. In 1719–1720, Campoflorido accused Treasurer Hinojosa of organising the sale of provisional receipts through (unreliable) stockbroker friends, instead of trusting his own chief cashier and the tax farmers of the provincial revenues. At the end of 1724, Verdes Montenegro was suspected, in his capacity as former Treasurer, of having deliberately postponed the payment of vouchers and other papers of his Treasury so that friends would purchase them at a discount and get them recognised, at the nominal price, in their accounts with the monarchy. In 1726, Ripperda and Hinojosa reformed the Treasury at the moment when denunciations of the traffic in papers and the discrediting of the institution were proliferating (Dubet 2015b). In these two cases, the accusation was motivated by conflicts over spheres of jurisdiction and rivalries between factions. It is difficult to ascertain to what degree the accusation was justified—the one brought against Verdes Montenegro was untenable for lack of proof; that against Hinojosa gave rise to no judicial proceedings. The use of the same arguments by rival groups nevertheless lends backing the view that the difficulty in controlling the Treasurer's promissory notes was real.

The monarchy's response was hesitant. In the 1720s, the king had to choose between two opposite projects promoted by men whom he had trusted since the War of Succession, Hinojosa and Ripperda, on the one hand, Verdes Montenegro and Patiño on the other. Whereas the former seemed to count on the banking houses to maintain the circulation of the General Treasurer's promissory notes, the latter preferred the tax farmers (Dubet 2012). The solution imposed by Patiño in 1726, as seen above, was to give the Finances Minister authority over the Treasurer. The Minister was henceforth the only one able to issue to the Treasurer orders for payment in the king's name. This solution was more ambiguous than it looked. Actually, Campoflorido and Patiño were aware of the fact that the monarchy's ability to pay depended on the outflow of promissory notes from the Treasury, which had become the chief form of debt since the liquidation of the 'juros' (perpetual loans) in the previous century, to which Patiño had actively contributed (Toboso Sánchez 1987; Torres Sánchez 2008). It is not unlikely that, in order to obtain funds, they had urged the General Treasurer to distribute to the king's creditors a volume of promissory notes larger than the fiscal revenues expected. At the same time, they were intent on knowing each year the precise volume of payments entered and made and the value of promissory notes in circulation. The solution they found had not only to do with accounts but with politics. Since October 1726, it have been up to the Minister's job, at each changeover of Treasurer, to put or not to put into circulation those promissory notes left unpaid by the outgoing Treasurer by inscribing on each one of them that he deemed still valid an order to pay them signed with his own hand—an idea, put into practice by Patiño, that stemmed from Verdes Montenegro. It was therefore the Minister who acted as guarantor of the debt, not the Treasurer, as Hinojosa wanted. In 1739, the Treasurer Francisco Lobato asked to be able to decide by himself which promissory notes passed on by the preceding Treasurer remained valid: the Minister, Iturralde, did not condescend to reply. It is thus easier to understand why these men at the helm wanted a Finance Minister who was 'intelligent' in financial matters. It was not a question of suppressing the traffic in promissory notes altogether, but of seeing to it that the operations did not escape the Minister and were not carried out to the detriment of the king.

The use to which the General Treasury was put during the ministries of Patiño and is successor Torrenueva illustrates the limits of this solution. Since 1734, the General Treasurer (Torrenueva under Patiño, and Lobato under Torrenueva) had been prompting Martín de Herce, who called himself 'chief agent' of the Treasury—although he did not figure on its lists of employees—to sell publicly in Madrid promissory notes appertaining to the Treasurer and to the latter's cashier, with the Minister's backing. The procedure enabled advances of funds to be made to the monarchy, two-thirds at least of those obtained between 1738 and the beginning of 1739. But it caused a shock. Iturralde, succeeding Torrenueva, suspended payment of part of the promissory notes given to the king's creditors (10 million of *escudos*), and less than half the ordinary revenue in any one year. It promised the eventual reimbursements of capital loaned, but not interest, except for the honest lenders. The decree of suspension of 21 March 1739 indeed set those who had lent in order to be of service, not in any mercenary spirit, i.e. the tax farmers and private individuals not engaged in any business dealings with the monarchy, against those who had given 'credits'. In 1752, Vega, a former client of Iturralde, explained what made the operations of the second group illegitimate. Not only had they aroused the greed of the inhabitants of Madrid by selling them the orders to pay at a discount—which amounted to a return to usury. But in addition, the operation had turned out to be to the detriment of the king, not to his benefit.[13] Herce had also bought out prior promissory notes in order to get them reimbursed at a high price. The real culprit was, however, the Minister: the 'broker' did under the eyes of an unwitting and negligent Patiño what the businessmen did in the shadows, conscious of defrauding. The remedy was not, however, to stop using the Treasurer's promissory notes to ensure payments to the monarchy and give it credit. Vega envisaged tightening the control exercised over the chief cashier of the Treasurer at Madrid, through which the promissory notes passed, by placing him under the eyes of both the Treasurer and the Finance Minister. This Minister, honest and 'intelligent' in financial matters, would not be content to establish more rigorous accounting procedures. The main threat that he could bring to bear on dishonest businessmen depended on royal arbitrariness: things would be arranged in such a way that those who had dealings with the king did not obtain closure of their accounts until they had become involved in some fresh service. It was a question of threatening them with seeing the profits made on previous contracts confiscated, or with not being reimbursed for the services they had performed within the framework of these contracts—on the pretext of fraud—for as long as these businessmen did not undertake fresh commitments (Dubet 2017).

***

During the reign of Philip V, the prevention of fraud on the part of the monied men consisted in regulating, by agreement with trusted financiers, the lawful profits which were acknowledged as owing to them, by restricting them to a few domains (those of tax-leasing, contracts of supply and exchange), and in depriving them, in principle, of profits derived from the distribution of the king's funds, notably the traffic in assignations. It was not a question of turning a blind eye to fraud, because what fraud consisted of in the eighteenth century is not the same as the modern definition. Vega and Campoflorido allowed to only those remunerations tolerated by moral standards: administrative expenses, monetary exchange, transport costs. Plus the profits accruing from social relationship in an unequal society every time a treasurer, a paymaster, or a tax farmer received gifts from 'friends' (soldiers, people with private incomes, employees of bureaus, courts of law, or financiers) to whom he

[13] Unlike the affair negotiated with Iturralde in 1725, if one believes Campillo.

had to pay the king's debts. In the end, the gifts made by the king to the financiers were liable to transform an illicit profit into a favour.

The doctrine was not new, but it was oriented by the effort to systemise the agreements made with a limited group of businessmen. Negotiation with them rested on trusted agents of the king able to speak their language and guarantee them solid reimbursements, always, however, subject to revision. The traffic in promissory notes of the General Treasurer, which followed that in assignations, nevertheless endangered the edifice built up, because anyone could indulge in it, particularly the powerful monied men. Recourse to the bank, the most radical alternative envisaged, was dismissed in the 1720s. The only way of preventing fraud on the part of financiers and, if the case arose, that of the General Treasurer, was to place them under the vigilant and informed eye of the Minister, while trying by various means to ensure their loyalty. One of the risks was that the Minister might encourage corruption, a reproach made against Verdes Montenegro and Patiño.

In this respect, after the death of Philip V, Ensenada wanted to break with the past. He effectively separated the handling of the debt left by this sovereign from the General Treasury and confided that debt to another repository supervised by a 'junta', in 1748. By doing so, he intended to divide the Ministry of Finances in two in order to put a stop to the 'collusion' linked to the payment of 'credits' in previous reigns. He explained in effect that hitherto nothing prevented the Minister from engaging in fraud along with the Treasurer.[14] At the same instant, the benefits allowed to the monied men were reduced by placing all the *Rentas Provinciales* under the state control (1748), thus bringing significant change to existing relations with financiers, especially those from Navarra. This move modified the basis of the General Treasurer's credit and obliged the monarchy to seek others, as González Enciso explains in this book. From this point onwards, speculation on the value of the General Treasurer's promissory notes probably became less interesting for private individuals that it had been in the first half of the century. The lack of scandal provoked by trafficking in the promissory notes of the Treasurer or of the Minister, in the second half of the century, possibly had less to do with the virtue of these office holders and their agents than with the fact that people could get rich by other means.

[14] Representations to the king, 27 May 1748 and 1751. Rodríguez Villa (1878: 85–91, 113–142).

Bibliography

Andújar Castillo, F. 2000. La reforma militar en el reinado de Felipe V. In *El cambio dinástico y sus repercusiones en la España del siglo XVII*, ed. J. Fernández García, M.A. Bel Bravo, and J.M. Delgado Barrado, 617–640. Jaén: Universidad de Jaén.

———. 2004. *El sonido del dinero. Monarquía, ejército y venalidad en la España del siglo XVIII*. Madrid: Marcial Pons Historia.

———. 2005. La hacienda real en tiempos de crisis: 1739–1741. In *Estudios en homenaje al profesor José Szmolka Clares*, ed. A.L. Cortés Peña et al., 537–546. Servicio de Publicaciones.

———. 2008. *Necesidad y venalidad. España e Indias, 1704–1711*. Madrid: Centro de Estudios Políticos y Constitucionales.

Aquerreta, S. 2001. *Negocios y finanzas en el siglo XVIII: la familia Goyeneche*. Pamplona: EUNSA.

Cavillac, M. 1983. *Gueux et marchands dans le Guzmán de Alfarache (1599–1604)*. Bordeaux: Institut d'Etudes Ibériques.

Clavero, B. 1991. *Antidora. Antropología católica de la economía moderna*. Milán: Giuffrè Editore.

———. 1996. La monarquía, el derecho y la justicia. In *Instituciones de la España moderna. 1. Las jurisdicciones*, ed. E. Martínez Ruiz et al., 15–38. Madrid: Actas Editorial.

de Castro, C. 2004. *A la sombra de Felipe V. José de Grimaldo, ministro responsable (1703–1726)*. Madrid: Marcial Pons Historia.

Dedieu, J.P. 2010. *Après le roi. Essai sur l'effondrement de la monarchie espagnole*. Madrid: Casa de Velázquez.

———. 2012. Les intermédiaires privés dans les finances royales espagnoles sous Philippe V et Ferdinand VI. In *Crédit public, crédit privé et institutions intermédiaires*, ed. V. Meyzie, 223–239. Limoges: PULIM.

Delgado Barrado, J.M. 2007. *Aquiles y Teseos. Bosquejos del reformismo borbónico (1701–1759)*, Granada and Jaén: Universidad de Granada and Universidad de Jaén.

Dictionnaire des finances, ed. J. Josse, Th. Le Gras, G. Cavelier, and La Veuve Saugrain. Paris, 1727.

Dubet, A. 2000. *Réformer les finances espagnoles au Siècle d'Or: le projet Valle de la Cerda*. Clermont-Ferrand: Presses Universitaires Blaise-Pascal.

———. 2009. *Jean Orry et la réforme du gouvernement de l'Espagne (1701–1706)*. Clermont-Ferrand: Presses Universitaires Blaise Pascal.

———. 2011. Los intendentes y la tentativa de reorganización del control financiero en España, 1718–1720. In *Más Estado y más mercado. Absolutismo y economía en la España del siglo XVIII*, ed. G. Pérez Sarrión, 103–136. Madrid: Sílex.

———. 2012. Entre dos modelos de gobierno de la hacienda militar. Las reformas de la Tesorería Mayor en España en 1721–1727. In *Un Estado militar. España, 1650–1820*, ed. A. González Enciso, 255–290. Madrid: Actas.

———. 2014. Control y negocio de la deuda real en el primer siglo XVIII: la Tesorería Mayor. *Obradoiro de Historia Moderna* 23: 94–138.

———. 2015a. El gobierno de la Hacienda real de Felipe V y los interesados según Alejandro de Vega. *Tiempos Modernos* 30: 2015/1.

———. 2015b. *La Hacienda Real de la Nueva Planta (1713–1726), entre fraude y buen gobierno. El caso Verdes Montenegro y las reformas de la Hacienda*. Madrid: Fondo de Cultura Económica.

———. 2015c. Entre razón y ciencia de la Hacienda: la conflictiva construcción de un modelo de buen gobierno de la Real Hacienda en España en la primera mitad del siglo XVIII. *Espacio, Tiempo y Forma* 28: 187–209.

———. 2017. La suspensión de pagos de 1739: ¿una medida de 'buen gobierno' de la Hacienda?. *Espacio, Tiempo y Forma* 30: 19–56.

———. 2018. El cambio en el gobierno de la Hacienda española en la primera mitad del siglo XVIII. In *Estado, poder, administración y élites en la monarquía hispánica*, ed. F. Andújar Castillo, M. Bertrand, and Th. Glesener, 217–232. Valencia: Albatros.

Egido López, T. 2002. *Opinión pública y oposición al poder en la España del siglo XVIII (1713–1759)*, 1st ed.: 1971. Valladolid: Universidad de Valladolid, Fundación Española de Historia Moderna.

Esteban Estríngana, A. 2003. Autopsia del despacho financiero. Ejecución y control de pagos en el tesoro militar del ejército de Flandes (siglo XVII). *Obradoiro de historia moderna* 12: 47–78.

García García, B. 1996. *La Pax Hispanica. Política exterior del Duque de Lerma*. Leuven: Leuven University Press.

Garnot, B., ed. 1996. *L'infrajudiciaire du Moyen-Age à l'époque moderne*. Dijon: EUD.

Garriga, C. 2006. Sobre el gobierno de la justicia en Indias (siglos XVI–XVII). *Revista de Historia del Derecho* 34: 67–160.

Gómez Centurión, C., and J.A. Sánchez Belén (eds.). 1998. *La herencia de Borgoña. La hacienda de las Reales Casas durante el reinado de Felipe V*. Madrid: Centro de Estudios Políticos y Constitucionales.

Graham, A. 2013. Auditing Leviathan: Corruption and State Formation in Early Eighteenth-Century Britain. *English Historical Review CCXXVIII* 533: 808–838.

Guerrero Elecalde, R. 2012. *Las elites vascas y navarras en el gobierno de la Monarquía borbónica*. Bilbao: Universidad del País Vasco.

Guerrero Elecalde, R., and J.M. Imízcoz Beunza. 2012. Negocios y clientelismo político. Los empresarios norteños en la economía de la monarquía borbónica. In *Empresas y empresarios en el norte de España (siglo XVIII)*, ed. J. Ocampo Suárez Valdés, 331–362. Trea: Somonte-Cenero.

Hanotin, G. 2009. *Jean Orry, un homme des finances royales entre France et Espagne (1701–1705)*. Córdoba: Universidad de Córdoba.

———. 2011. *Au service de deux rois. L'ambassadeur Amelot de Gournay et l'union des couronnes (1705–1709)*. Doctoral thesis, Université de Paris-Sorbonne.

Herzog, T. 2004. La comunidad y su administración. Sobre el valor político, social y simbólico de las residencias de Quito (1653–1753). *In Mélanges de la Casa de Velázquez* 34 (2): 161–183.

Hespanha, A.M. 1993. *La gracia del derecho. Economía de la cultura en la Edad Moderna*. Madrid: Centro de Estudios Constitucionales.

Kamen, K. 1964. El establecimiento de los intendentes en la administración española. *Hispania* XXIV: 368–395.

———. 1974. *La Guerra de Sucesión en España, 1710–1715*. Barcelona, Buenos Aires, and México: Grijalbo.

Legay, M.L. 2011. *La banqueroute de l'État royal. La gestion des finances publiques de Colbert à la Révolution française*. Paris: Éditions de l'EHESS.

Malaprade, S. 2018. *Des châteaux en Espagne, mobilité sociale et gouvernement des finances au XVIIe siècle*. Toulouse: PULIM.

Mantecón Novellán, T.A. 1998. *La muerte de Antonia Isabel Sánchez. Tiranía y escándalo en una sociedad rural del Norte español en el Antiguo Régimen*. Alcalá de Henares: Centro de Estudios Cervantinos.

Ozanam, D. 1989. Jean Orry, munitionnaire du roi. *Etudes et documents*. Paris: CHEFF.

Peytavin, M. 2003. *Visite et gouvernement dans le royaume de Naples (XVIe–XVIIe siècles)*. Madrid: Casa de Velázquez.

Rodríguez Villa, A. 1878. *Don Cenón de Somodevilla, marqués de La Ensenada*. Madrid: Librería de M. Murillo.

———. 1882. *Patiño y Campillo*. Madrid: Sucesores de Rivadeneyra.

Rowlands, G. 2002. *The Dynastic State and the Army under Louis XIV. Royal Service and Private Interest, 1661 to 1701*. Cambridge: Cambridge University Press.

Ruiz Martín, F. 1975. Crédito y banca, comercio y transportes en la etapa del capitalismo mercantil. In *Actas de las I jornadas de metodología aplicada de las ciencias históricas*, III, 725–749. Santiago de Compostela: Universidad de Santiago de Compostela.

Sanz Ayán, C. 2013. *Los banqueros y la crisis de la monarquía hispánica de 1640*. Madrid: Marcial Pons.

Solbes Ferri, S. 2014. El control del gasto de la Marina española en las Secretarías de Estado y del Despacho. Los pagos dependientes de la Tesorería General en la primera mitad del XVIII. In *El Estado en guerra. Expediciones navales españolas en el siglo XVIII*, ed. M. Baudot, 147–194. Madrid: Polifemo.

Teijeiro de la Rosa, J.M. 2002. La intervención de la Real Hacienda militar en el siglo XVIII. In *La Hacienda Militar. 500 años de Intervención en las fuerzas armadas*, ed. J.M. Teijeiro de la Rosa, 153–294. Madrid: Ministerio de Defensa.

Téllez Alarcía, R. 2015. *Represión política y víctimas del absolutismo ilustrado en España: la conspiración del marqués de Tabuérniga*. Madrid: Endymion.

Toboso Sánchez, P. 1987. *La deuda pública castellana durante el Antiguo Régimen (juros)*. Madrid: Instituto de Estudios Fiscales.

Torres Sánchez, R. 2002. Cuando las reglas del juego cambian. Mercados y privilegio en el abastecimiento del ejército español en el siglo XVIII. *Revista de Historia Moderna* 20: 487–512.

———. 2008. Incertidumbre y arbitrariedad. La política de deuda pública de los Borbones en el siglo XVIII. *Estudis* 34: 263–282.

———. 2012. *La llave de todos los tesoros. La tesorería general de Carlos III*. Madrid: Sílex.

———. 2013. Administración o asiento. La política estatal de suministros militares en la Monarquía española del siglo XVIII. *Studia historica. Historia moderna* 35: 159–199.

Vallejo, J. 1998. Acerca del fruto del árbol de los jueces. Escenarios de la justicia en la cultura del ius commune. *Anuario de derecho de la UAM* 2: 19–46.

Vázquez Gestal, P. 2013. *Una nueva majestad. Felipe V, Isabel de Farnesio y la identidad de la monarquía (1700–1729)*. Madrid: Marcial Pons.

Waquet, J.C. 1984. *De la corruption. Morale et pouvoir à Florence aux XVIIe et XVIIIe siècles*. Paris: Fayard.

CHAPTER 5

Forgery of the French Coinage: The Question of the Counterfeit Money in the Southern Low Countries, 1710–1730

Marie-Laure Legay

In medieval and early-modern Europe, the ruler, as a representative of civil power, possessed *jus monetae*, as was the case for Roman emperors.[1] At the end of feudalism this right, until then limited to the ruler, was extended to lords on a given fief. This change did come with occasional difficulties, but always in line with the affirmation of the superiority of civil power over seigneurial or communal law. The main effect of the ruler's control over currency lay in his fiscal prerogative through seigniorage: the king determined the value of the currency, in the money of account. He taxed the metals and the coins, and used them as a source

[1] For a criticism of the domanial origin of the right to issue currency as presented by Bridrey (1906), see Babelon (1908).

M.-L. Legay (✉)
University of Lille III, Villeneuve-d'Ascq, France
e-mail: marie-laure.legay@univ-lille3.fr

J. Félix and A. Dubet (eds.), *The War Within*,
Palgrave Studies in the History of Finance,
https://doi.org/10.1007/978-3-319-98050-8_5

of revenue by changing, at will, the title, weight and purchase price, and he was the only person authorised to do so. Consequently, a counterfeiter, guilty of lese-majesty, was severely punished, condemned to death by boiling water and oil (Cauchies 1976). However, forgers of foreign currency were dealt with differently, as they did not affect their sovereign's interests but those of their competitors (Feller 1986). But were they actually counterfeiting? A number of recent works on the subject show that the notion of counterfeiting is not easy to define, that it exists in various forms, depending not only on the processes used, but also on the intentions of the manufacturer (Béaur et al. 2007).

This chapter aims to analyse the attitude of Brussels' political authorities with regard to counterfeiting French money during the years 1710–1730. The context of Louis XIV's last wars was characterised by a severe scarcity of cash and a monetary policy which resulted in a complete disorganisation of currency markets. Analysed, among others, by Bloch (1953), Lüthy (1960) and, more recently, Rowlands (2012) and Félix (2018), successive devaluations of the French currency by re-stampings of the existing coinage gave rise to massive smuggling of species out of the kingdom. It became tempting to buy the old coins—if necessary at a higher price than that which the French mints were willing to pay—and to re-stamp them to pocket the higher value set by the king. The process was used many times by the neighbours of the kingdom of France, including the inhabitants of the Habsburg Netherlands (or, Southern Low Countries), who, furthermore, could buy coins from the United Provinces (or Netherlands).

The Brussels and Paris archives offer the opportunity of analysing the magnitude of the fraud. They reveal that banking houses in the Low Countries did not only intervene on the markets, but also got involved in the production of counterfeit money. The merchants turned into manufacturers of gold coins, shamelessly taking possession of sovereign power to restore, by themselves, the law of *jus gentium*, i.e. international law (Alland and Rials 2003: 463–467; Renoux-Zagamé 2003). It is primarily in light of the freedom of nations to trade that the phenomenon of money counterfeiting must be examined. The international trade laws required that each 'nation' define its monetary identity: it is what economists would nowadays refer to as 'anchoring'. In the absence of a central bank, it was the Sovereign's responsibility to define a coherent monetary system articulated with the value of neighbouring currencies, in order to ensure price stability. In this respect, the monetary identity of the Southern Low Countries (now Low Countries), confined between the prosperous maritime powers, to the north-west, and the kingdom of the Bourbons, to the south, remained unclear. For a long time, the currency of the Low Countries was pegged onto that of foreign nations. It is therefore important to consider the fraudulent episode of counterfeit money in relation to a political as well as an economic necessity. As we will see, the interim Governor, the Marquis de Prié, encouraged it in the 1720s, and a commission of enquiry on counterfeiting of French money proved relatively lenient in this respect.

1 The Violation of People's Rights

The Belgians, or the population of the Low Countries, considered the monetary ordinances of their Habsburg sovereigns as inapplicable (Legay 2016). What is more, most of them did not in the least feel concerned by the legislation: the merchants in Antwerp had always regarded the monetary ruling (*placard*) of 1652 'as not compatible with the necessary freedom in trade'.[2] Thus the challenge for the Habsburgs resided in the necessity to defend the royal rights while some of the elites believed that the sovereign was merely delegated to uphold the people's rights: 'The seigneurial right and the manufacturing costs have always been handed over to the sovereigns of these Low Countries out of an ardent desire on the part of their subjects to see their coinage illustrious in their realms, and this right is allowed to be accepted through the concession of the people that we call *jus gentium*'.[3]

The large trading houses in the Low Countries demanded the valuation of foreign coins, but also the freedom to deal in bullion metals and coins. By the royal decree of 8 February 1686 Charles II of Spain recognised that freedom.[4] He did not force the traders to take the precious metals that were not considered legal tender to the mints. On the contrary, they were authorised to deal in those metals without being subjected to payment of tax. Later, on 9 December 1687, the king restricted the right to export bullion as well as coins with no legal tender status.

[2] Archives générales du royaume, Brussels [now: AGR], Jointe des Monnaies [now: JM], 58, Remontrances du Magistrat d'Anvers, 1725; and Conseil des finances, 8635, Note sur l'édit général de 1652.

[3] AGR, JM, 44 bis, letter from de Wautiers, 13 February 1710.

[4] AGR, JM, 58, Remontrances du Magistrat d'Anvers, 1725.

Yet in ordering that they had to be brought to the mints after a period of three months following entry, he recognised freedom of trade. This legislation created a legal precedent by voiding the *placard* of 1652. The attempt to revive the old legislation with the new ruling of 3 January 1698 was a failure due to the massive circulation of foreign currencies, both under the French occupation and that of the seafaring powers. In fact, as the century drew to its close, the ruler of the Low Countries took on board the obvious truth that would later be confirmed by eighteenth-century theorists like Ferdinando Galiani: 'Currency should be treated like a commodity, and if universal consent happens to differ from the price offered by the mint, that of the multitude who, when they are in possession of freedom always follow truth, should prevail' (Tutin 2009: 109).

The monetary practices of the Low Countries were characterised by a dual system of values, with a currency of exchange (legal tender as per ordinances) and current money (tied to the commercial rate). Let us remind ourselves that foreign currencies were not allowed in France, and that in Holland they were only accepted at the price merchants were willing to give for their intrinsic value. In parallel with the strong currency, whose value depended on the fineness of the metal used, people employed a weak currency. As Wervecke (1934) noted, the Belgian authorities were, at the most, able to have some influence on the money of account by designating the standard coin base on which the account values were established, but 'they were unable to impose a given ratio between the standard coin on which was based the account system and other real currencies'.

Indeed, implementing a current appreciation of foreign currencies had some drawbacks from an accounting perspective, but also in that it presented usury risks when the parties in a transaction wished to be paid either in current money or in currency of exchange, depending on the benefits to be gained at the time of payment. Overall, however, the ratio between the two value systems remained stable. In 1704, the ratio of current money to exchange currency was fixed at 7 to 6 and remained stable, so that the supporters of freedom could continue to defend their arguments. The magistrates of Antwerp, eager to defend the town's merchants who had been involved in the traffic in specie between 1710 and 1720, emphasised that 'owing to changes over time, one can no longer go along with the speculations of the authors of these old placards, who were sometimes more attached to rigorous canon law than necessity permits'.[5] The Ordinance of 21 April 1725 eliminated the appreciation of current money, but there again, the attempt was short-lived and lasted exactly nine days! The credo remained unchanged: 'Gold and silver coins are not a sufficiently solid mass to be held back or halted by a decree or by the most rigorous law just as long as they have an outlet elsewhere offering the slightest advantage. We even observe that every trading nation is so convinced of this fact that its government pays little attention to their entry and departure'.[6]

It was one thing to recognise the current value of money, it was another to let the market drift because of the neighbours' practices. The arbitrary depreciations implemented by the French rulers became intolerable to the Belgians: 'It can very truly be said that France, where currency is concerned, rules roughshod over all divine, human, and political laws'.[7] During the War of the Spanish Succession (1702–1714) French monetary policy seriously prejudiced the interests of the inhabitants of the Low Countries. In 1709, Louis XIV devaluated the national unit of account by raising the value of the golden *louis* to 20 livres and the *silver écu* to 5 livres. Then, between 1 December 1713 and 1 September 1715, a succession of re-evaluations restored the *louis d'or au soleil* to 14 livres (or 420 livres to the mark). With the Regency, a policy of devaluation resumed (Lévy 1977). Following the peace treaties of Utrecht and Rastadt, the maréchal de Noailles, president of the Conseil des Finances, in late 1715, and the comte d'Argenson, finance minister, in June 1718, returned to Louis XIV's practices of balancing the budget and paying off debts by tampering with the coinage. This policy took an even more radical turn during John Law's System (Lévy 1977). The natural order of things was so disrupted that the 'false reform' of French coins that took place in the neighbouring foreign countries became almost industrial.

The Low Countries legally benefited from the massive quantities of bullion, but which were legal tender in Brussels. A report on the coinage explained that 'having debased and adulterated the preceding coins for all purposes of circulation and outlay, and not having paid their intrinsic value in new coins at the mints, but paying instead their extrinsic value by means of an exorbitant increase in the circulation of the said new

[5]'AGR, JM, 58, Representations, 1725.

[6]AGR, JM, 46, Letter, ca. 1722.

[7]AGR, JM, 58, Document 2.

coins, certain French citizens and merchants have transported into these lands a large number of the said discredited coins, which we have drawn upon ourselves because of a circulation and value more advantageous than France paid at the mints for the depreciated coins'.[8]

Yet the risk of being invaded by the debased currency forced the Belgian bankers and merchants to respond by reforming the currency themselves. On 10 January 1718, the Low Countries authorised the appreciation of the *louis d'or* in exchange currency (11 florins and 4 sols) as in current money (13 florins and 1 sol). Two years later, the *louis* was devalued to 10 florins, 16 sols and 2 liards (exchange value) and to 16 florins and 12 sols and 2 liards (in current value). The depreciation of the French currency most definitely created 'an opportunity for the counterfeiting of those new species'.[9] The first *louis d'or* of Louis XV, also called *louis d'or de Noailles*[10] (1716), followed by the production of gold louis with the Cross of Malta (1718), the *quinzain* (1719), the 'LL' *louis* (1720) and the *mirliton* (1723) were all opportunities for the Regent to liquidate the war debts, and for the Belgians—more or less encouraged by their political authorities—to manufacture counterfeit French currency.

Did that constitute a serious crime? Did the *Roi Très Chrétien* deliberately violate *jus gentium*? Judging by the subsequent remarks of Ferdinando Galiani, there is little doubt about it. In an essay on value, the famous Italian economist, building on the events of 1720, claimed that by minting coins, the king could only reveal the intrinsic value and that he should therefore act fairly and with rectitude: 'It is not up to the king to arbitrarily impose on minted metal any value he likes, but it is proper, as a general rule, that the value should be made consonant with the inherent value' (Tutin 2009: 108).

The king could not absolutely control the value of currencies to such an extent as was 'unnatural', lest he be considered a tyrant. By not respecting the rules of fair trade supposed to be established between

[8] AGR, JM, 18, Reflections sur les causes de la décadence des monnoyes dans ces Pays-Bas autrichiens.

[9] AGR, JM, 58, Document 2.

[10] 20 were struck in a gold mark with a legal tender value of 30 livres, which gave the gold mark a value of 600 livres.

nations, the King of France released the other princes of Europe from their obligations, including from the mutually agreed legislation prohibiting the manufacture of, and trade in, counterfeit currency. Currency counterfeiting thus became a natural weapon of defence. It was little more than an imitation of re-formed coins which, provided they had the same title and alloy as the real coins, could be seen in the Belgian provinces as compensation: 'if by chance some [of the counterfeit coins] leave this country for France, this will not constitute any injustice towards that realm, but compensation for ourselves and our subjects. France must blame herself; it is she who began violating the right of nations'.[11]

In truth, the kings of France did cause a war to be justly waged against themselves, a war which 'God, the personification of justice and protector of the oppressed, would assist with his all-powerful arm in order to repel the audacity of France'.[12] Furthermore, it was argued that a counterfeiter attacking a foreign currency could not be equated to a criminal of lese-majesty. According to ancient laws, reintroduced by Charles V in 1526 and 1531, the culprit was not subjected to torture by the boiling water or oil sentence reserved for the counterfeiter of the reigning sovereign's currency, but only to exile. The use of counterfeit money also had to be considered: if the coins manufactured with the die of a foreign sovereign had legal tender only in that land, and were used for the purpose of local trade, and without leaving the territory in question, the fraud became more relative still. No prejudice was caused to the king whose effigy was usurped.

Better still, according to the decree of 31 May 1564 issued by Philip II of Spain regarding the coins that were then manufactured in the Low Countries with the coat of arms of Portugal, it appears that the offenders were only considered counterfeiters if the specie coins they manufactured contained less precious metal that their legal counterparts. It is in light of this argument that the counterfeiting that took place in the Belgian provinces during the Regency period must be assessed. The faking of 'reformed' French *louis* coins, with the same title and alloy as the real ones did occur, but underweight *louis* coins were also manufactured, which was a monetary crime.

[11] AGR, JM, 58, Document 2.

[12] Idem, Document 1.

2 *The Fake* Louis d'or *of the Governor, Marquis of Prié*

The treaty of Utrecht (1713) oversaw a transfer of sovereignty in the Low Countries from Philippe d'Anjou, Louis XIV's grandson, and king of Spain under the name of Philip V, to the house of Habsburg, The early years of Austrian sovereignty in the Low Countries were rather chaotic. A decade of war had brought unspeakable havoc. Emperor Charles VI was very suspicious of the authorities appointed by his predecessor, including John Brouchoven of Bergeyck, a competent minister who presided over a reform of the finances under Anjou (de Schryver 1965),[13] A distant ruler, the emperor had to deal with the local elites and the government in Brussels managed affairs independently (Van Gelder 2011). Hercule Louis Joseph Turinetti, marquis de Prié (1658–1726), served as Governor *ad interim* with great freedom between 1716 and 1724, involving the Southern Low Countries in the shoddy affairs of fraud. For the operation on French money, 'absolute secrecy was required from [him] as well as from the government and several other people'.[14] It was deemed necessary in order to tackle the monetary aggression launched by the French in May 1718, and which was particularly potent in Belgian cities.

Indeed, that year, France undertook a new recoinage. First, the price of the 22 carat gold mark (the carat being the common unit of measure of gold purity) was raised from 480 livres to 600 livres. Second, the weight of the gold *louis* was increased to 6 *esterlins* and 12 *as*, and its value was increased to 36 livres. The weight of the silver *écu* was also changed to 16 *esterlins* and its value increased to 6 *livres*. Associated with a conversion of bearer bonds, this new devaluation of the *livre tournois* was widely contested by French Parlements (Lüthy, 310–311). It led to a massive drain of Belgian specie towards Louis XV's kingdom and gave rise to fears concerning its effects on trade: 'By its May 1718 declaration,

[13] In 1700–1701, the revenue from *aides* and *subsides* in the Low Countries provided the duc d'Anjou with a net return of 1.74 million florins (2.78 million in total revenue minus 1,034,490 in annual expenses). Overburdened with rents, the domain generated next to no revenue, while maintaining the troops in the field cost between 2.7 to 2.8 million florins. Archives nationales, Paris [now: NA], G^2 210, dossier 2: 'Etat général des aides et subsides que les provinces des Pays-Bas fournissent annuellement à SMC', 1701.

[14] AGR, JM, 58, Document 7.

France has just imposed on us a fresh loss of 30 percent by which not only is the course of trade interrupted, but also the thorough ruin of the State and the country is threatened'.[15]

In the face of the 'exchange rates [France] tyrannically imposes upon gold and silver coins' the reaction was swift: the English, Dutch, Liegeois, Genoese and Venetians resorted to counterfeiting the new French coins. The Marquis de Prié also engaged on this path, secretly securing support from Trossy, a finance adviser, and Jean-Charles Wautier, *maître général des monnaies*. It must be noted that the governor took the precaution of consulting the Society of Jesus on the appropriateness of such an operation. For the examples of the English and the Dutch, who were regarded as being marred by Protestantism, and the case of the Italian republics, which were not ruled according to the divine right of kings, seemed insufficient to morally justify counterfeiting. However, the Jesuits van Eyl and Guyot unburdened the conscience of the governor by giving their approval. Buoyed up by this encouragement, the Marquis de Prié launched the operations.

In September 1718, Wautier recruited Jean d'Arme (or Gendarme), a smelter, and Gilles Delmotte, a 43-year-old gold washer from Brussels, 'to prepare a machine to [work] gold and to mend a press that lay under the Palace's clock tower in this city'.[16] These instruments were moved into the stables of Wautier's residence. The latter also had in his possession the necessary smelting furnaces. Wautier's actions were therefore in complete contradiction with the decrees which naturally prohibited the minting of coins outside the mints. Van der Borght, another *maître des monnaies*, was also informed of the operation, as well as several members of the *Chambre des comptes*. Indeed, for his supplies of ingots Wautier relied on Van der Meeren, advisor at the *Chambre des comptes*, and the merchants Van der Mandere and Beauchamps. Prié entrusted them with a chest of 50,000 florins to start the operations, as per a contract passed in Bruges on 25 August 1718.

These suppliers, however, raised difficulties concerning the price of the gold. Their offer exceeded by 19 florins and 3 sols the rate of the 1652 decrees.[17] The merchants wished to force the sale by any means

[15] AGR, JM, 58, Document 2.

[16] Idem.

[17] Instead of 356 florins 13 sols for the *marc fin* of 24 carats, the price was 375 florins 16 sols.

and to accelerate production, a cause of trouble for Wautier who was waiting for Vienna's approval. When he heard that the Marquis de Prié was prepared to proceed with production without the Court's permission. Further to an alleged row with Van der Mandere and Beauchamps, Wautier denounced the whole operation to the fiscal councillor, hoping thereby to benefit from the immunity accorded by Article 41 of the 1652 decree, to any person who reported the perpetrators of counterfeiting, even if they were an accomplice in the operation.[18]

The new Austrian authorities had not yet taken the full measure of the Belgian concerns over the impact of French monetary policy. They seemed more preoccupied with the management of the elites. To the subjects of the southern Low Countries, their worries confirmed as 'a certain fact that public calamities had resulted from the lack of attention paid to currency which has always merited, because of its importance, the vigilance of Philip of Anjou and his officials, predecessors of Your Majesty'.[19] The Marquis de Prié might indeed not have been the man for the job of governor. The complaints against him reported in a secret memorandum written in Vienna in 1725 depict him as a greed y man.[20] Eleven charges were made against him. Not only had he failed to supply the Viennese authorities with the requested financial statements, but he had also omitted to submit each year a 'specific and accurate account of all funds, of any nature whatsoever, moved in and out of the royal treasury'. Furthermore, he was suspected of having unlawfully collected taxes, of having engaged in excessive borrowing, of having received bribes in return for offering posts in both secular and clerical institutions, and of having interests in the revenue from tax farms. Finally, he was accused of allowing the counterfeiting of coinage:

> The Marquis de Prié is said to have permitted, at Antwerp, the public minting of currency with the French die for the sum of 40 million, and when the members of the Chamber of Accounts have been authorised to investigate this disorder, the Marquis de Prié ordered the fiscal officer and

[18]AGR, JM, 20.

[19]AGR, JM, 58, pièce 4.

[20]AN, G^2 214, 'Examen de la Régence du Marquis de Prié; Mémoire secret touchant les omissions d'une part, et les excès de l'autre, que l'on peut supose [sic] de divers endroits avoir été practiqués pendant la régence du Marquis de Prié aux Pays-Bas, conséquemment au plein pouvoir de Sa Majesté', Vienna, 29 January 1725.

> secretary of the said tribunal back to Brussels. There is talk of 14 Brabant sols being made on every pistole, and of currency still being minted, less publicly, at Antwerp and Malines, with neither the Councillors nor the tribunals daring to speak of it.[21]

In other words, having failed to implement a counterfeiting operation in Brussels, Prié ensured that it would be done in Antwerp and prevented the councillors and judges of the Southern Low Countries from thwarting the new undertaking.

3 Pietro Proli and the Antwerp Connection

Backed by the leading businessmen in the Southern Netherlands and yet unable to use his Brussels network, the Marquis de Prié exploited the Antwerp connection by entrusting the counterfeiting operations to Pietro Proli, who played an active part from 1717 until 1723, if not later. Originally from Lombardy, Proli had settled in Antwerp as a merchant and banker, before he was appointed director of the Ostend Company in 1721 (Houtman-Desmedt 1983).[22] He had already been involved in currency trafficking. When the French government ordered the old *pistoles au soleil* to be re-stamped with the three *fleurs de lis* (1717) he had large quantities of the coins refashioned in Antwerp. For this purpose he partnered with several counterfeiters, including Guillaume Joris and Pierre Carpentier, assisted by an engraver called Boogh. Joris and Carpentier had use of minting presses at their residence. Following a dispute between Pierre Carpentier and his sister, wife of counterfeiter Nicolas-Joseph Madou, the re-stamped and old coins were delivered to Proli. The latter then proceeded to look for other minting presses, particularly in Isenghien. On this occasion, he attempted to get rid of his former associates. He summoned them to a meeting beneath the tower of the cathedral and pretended that they had been reported to the Mint of Antwerp. The manoeuvre did not work.

The scale of the counterfeit trafficking in Antwerp was considerable. To this day, no historian has been able to assess the precise extent of the traffic. Virtually all the bankers in the city were involved, shielded by

[21] Idem, 9th point in the *Mémoire secret*, 1725.

[22] Pietro Proli (1671–1733) was Charles' father.

Antwerp's privileges, by virtue of which the city stock exchange was exempt from any investigation—by order of His Majesty. Thus the members of Antwerp's bourgeoisie were not obliged to declare where their specie money originated from. However, it is important to distinguish between the different networks. Proli tended to work for the bankers of the Low Countries and the United Provinces. He did, however, smuggle *louis* into France, but in far lesser proportions than banker Baetans, the other important actor in Antwerp's network. As we shall see, contrary to Proli's semi-public trafficking, Baetean's fraud consisted in overstating the weight of *louis*, and then smuggling them back into France.

It is difficult to determine whether the fraud operations conducted in Antwerp were all commissioned by Prié or whether some served only the interests of bankers. Although Proli was associated with banking houses in Antwerp (Andre Pieters, Jean Charles van Heurck), Brussels (Charles Triponetti), Amsterdam (Andrioli) and Rotterdam (Crommelin and Commelijn), he also acted for his own account. Proli's partners ordered coins from him, having plates delivered from Holland. He took a commission of 15–30 sols per coin and sent the goods to his correspondents using complicit carriers. Jean-Pierre Gilbert and Adrien Coolens were paid one sol per new coin delivered. They sometimes took responsibility for the delivery of the plates. Jean-Pierre Gilbert was helped by his sisters who carried the plates from banker Pieters's home to Gilbert's. The plates were forwarded on by couriers—still on behalf of Pietro Proli—to all kinds of counterfeiters who had minting presses hidden in their Antwerp homes, or elsewhere. Among those counterfeiters were Charles Acquart, Pierre Carpentier, Guillaume Joris and Nicolas-Charles Madou. Some of the carriers became counterfeiters themselves: from 1723 onwards Jean-Pierre Gilbert minted *louis au soleil* coins in the village of Roesendael.

In 1718, the gold plates supplied by banker Andrioli were formed by Baerts, the assayer of the Mint of Antwerp, in Proli's mansion located to the south of Berchem's harbour. Proli hired Gilbert to deliver the plates to Isenghien in Flanders. There, he gave the gold plates to two Flemish counterfeiters, Jean-Baptiste and Nicolas Verhulst van Severen, who marked the plates with the six-crown French die, using a press manufactured in Amsterdam. The press was transported from Amsterdam to Isenghien by a goldsmith from Brussels known as Stevens, and acting on orders from Proli and Andrioli. Five chests were needed to transport the press in a journey overseen by Jean-Louis Pirson. An etcher known by the name of Liègeers was hired for the operation and was paid over 1800 florins for his services. Once marked, the coins were handed over to Gilbert who delivered them to Proli. This complex operation involved not only men with close connections to the government, but also a significant number of counterfeiters from Antwerp.

After Liègeers, the etcher, left, Pietro Proli hired a new production team based in Liège. The Prince-Bishop of Liège had already rendered himself notorious in the massive production of counterfeit French currency. Far from being inclined to fight the criminals, the prince-bishop of Liège, Joseph Clement of Bavaria, had the regrettable tendency to profit from the trafficking, with the complicity of the aldermen of Liège and the Canto brothers (Dumoulin 1992). The plates were transported to Liège by the carrier Gautier. The latter was joined by citizens of Holland: Adrien Adrianssens and Camille Florens, who resided in Rijsbergen in the barony of Breda, and by Adrien and Gerard van Opdorp, who lived halfway between Antwerp and Moerdijk. They delivered the goods to a stranger at a tavern. While the plates were being minted at the den in Liège, the carriers hid in wait, before getting on their way again to deliver the counterfeit coins to Proli either in Antwerp or Berchem. Towards the end of 1718, a Lombard banker changed Proli's plans by entrusting Adrien Coolens with transport of'a large quantity of gold plates' to Malperdy Castle, situated on a moor, one league away from the village of Westwesel. There, the plates were delivered to Proli's employees—including the Opdorp brothers—and pressed with the Cross of Malta, the French die. Coolens waited there as long as was necessary before returning to Antwerp with the coins.[23]

4 The Counterfeiting of Gold Louis with Two Ls

Proli conducted this new venture in the counterfeiting of French coins, and remained safe from prosecution until his activities were discovered and led to the high profile trial of 1723–1725. If one is to believe several testimonies, clandestine minting presses for manufacturing counterfeit specie had been flourishing in Isenghien, Liège, Malperdy, and other places. Meanwhile, the counterfeiters experienced a few scares, for example in 1720 when a press ordered by Andrioli and Proli was seized

[23] AGR, JM, 58, Comparution et déposition d'Adrien Coolens, 11 July 1725.

in Brussels. On this occasion, Andrioli lost 945 gold plates, which gives an indication of the magnitude of the trafficking. Etcher Lambert and minter Pierre Dubois were arrested, while Pietro Proli, in a panic, tried to get rid as quickly as possible of the 900 plates with the Cross of Malta. The banker begged Jean-Pierre Gilbert and Adrien Coolens to 'hide or burn all papers and documents they and others had in their possession pertaining to his commerce in specie coin and currency".[24] Proli did not, however, stop his fraudulent trafficking activities. Indeed, he employed Guillaume Joris to mint French pistoles with two Ls. He also bought coins from Coolens and his associate Gilbert and sent the lot to France.

Transporting counterfeit currency into France was a different affair and it bore much resemblance to the activities conducted in Antwerp by bankers such as Baetens, Devos or Vandaele concerning the production of underweight *louis d'or* coins. It was one thing to counterfeit money with a view to protecting from the French devaluations by re-stamping genuine *louis* while maintaining the extrinsic value of the specie. It was quite another one to manufacture underweight coins and to resell them in France. As can be seen from the list below, Gilbert and Coolens did not only work for Pietro Proli but had other clients (Table 1).

Gilbert and Coolens also supplied the metals and tens of thousands of *louis* coins which they collected from Amsterdam with the help of the above mentioned carriers—Adrien Adrienssens, Camille Florens, Adrien and Gerard van Opdorp. A total of 277,870 pistoles were counterfeited between 1718 and 1723. 172,068 *pistoles* by banker Andrioli between 26 August 1718 and 19 May 1723, 23,594 by Jacques Scheltens between 20 April 1719 and 13 January 1721, and 82,208 by bankers Magistris and Ravelli between 13 March 1722 and 19 May 1723.

The Marquis de Prié does not appear to have been aware of this traffic before April 1723, when de Hemptines was instructed by the Chambre des comptes of Brabant to prosecute the counterfeiters, and informed him of the recent discoveries.[25] Hubert Baetens and his brother had in their cellar a large minting press and all the manufacturing equipment, moulds, crucibles, files, etc. There, the operations were simple:

[24] Idem.

[25] AN, G^2 220, dossier 24, Correspondance du procureur général de Hemptines au sujet des perquisitions et informations contre les faux-monnayeurs.

Table 1 List of purchasers of *louis* with a double L working with Adrien Coolens

Name	*Occupation or location*	*Period of purchase*	*Quantity of coins*
ACQUART Charles	Counterfeiter		1633
BAL Gilles	Merchant, Antwerp	18 March–22 May 1721	310
DONCKER de Jean	Cashier, Antwerp	22 November 1721–17 March 1722	560
BOSSARD Jean-Baptiste	Ypres		2211
CLE Pierre de	Banker, Antwerp		2437
COOVERS Alexandre	Messenger from Antwerp to Brussels		600
GRAS	Brussels	15 May 1719–12 August 1723	91,461
HELLIN Antoine and Noë		23 September 1721–14 March 1723	70,943
HELLIN A. and POITIER assoc.		9 January–19 July 1723	32,446
LAROSE Jacques	Merchant, Antwerp		1125
MASQUELIER Joseph	Banker, Antwerp	29 April 1721-25 May 1723	54,942
MASQUELIER Joseph	Banker, Antwerp	7 January 1724	319
MILON Joseph	Merchant—Mons		5470
PIETERS André	Banker, Antwerp	6 April 1723	1800
PROLI Pietro	Banker, Antwerp	3 March–15 November 1721	1349
SCHWARTS	Banker, Antwerp		8400
SMITS Jean-Gaspard	Merchant, Lille		1244
STEPHANO Jean	Antwerp		1918
VAN SEVEREN Nicolas	Counterfeiter, Dixmuden, pays de Was		5568
VANDENABECKEN	Messenger from Ghent to Brussels		3420
VAN DEN PIT Jacques	Pays de Was		100
VRYLINCKS	Banker, Antwerp		150
TRIPONETTI Charles	Banker, Antwerp	30 January–15 September 1721	11,683
VERHULST Jean-Baptiste	Counterfeiter, Isenghien		12,582
WILLEMS Michel	Banker, Ghent	11 September 1718–13 May 1721	14,554
Total			**326,906**

> The English guineas, without being melted, were stamped with the LL of the French die as well as the guineas of Malta. The *pistoles* of France and Spain were melted, making a profit of 42 to 43 sols per coin because the said coins were lighter by approximately 13 *as* than those minted in France, the alloy used being different to the one used to make the coins in France.[26]

Baetens claimed that between 1720 and 1723 almost 50 million florins in gold coins were smuggled into France. He operated especially on Sundays, Sunday being the day of the Eucharist. 'In the morning during High Mass', he minted 400 coins, watched by Jacob Goemare, a witness and middleman. Bankers Devos, Vandaele and de Clé did the same. Altogether, Hemptines charged 25 people with manufacturing double Ls *pistoles*, as well as 8 of the "manufacturer's" direct accomplices and 25 other people with having traded the metals and corresponded with these counterfeiters (Table 2).

It is important to bear in mind that a considerable number of Antwerp residents were involved, one way or another, in trafficking operations: so much so that it is difficult for historians to identify every relationship and disentangle the network of complicity. For example, Cooymans, one of the most famous merchants of Antwerp, became involved in the business of minting *pistoles au soleil*. He was associated with his brother, who lived in Breda, as well as with Christien van Ham, who lived in the municipal jurisdiction of Sundert, also home to the States General. In November 1723, at the home of Adrian Coolens, Cooymans met Cormille Walkiers, the Receiver General of the Domains, who was fully aware of the merchant's activities. Walkiers was himself in the business of printing plates on Carpentier's press and purchased a new press screw when it broke down. Bernard van Rietbeeck, also from Antwerp, was involved in transporting counterfeit *pistoles au soleil*. Those activities were so extensive that the city's magistrates were suspected of participating in the traffic, including the burgomaster de Kuyff who possessed a press for striking medals at his home. Interestingly, De Kuyff ended his career by taking the ecclesiastical habit and joining the cathedral chapter of his city. The general prosecutor listed the most prominent accomplices, among whom were de Kuyff, but also Baron de Cloots,

[26]Id., dossier 1, Informations prises par le conseiller et procureur général dans la ville d'Anvers sur les faux-monnayeurs, déclaration de Jean-Baptiste Derez, 27 July 1723.

Table 2 List of counterfeiters of *louis* with double L in Antwerp[a]

Name	*Role*	*Occupation*
ANDRIENSSENS Adrien	Bookkeeper of the counterfeiters	
BAETENS Hubert and Lambert, brothers	Manufacturer of coins	Bankers
BAL Gilles	Supplier of species	Merchant
BOTEROL		
BUNEL		Merchant
CANNEKENS		
CARPENTIER Pierre	Manufacturer of coins	
CLE Pierre de	Manufacturer of coins and plates	Banker
COGELS	Cashier of the counterfeiters Carpenter	
COOLENS Adrien	Manufacturer of coins	
COOVERS Alexandre		Carrier
DEBESCHE Jean-Baptiste		Goldsmith
DEVOS	Manufacturer of coins	Banker
DONCKER Jean de	Cashier	
GENDARME Jean	Manufacturer of coins	Smelter
GILBERT Jean-Pierre	Manufacturer of coins	Glass vendor
HAECK Charles	Receiver	
HELLIN Antoine	Manufacturer and seller of plates	Banker
HELLIN Noé	Receiver	
HUYBRECHTS Martin	Manufacturer of coins	Cloth merchant
JANSSENS		*Cipier du consitoire*
LAGAES		Apple seller
LANWERYSSENS		
LAROSE Jacques	Supplier	Merchant
LAVIGNE Corrmille	Manufacturer of coins	Goldsmith
LENAERT Pierre	Receiver and supplier of material	Merchant
LIESSY	Receiver	*Tireur d'or*
MATTHYSSENS		
MERTENS Jacques		Goldsmith
NEVIS Jacques		
NAEFF Jean de		
PEYTIER	Manufacturer of plates and supplier	Banker
POITIER, brother-in-law of the Hellins	Receiver	
SAEYS Charles		
SCHARENBERGH Jean	Manufacturer of coins	Goldsmith
SCHRENAERTS	Supplier of material	Banker
STEPHANO Jean	Supplier of material	Banker
VANBENGHEM		Goldsmith

(continued)

Table 2 (continued)

Name	*Role*	*Occupation*
VANBENGHEM		
VANDAELE	Manufacturer of coins	Banker
VANHEURCK Jean-Charles		
VAN PRUYSSENS Jean-Baptiste		Banker
VERACHTER Jean M.		
VERACHTER Guillaume		
VIGE, brother-in-law of Matthyssens		
VRYLINCKS	Supplier of metals	Banker
ZEGERS		

[a]AN, G^2 220, dossiers 9 and 10

the Pensioner Van Kessel, bankers Jean Van Delft and Jacomo de Cleves, silk merchant Devos, wine merchant Cormille de Winter, and cashier Maes.[27]

5 Liège's Manufacture

The market for counterfeiting the *louis* coins with 2 Ls was also exploited by the population in Liège. Jean-Louis Pirson's testimony and the analysis of his coded correspondence help better understand how the counterfeiter Nicolas Canto, ringleader of a network that was already well known in the Principality of Liège and beyond, together with Florkin, another counterfeiter, worked with François Dufour, a merchant in Luxembourg. Dufour provided Canto with old gold *louis* and old silver *écus* and other coins. The coins were re-stamped in clandestine workshops in Attert and Martelange. Jean-Louis Pirson was the go-between.[28] He was 45 years old in 1725 and he had worked for many years as the purchasing agent and Brussels correspondent of the widow of the governor of Liège. In exchange for old coins, he delivered fake *louis* with 2 Ls to

[27]AN, G^2 220, dossier 20, Noms de ceux que l'on soupçonne de coopérer à la fabrique et négoce des espèces dans ladite ville d'Anvers et que l'on pourroit bien convaincre en cas de recherche ultérieure'.

[28]Id., dossier 8, 'Examen du prisonnier Jean-Louis Pirson', February 1728; AGR, JM, 59, Procès-verbal, 1725.

Dufour, but also to all those who promised him bills of exchange, as Le Coultier Le Brun, 'so as not to be affected by the reduction in value of specie which [Pirson] believed would be reduced according to public rumours'.[29]

During his testimony on 23 April 1725, Pirson supplied the list of his accomplices. The list included the following names: Théodore Hacquier, Pierre Thomas, Henry Debruyne (residents of Brussels), Dufour and Ingelbien (residents of Luxemburg). Among the names mentioned in the coded correspondence are those of the famous French financier Paris de Montmartel, and Andrioli who supplied the planchets. The names of Dodemont—who was Hacquier's brother-in-law and accomplice—of the Marquis de Rossi, of Jacquet, receiver general of the Low Countries and his clerk, Brocard, also featured on the list.[30] The receiver general was charged, following the examination of an incriminating letter written by Brocard, dated 17 September 1724, in which he made mention of the *louis* with 2 Ls: 'I earnestly desire that they be put in circulation like those bearing the cross of Malta, as much because they can be put to use as because you have in your coffers a good supply of them, as you know. I have been told that 15 contrivances have been sold for a quarter in advance and 5 at face value, but that because of the absence of certain persons, they have not yet been transported'.[31]

Given that the sovereign of the Low Countries had not authorised the circulation of *louis* coins with 2 Ls on his territory, Jacquet could not have gathered a good supply through honest trade. The word 'contrivances' also reinforced the suspicion of fraud. It was eventually established that Jean Baudin Jacquet, born in Liège and receiver general of finances appointed by Eugène de Savoie in 1721,[32] had commissioned Pirson to trade 20,000 livres in Paris, with banker Cottin, in return for gold and silver specie to be brought back to Brussels.

[29] AGR, JM, 60, 'Note sur la correspondance de Jean-Louis Pirson, commençant par: 'Son Altesse sera informée que dans les lettres écrites à Jean-Louis Pirson, prisonnier...', n.d., ca. 1725. Pirson's interrogation revealed that a certain 'Ingelbien wanted to abet Pirson in his escapades by writing to the Liège bankers along the lines of model letters sent to him by... [Pirson] on the basis of legal objections allegedly made by the said bankers to bills of exchange'.

[30] Idem.

[31] AGR, JM, 61.

[32] AGR, JM, 60. Patents, 21 December 1721.

6 Counterfeiters and Royal Pardon

A few weeks before his sister, Marie-Elisabeth, became governor of the Netherlands by letters patent of 1 September 1725, Emperor Charles VI had tried to restore his monetary authority. Indeed, on 21 April, he eliminated the appreciation of silver coins in current value. Furthermore, he wished to devaluate the exchange rate of the gold *louis* of France to 10 *florins* and 16 *patards*, and that of the silver *ryder* of Holland to 3 *florins*. But the turmoil this caused in the country was such that the ordinance was repealed on 30 April.[33] Thus, both currencies survived, reflecting the subordinate position of the Low Countries in the North-West European trade. Marie-Elisabeth and the three councils re-established on 19 September 1725 were left to deal with that reality.

The restoration of authority required, above all, the dissolution of the counterfeiting networks that had been rampant during the governing years of the Marquis de Prié. On 14 April 1725, the Count Wirich von Daun, appointed Governor of the Low Countries in February, ordered a preliminary investigation and preparation of the 'prosecution of those who had the temerity to forge coins in Antwerp and elsewhere'.[34] He appointed two commissioners of the Council of Brabant and demanded that the criminal trial be conducted with 'as much diligence as may be'. Following investigations by Hemptines, General Prosecutor of Brabant,[35] the sentences were passed: the Council of Brabant ordered the banishment of many of the accused and asset forfeitures. The forgers themselves were executed with boiling oil and water and their property was confiscated and sold. Hubert Baetens and Adrien Coolens were among those. The sale of the latter's property raised a total of 90,000 florins. Pierre Carpentier was also sentenced, on 8 March 1726, 'to be executed in a cauldron of boiling oil and water, and to have all his property confiscated'. But he fled and so could only be executed in effigy. The authorities, meanwhile, attempted to recover the proceeds of the sale of his chattels, in total 87,278 florins.[36] The Council, however, was

[33] On 11 May 1725 the French louis were raised to a uniform exchange rate of 11 florins de change, or 12 florins and 16 ½ sols for current money.

[34] AGR, JM, 60, letter from Wirich Philippe Laurent, comte de Daun, prince de Thiano, 14 April 1725.

[35] Guillaume François Joseph, baron of Hemptines, died in 1766.

[36] Ordonnance of 24 April 1726 (Génard 1872: 161–162).

soon overwhelmed by the number of cases and failed to process them quickly.[37] Furthermore, the counterfeiters were part of the *crème de la crème* of the banking and trading sectors, which made it difficult to condemn all the protagonists without dealing a serious blow to Belgian trade. In Antwerp, the businessmen exercised their rights by reminding that the '[city's] sovereigns, notably the duke, Jean, have always been lenient and moderate in their dealings with the merchants, reassuring them with various privileges [...] among which it is said that the inhabitants of Antwerp could not be brought to justice before judges other than their laws'.[38] They argued that the investigations made against the Antwerp merchants between 1605 and 1608 had been over-rigorous: 'the obligation imposed on the merchants to supply their account books pertaining to the East India trade chased the main merchants out of the city of Antwerp to the United Provinces'.

Thus, following the arguments presented by the Magistrate of the city in support of his bourgeois citizens, most of the sentences were commuted to fines through acts of amnesty passed between May and December 1725.[39] The 'forgers' were released from prison but made to pay high fines. Guillaume Joris, pardoned on 20 May, was fined to the tune of 84,000 florins. Nicolas Joseph Madou had to pay 50,000 florins and Jean-Pierre Gilbert 42,000 florins, which the authorities also exacted from Mathias Nettine. Charles Acquart was fined 22,000 florins. Cornille de Winter appears in the list of those forced to disgorge 10,000 florins; Jean-Baptiste Debesche was fined 7000 florins, Jacques Mertens 6000, Martin Huybrechts 4000, etc. Most bankers were left alone by the authorities: Charles Triponetti, for example, was granted a moratorium from prosecution, while Pietro Proli got away with an act of silence established on 3 October. They all wished to clear their names so as to be able to continue their business lawfully. Joris and Gilbert even went so far as to tender for the running of the Antwerp Mint in 1727.

[37] In December 1725, Antoine-Joseph de Herzelles, member of the States of Brabant, sent to Vienna a 'Mémoire où l'on donne une idée de l'impossibilité où se trouve le Conseil de Brabant d'administrer la justice aussi promptement que les loix l'ordonnent'. 4908 trials were being conducted concurrently in the Tribunal (Mortier and Hasquin 1999: 58).

[38] AGR, JM, 58, Remontrances du Magistrat d'Anvers, 22 September 1725.

[39] AN, G2 220, Actes de grâce; AGR, JM, 58 et 61.

Similarly in Liège, the new prince, Georges-Louis de Berghe, took firm measures, in contrast to his predecessor. He had Pirson arrested on 21 February 1725. The latter was banished from Liège for 30 years. Count Wirich van Daun ordered investigations against many people in Liège, including high-ranking officials such as Receiver General Jean Baudin Jacquet who was suspected of fraud.[40] The Prince of Liège did not fail to supply Daun with the incriminating documents. Without any preparatory inquiry from any judicial institution and without any decree from any council, Daun issued orders of committal and for the seizure of assets against the Receiver General and his clerk, Brocard, in Brussels and Mechelen as well as in Ypres.

In both Liège and Brussels, the political will to put a definitive end to the activities of the 'counterfeiters of French coins' dealt a blow to business. In 1726, following the example of Charles VI who issued an ordinance to condemning the counterfeiters to death by hanging (21 January), the prince of Liège confirmed the impossibility of claiming any privileges whatsoever intending to prevent the arrest of a counterfeiter; and he issued an order prohibiting the possession of presses, coining mills and dies for the manufacturing of specie coins. He called on the population to inform the authorities about any suspected counterfeiting activities, promising 100 *écus* in addition to one-third of the value of the confiscated coins. The ringleader of the network, Nicolas Canto, was arrested in December 1726.

Many grey areas subsisted, however, as to the principles of law on the basis of which the sentences were passed. There is no doubt that the necessity to defend the Belgian currency prompted the judges to temper the sentences. The leniency of the sentences lies at the heart of the administration of the Low Countries because the French monetary policy remained a major stumbling block for the economy. The temptation to produce coins imitating French coinage remained. At the end of 1726, Marquis de Rialp[41] and Baron Adam Joseph Sotelet signed an agreement for the manufacture of gold coins similar to those 'that will be minted in France'.[42] Sotelet was entirely free to procure precious

[40]AGR, JM, 60. Patents, 21 December 1721.

[41]The marquis of Rialp, don Ramon de Vilana Perlas (1663–1741), was the head of the Spanish Secretariat of State in Vienna. He served as intermediary between Emperor Charles VI, of whom he was an intimate, and the supreme Council of the Netherlands.

[42]The text of the convention in Bigwood (1903: 372–374).

metals and to circulate the counterfeit species wherever he wished, but he had to bear the costs of the operation. The profits, however, were to be shared equally with the sovereign. This agreement was never put into practice because the French monetary reformation of 1726 produced positive effects on European trade. Sotelet nevertheless incurred expenses and invested large sums in the operation for almost two years. As in 1718, the key actor in this manufacture of foreign currency had to procure the metals and the necessary equipment, and had to surround himself with competent people, both workers and carriers.

It is difficult to ascertain to what extent Marie-Elisabeth was aware of that arrangement, overseen by her brother from Vienna. Whatever the case might be, she was not able to defend the Baron when he was apprehended by the Magistrate of Brussels for various acts of misappropriation he was alleged to have committed. Sotelet, who was in possession of the compromising agreement, negotiated a safe passage. Similarly, Marie-Elisabeth granted Receiver General Jacquet a safe conduct for himself on 30 October 1725 and the release of his assets on 8 July 1726.[43] Jacquet had opportunely recalled the services he had rendered to meet the emperor's pressing needs, in particular the funding of Charles VI's troops and the 120,000 florins that were still owed to him, and also the 100,000 florins still due to him for his services as public receiver. The governor also discharged Théodore Hacquier and François Dufour. All this is understandable if one bears in mind that the Low Countries reacted belatedly to the new context of European foreign exchange.

7 Conclusion

The monetary policy of the Sun King, who flouted the right of nations to trade according to principles of fair exchange, put all his neighbours on alert. Unless the Belgians were prepared to suffer considerable losses, it was impossible for them not to react to the impact of the French devaluation by forging massive quantities of *louis*. The public authorities turned a blind eye to the actions of the merchants who had the capacity to re-stamp the French coins. The Minister Plenipotentiary of the Austrian Low Countries himself, the marquis de Prié, was involved in the trafficking and without too many scruples. The leniency of Marie-Elisabeth makes sense if one bears in mind that the judges of the special

[43] AGR, JM, 60, Orders of 30 October 1725 and 8 July 1726.

commission distinguished imitators from real counterfeiters. The latter were sentenced to death by boiling oil and water, while the former were merely made to pay fines. There was great risk in wiping out the *crème de la crème* of the Antwerp mercantile sector by passing overly harsh sentences.

The production of counterfeit currency in Antwerp made the authorities aware of the need to intervene in the monetary concert of nations by implementing measures other than maintaining the double system of money of exchange and of current money. The system as a whole had to be redefined, and not just the gold-silver parity, but also the legal value of currencies, so as to harmonise them with that of neighbouring countries. The establishment under Marie-Elisabeth of a new monetary institution, the *Jointe des Monnaies* (1730), was followed by the great reform undertaken by Maria Theresa of Austria in 1749. These successive efforts enabled the Belgian nation to regain its monetary identity, and gave the nation the means to trade peacefully (Legay 2016). The arbitration function of the sovereign became decisive. This was a new role for the political authorities, who now had to shift from using currency as a source of tax revenue to using it for mercantilist purposes. While businessmen naturally mastered the markets of precious metals and currencies and often acted without taking into account the legal tender defined by the legitimate ruler—sometimes to such an extent as to usurp monetary sovereignty (Rachline 1993: 72)—it was important to reduce their capacity to intervene on the market by defining a coherent system to stabilise commerce. Currency was an asset which engaged the whole of society, and, according to Simmel (1987), which required validation on which trust was to be based, and which unified the community. In the absence of a central bank, the first of which was to be set up in Belgium in 1850, it was the sovereign's responsibility to voluntarily peg his currency to that of his neighbours.

References

Alland, D., and S. Rials. 2003. *Dictionnaire de la culture juridique*. Paris: Lamy-PUF.

Babelon, E. 1908. *La théorie féodale de la monnaie*. Paris: Imprimerie nationale, C. Klincksieck.

Béaur, G., H. Bonin, and C. Lemercier. 2007. *Fraude, contrefaçon, contrebande de l'Antiquité à nos jours*. Genève and Paris: Droz.

Bigwood, G. 1903. Fabrications clandestines de monnaies d'or françaises sous Charles VI dans les Pays-Bas autrichiens. *Revue belge de numismatique* 59 (77–97): 356–376.

Bloch, Marc. 1953. Mutations monétaires dans l'Ancienne France. *Annales Economies, Sociétés, Civilisations* VIII: 145–158.

Bridrey, E. 1906. *La théorie de la monnaie au XIVe siècle. Nicole Oresme*. Paris: V. Giard et E. Brière.

Cauchies, J.-M. 1976. Faux-monnayeur et justice du chaudron à Valenciennes (1438), *Valenciennes et les anciens Pays-Bas, Mélanges offerts à Paul Lefrancq*. Valenciennes, Publication du Cercle archéologique et historique de Valenciennes, IX: 81–93.

de Schryver, R. 1965. *Jan van Brouchoven, graaf van Bergeyck (1644–1725): Een halve eeuw staatkunde in de Spaanse Nederlanden en in Europa*. Brussels: Paleis der Academiën.

Demoulin, B. 1992. Le faux-monnayage dans la Principauté de Liège au temps de la Régence 1715–1726, *Bulletin de l'Institut archéologique liégeois* CIV: 335–342.

Félix, J. 2018. 'The Most Difficult Financial Matter That Has Ever Presented Itself': Paper Money and the Financing of Warfare Under Louis XIV. *Financial History Review* 25 (1): 43–70.

Feller, L. 1986. *Faux-monnayeurs et fausses monnaies en France à la fin du moyen âge*. Paris: Le Léopard d'Or.

Génard, P. 1872. *L'hôtel des Monnaies d'Anvers*. Anvers: C. Muquardt.

Houtman-Desmedt, H. 1983. *Charles Proli, Antwerps zakenman en bankier, 1723–1786*. Brussels: Verhandelingen.

Legay, M.-L. 2016. *La souveraineté monétaire dans les Pays-Bas méridionaux XVIe–XIXe siècle*. Turhnou: Brepols Publishers.

Lévy, C.-F. 1977. Finances et spéculation sous la Régence. *Bulletin de la société d'histoire moderne et contemporaine* 20: 10–17.

Lüthy, H. 1960. *La banque protestante de la Révocation de l'édit de Nantes à la Révolution*, t.1. Paris: SEVPEN.

Mortier, R., and H. Hasquin. 1999. *La haute administration dans les Pays-Bas autrichiens, Etudes sur le XVIIIe siècle*, vol. XXVII. Brussels: Éditions de l'université de Bruxelles.

Rachline, F. 1993. *Que l'argent soit. Capitalisme et alchimie de l'avenir*. Paris: Calmann-Lévy.

Renoux-Zagamé, M.-F. 2003. *Du droit de Dieu au droit de l'homme*. Paris: PUF.

Rowlands, G. 2012. *The Financial Decline of a Great Power. War, Influence and Money in Louis XIV's France*. Oxford: Oxford University Press.

Simmel, G. 1987. *Philosophie de l'argent*. Paris: PUF.

Tutin, C. 2009. *Une histoire des théories monétaires par les textes*. Paris: Flammarion.

Van Gelder, K. 2011. L'empereur Charles VI et l'héritage anjoin dans les Pays-Bas méridionaux (1716–1725). *Revue d'histoire moderne et contemporaine* 58: 53–79.
Van Werveke, H. 1934. Monnaie de compte et monnaie réelle. *Revue belge de philologie et d'histoire* 13 (1–2): 123–152.

CHAPTER 6

The Talhouët Affair: Graft and Punishment in 1723 France

François R. Velde

The "Talhouët Affair" was the most serious corruption scandal of eighteenth-century France. It arose in the context of a major restructuring of the public debt (the "Visa" of 1721–1723) and was handled by a special court which meted out exemplary punishment. Both the Affair and its context (the Visa of 1721) are known, but have not been studied in detail (Combeau 1999; Deschamps 2015).[1] In this paper I will begin with a summary the Visa and then recount the Affair, with some concluding comments.

[1] The comte d'Argenson, who was the investigating magistrate, kept considerable material on the affair (Bibliothèque de l'Arsenal, mss 2848–2849; see also the diary of the court in Bibliothèque du Sénat, mss 139–140).

F. R. Velde (✉)
Federal Reserve Bank of Chicago, Chicago, IL, USA
e-mail: fvelde@frbchi.org

J. Félix and A. Dubet (eds.), *The War Within*,
Palgrave Studies in the History of Finance,
https://doi.org/10.1007/978-3-319-98050-8_6

1 French Finances from 1715 to 1720

As is well known, the second half of the reign of Louis XIV left France saddled with a huge debt (around 50% of GDP, or ten times fiscal revenues). At his death in 1715 his five-year old great-grandson Louis XV succeeded him under the regency of the sun-king's nephew, the duc d'Orléans.[2] The Regent had to deal with the financial situation. In a first phase, under the leadership of the duc de Noailles, the budget was brought under control using old-fashioned methods: namely, a combination of partial defaults (cuts on interest payments, "renegotiation" under duress of the short-term debt), tax increases (including heavy monetary taxation) and spending cuts. By 1718 the budget was not too far from balance, but little had changed in the structures and methods of public finance, and Europe remained a dangerous place, with war threatening to break out at any time and leave France either to forfeit the fight or risk bankruptcy.

It is in this context that the Scotsman John Law proposed to give France better fiscal and financial tools, and convinced the Regent to let him set up in succession a series of institutions and policies that held the promise to transform French public finance. First (in 1716) he created a Bank that could issue notes, lend cheaply and stimulate the economy. Then (in 1717) he founded a trading company that would earn profits on overseas trade and undeveloped colonies, as well as collect taxes more efficiently. Finally, in 1719, he launched a massive debt conversion that promised to lower the government's borrowing costs: the Company lent to the government enough to repay the whole national debt and financed this loan by issuing equity, effectively turning government bondholders into shareholders of the French Indies Company. As is also well known, Law's "System" (as the scheme became known) didn't work out. Law used the Bank to support the price of Indies Company shares, unleashing inflation. His attempts to reverse the inflation led to a crisis of confidence and a run on the Bank in May 1720. For the next six months he sought to reduce the quantity of outstanding notes by issuing various securities, without success. At the same time, the debt conversion was halted and reversed, with new perpetual annuities issued to buy back

[2] When Louis XV came of age in February 1722 the duc d'Orléans ceased to be Regent but his right-hand man the cardinal Dubois became prime minister.

the old debt certificates. When Law fled France in December 1720 the Company was insolvent and public finances were in disarray.

In January 1721, the Company and the Bank are insolvent. There were 2,200,000 livres (L) in securities of various kinds, all issued in 1719–1720. Of those 1,200,000 L were the King's debt (annuities issued from June 1720) and the rest were debts of the Company and the Bank. These securities were very heterogeneous in terms of their legal characteristics, collateral, interest, value at issuance, current market value, liquidity, ownership, etc. Who (the King, the Company) owed what was unclear. At a meeting in January 1721 the major decisions were taken to deal with the situation. First, the government chose not to walk away. All debts would be assumed by the King, his own as well as that of the Company, although doing so at par was financially impossible. Thus, based on the structural primary surplus, the government decided how much debt was sustainable: this provided the total aggregate value of debt that would be taken on. Next came the question of reducing the existing claims down to this aggregate value. Rather than impose uniform haircuts, the government adopted a plan put forward by the Paris brothers, longtime financiers. Their objective was to recreate the public debt at a sustainable level as described, redistribute among claimants in a transparent manner based on principles of fairness, and save the Indies Company. This required an examination and revision of all the claims: in other words, a "visa".

2 The Operation of the Visa, 1721–1723

To carry out this plan they proceeded in three steps. The first was the submission of all securities issued from Law's System. The second was the reduction of claims. The third was the issue of a new security.

1. Submission

In the first step, starting in January 1721, all individuals and corporations who held any of the securities generated by the System between 1719 and 1720 (shares and bonds of the Indies company, notes and bank accounts of the Bank, annuities issued by the king, vouchers issued during the debt conversion of 1719, etc.) were required to submit them for inspection ("visa"). Along with the securities they were required to provide their name, status or employment, and address, but no other personal information. In addition, they were to submit an itemised list of the securities as well as a statement of "origin," i.e. how the securities came into their hands (inheritance, exchange, reimbursement, purchase, commercial transaction, etc.). The submissions were registered and securities returned to the owners. A total of 500,000 claims were filed (the number of households in France was about 4.5 m), half for less than 500 L. In the offices of the Visa, the information was carefully processed, compiled and aggregated. The submissions were registered multiple times: at the time submission (in a diary), on the general ledger, and on special ledgers by origin and by nature of securities. In addition a dictionary of all claimants was compiled, with cross-references to all the ledgers and diaries.

The self-reporting of origins obviously problematic: after much opposition within the government, the Paris brothers were able to require all notaries in France to submit extracts of all financial transactions between July 1719 and December 1720. To assuage the fears raised by so much private information in the hands of the government, it was solemnly promised that all the documentation would be publicly burned at the conclusion of the Visa. The extracts were crossed-checked with the submissions through the dictionary, and when discrepancies were found the claimants were asked to provide clarification.

2. Reduction

The second stage was the reduction of claims, or imposition of haircuts. The aggregate amount of sustainable debt had been decided, and now aggregate amounts by nature and origin of securities were available. First, the shares in the Indies Company were separated from all other securities. Then, in November 1721 a matrix was devised, with rows and columns by nature and origin: the cells of the matrix were the coefficients of reduction. Since the total amount resulting was already fixed, "reducing" was really redistributing, a zero-sum operation. Notably, claims under 500 L were not reduced. Even claims without a proven origin received at least 5%.

The guiding principles were to use available the information to infer how "deserving" each claim was. At one extreme a government debtholder who had been forced to receive a reimbursement was considered the most "innocent"; at the other extreme, the speculator who had bought securities on the cheap at the last minute, the eighteenth-century equivalent of modern "vulture funds," were the least deserving. The bulk of the work was done between November 1721 and August 1722. For the most part, it consisted in a mechanical application of the rules. Of course many special or difficult cases arose, and there was a multiple-tier process to handle them. Four committees handled questions, a general committee chaired by the Contrôleur Général handled more difficult cases, and sensitive claims (princes, diplomats) and appeals were handled by the Contrôleur Général (minister of finance) himself.

The whole process was entirely outside the ordinary courts, under the authority of the Privy Council. The reductions were prepared by clerks, authorised by magistrates of the Council (8 councillors of State, 59 maîtres des requêtes, 45 councilors of the *Grand conseil*, a minor organ of the King's Council). The reductions began in December 1721 for small claims, in March 1722 for large claims, and in June 1722 for "sensitive claims." Every claim generated a "liquidation sheet" which served as the basis for the issue of new securities.

3. New securities

The last step was the issue of new securities, one for shares of the Indies Company and one for what would be part of the King's debt. In January 1722 a "special purpose vehicle" (SPV) was created which issued new securities to the public from March 1722 to early 1723. Those securities formed the liabilities of the Visa. Claimants were called in to bring in their old securities in exchange, and these formed the assets. Formally, the SPV consisted of a principal "comptable," 32 cashiers for each one of the 8 Paris bureaus and the various provinces bureaus, a chief comptroller and 16 deputy comptrollers.

The SPV was liquidated through three-way compensations with the King's Treasury and the Company. The profits of the SPV (from the reductions) accrued to the King, who gave them to the Company, as well as a further indemnity, in order to insure the solvency of the Company.[3] The Bank's books were balanced in November 1723, the Company was made whole (at the cost of increasing the King's debt), and all securities issued by the System had legally disappeared, putting the Company out of reach of any legal claims.

[3]The Company had been placed in receivership in April 1721. It emerged again as a free-standing Company in 1725 and continued to operate until 1769.

The extent of the operation was enormous. The 500,000 claims filled 3551 diaries. The notaries provided 1,393,000 extracts of financial transactions, although only those above a certain size were actually verified. The Visa sent 75,000 requests for clarification. At its peak the Visa employed 1900 clerks, and the total cost of the operation was 9 million L (in comparison, the total costs of the Royal Court amounted to 12 million L per year, out of a budget of around 200 millions).

3 The Affair

In late 1722, as the Visa was winding down, two commissioners conspired with cashiers to forge liquidation sheets, obtain certificates and sell them on the market. They were caught, tried by special court, and sentenced. The trial raised interesting legal issues and shed light on the government's stance toward corruption.

3.1 The Perpetrators

Let us now meet the five perpetrators, by order of precedence. The highest ranking was François-Joachim de La Pierre, seigneur de Talhouët (1687–1770). His grandfather was a wine merchant in Brittany who naturally became a tax collector of wine duties. He enriched himself by speculating on land, having been tipped off that the French Indies Company planned to build a port which is now Lorient on the coast of Brittany. This allowed him to buy an ennobling office and settle his children comfortably. François-Joachim's father bought him an office of councillor at the Parlement of Paris in 1710, and in December 1719 an office of *maître des requêtes*. In 1722 he married the daughter of Jean-Baptiste Bosc, *procureur général* of the *Cour des Aides* (attorney general of the Court of Excise), a close supporter of the Regent; the bishop of Sisteron, a close friend of Cardinal Dubois blessed the ceremony. He was therefore very well connected and on his way to a brilliant career. He was appointed as commissioner to the Visa in December 1721.

The other commissioner was Jean-Charles Clément (1689–1732), a younger son of Julien Clément, a famous "accoucheur" (man-midwife) who assisted in the births of Louis XIV's illegitimate children, and later all of the royal princes, including Louis XV and the reigning king of Spain. Destined for an ecclesiastical career he never took orders but received the commendam of a rich abbey in 1709. He was appointed in

1713 councillor to the *Grand Conseil*, a secondary royal court of justice. An amateur chemist, he thought he had found a way to produce saltpeter and had formed a partnership with an artillery officer and member of the Academy of Sciences; in December 1722 he had signed a contract with the War ministry to establish a factory near the Invalides. He was appointed commissioner to the Visa in March 1722.

The senior clerk, Jacques Daudé (c. 1673–1753), had served as war commissary in northern France under the Paris brothers in the early 1710s; the eldest Paris was godfather to his eldest son. He was taxed fairly heavily by the *Chambre de Justice* in 1716 but the Regent intervened to waive part of his fine. He was appointed chief comptroller of the Visa in January 1722. Jean-François Féburier (c. 1679–1728), son of a surgeon, came from the Paris bourgeoisie and started as a solicitor at the Parlement de Paris, but entered the world of war finance and spent most of the late war in the army provisioning business in Flanders. He married the daughter of a senior paymaster's clerk and sister of a future farmer general; widowed, he remarried with the daughter of the head of the high-warp tapestry workshop at the Gobelins. He was taxed fairly lightly by the *Chambre de Justice* in 1716 and was appointed cashier at the Visa in January 1722. The youngest clerk was Jean-Baptiste Gally (c. 1691–1743), born in northern France, secretary to the local *intendant* for a number of years, married in 1716 to the daughter of the treasurer of Maubeuge and a friend of Paris-Duverney. He was also appointed cashier in January 1722.

3.2 The Crime

As explained above, the main business of the Visa had concluded in September 1722, and indeed most of the documentation had been publicly burned, as promised, in October 1722. There still remained work to do. Some liquidation sheets and certificates remained unclaimed, and the deadline was extended to January 1723. Mistakes needed corrections, difficult cases were unresolved and a smaller group of commissioners were appointed to this task in August 1722. Finally, there remained sensitive cases (princes, high-ranking officials and foreign diplomats), handled personally by the minister of finance or the prime minister, who would order a supplementary liquidation sheet as needed. All of this meant a reduced personnel (most of the commissioners were discharged in September 1722) and perhaps less rigorous monitoring, especially since the sensitive cases were by their nature handled more discreetly. The final settlement and winding down of the Visa would not take place for a few months, and in the meantime the liquidation sheets remained in the custody of the cashiers, until such time as they gave accounts to the principal "comptable" (accountant).

The sequence of events can be inferred from the depositions of the defendants, with the limitation that Talhouët refused to answer and his version remains unknown; in addition the defendants occasionally contradicted each other, but on minor points. In September 1722 Talhouët approached Féburier, whom he had known for some years, and told him that he had been appointed to handle the liquidation of the sensitive cases and could create supplementary liquidation sheets, or supplements, as he saw fit. The idea was simple, but required both a cashier and a commissioner: the cashier would find claims in his custody that had been heavily reduced, the commissioner would revise them upward as if on government orders and issue supplementary liquidation sheets (backdating them) from which new certificates would be issued. The certificates would then be sold on the open market for cash.

Great minds thinking alike, at about the same time Daudé came up with the same idea. Gally, who had lost a fair amount in the Visa, had once approached him to ask if he could persuade one of the remaining commissioners to revise his liquidation sheet. Daudé thought not, but a few days later he went back to Gally and suggested to him the scheme, with Clément in mind as commissioner. Clément proved quite open to the idea.

The two sets of accomplices (Talhouët and Féburier on one hand, Clément, Daudé, and Gally on the other) eventually made contact, although how is unclear. At some point Daudé and Féburier came into contact, and Féburier provided Daudé with sheets to be signed by Clément. Later on, in late January 1723, Talhouët pressed an increasingly worried Féburier for more sheets, and the latter put him in touch with Gally, who became Talhouët's provider.

It was also around that time that Daudé improved the scheme: instead of revising existing liquidation sheets, they destroyed them and replaced with entirely fictitious ones under the same number. They bought shares on the open market and filed them under fictitious names and addresses. The names he took from the rolls of the French army's Irish regiments, under the belief that British claimants were better treated. This was an improvement because their method had been to identify claims that had suffered heavy reductions to produce false supplements. But large claims were likely to be have been filed by rich and well-connected claimants, who had either appealed without success or not appealed at all. When revisions went through the hands of various clerks (who were unaware that they were falsified), some of them conceived that informing claimants of their successful revision might be elicit gratitude and a reward. Thus word got around of the large revisions, as various individuals were stunned to learn that they were beneficiaries of revisions they thought denied of had never even requested. The individuals would inquire at the offices of the Visa and inevitably be referred to one of the accomplices, who would either brush them off or give them the run-around. But well-connected claimants were not so easily discouraged, and several escalated to Paris-Duverney, the Contrôleur general, or even the Regent.

In parallel the Visa operation was winding down, and the cashiers had to close their accounts. It became apparent to the Paris brothers that two bureaus had abnormal amounts of liquidations, and that the head cashiers were deliberately hindering the closure of their accounts. In late February Paris-Duverney requested an account of all the supplements issued since October 1722, a request that threw the cashiers into panic.

The cashiers stopped visiting the houses of the commissioners, and the accomplices met in other homes or even in the Tuileries gardens. Talhouët told them that he knew people in high places but had to bribe them, and demanded 100 shares from his accomplices. In early March the cashiers agreed to give him 25 each. Talhouët even proposed to create more fake sheets for Daudé's contribution but the cashiers refused and convinced Daudé to come up with 50 shares (Clément refused to participate, and only promised to give 10 shares after the end of the Visa). In exchange, however, they obtained from Talhouët written and signed receipts accounting for the certificates they had provided. This reassured the cashiers: Talhouët must indeed be well protected if he was willing to provide them such cover.

But the rumours kept growing and the cashiers were increasingly nervous, meeting constantly with Talhouët who assured them that he had been appointed to close their accounts and that it would be sufficient to bribe the clerks who were spreading rumours. Then Talhouët started asking the cashiers to return the documents he had signed, claiming that it was not in the right form to show to the Contrôleur général. Furthermore, when he learned that Gally had shown his receipt to one of the Paris brothers Talhouët became furious. The cashiers refused to give up their receipts, even after Daudé pleaded with them at Talhouët's insistence. To the end, however, Talhouët projected confidence. At one of their last meetings, Féburier asked Talhouët if he had any regrets: he had none.

3.3 *Arrest and Trial*

On 27 April 1723 an Englishman named Hartley went to the Visa offices to exchange a certificate for shares: the clerk suspected that something was wrong with the certificate and called the police. Hartley stated that he had purchased the certificate on behalf of a gentleman named Hayes from a broker. Gally, from whose bureau the certificate came, vouched for its authenticity. Two days later the Paris brothers met with the lieutenant of police Marc-Pierre de Voyer de Paulmy, comte d'Argenson, and orders were sent out to arrest the next morning Féburier and Gally, their clerks, Daudé, and another cashier named Pierre Sanson. All were sent to the Bastille and interrogated on 1 May. Daudé denied any irregularities; Gally did as well, but was contradicted by his clerk, and Féburier promptly claimed to have acted on the instructions of Talhouët and presented his copy of Talhouët's receipt. It quickly became clear that commissioners were involved, not mere clerks. The matter was presented to the prime minister and to the duc d'Orléans, who decided to establish a special court to handle the matter. Talhouët was arrested, but discreetly and properly: at 4 in the morning on a Sunday, by a police officer was a decorated army veteran, all gestures in consideration of his rank. The court, established by patents of 11 May was to investigate and try without further appeal fraud and wrongdoing committed in the Visa "to the great harm to our finances and the public interest," such crimes being under the king' sole jurisdiction (hence outside of the ordinary courts). The court held its sessions at the Arsenal, hence its name of *Chambre de l'Arsenal*, and was composed of four councillors of State and twelve maîtres des requêtes, colleagues of Talhouët. The king's attorney was Aubéry de Vatan and the investigating judge was the comte d'Argenson.

The court's first act was to issue a writ for the suspects, except Talhouët.[4] D'Argenson then proceeded along two tracks, searching for

[4]Their initial arrest on 30 April was by *lettre de cachet*; the king could detain them at his pleasure, but a writ was necessary to initiate criminal proceedings.

the testimonies of witnesses and for documentary evidence. Two dozen witnesses were deposed, mostly individuals in whose names the fraudulent liquidation sheets had been issued, to establish that they never received the certificates. Meanwhile the Paris brothers were using their machinery to single out all the suspect liquidation sheets, not only in the bureaus of Gally and Féburier but in all others. To that end the two cashiers were taken out of the Bastille at the end of May to their offices in order to close their books. All suspect documents were turned over to d'Argenson, who began to interrogate the suspects under investigation.

He started with Féburier on 2 June and interrogated three days in a row. Féburier brought up again the receipt signed by Talhouët and claimed to have followed orders; however privately he was despondent, as his police officer noted. On 7 June cardinal Dubois wrote to d'Argenson, instructing him to offer Féburier a complete pardon, and possibly no verdict, if he confessed and turned on his accomplices. But the investigation dragged on for another three weeks. The reasons are not entirely clear, but it seems likely that d'Argenson withheld the offer because he was at the time negotiating through Talhouët's father-in-law Bosc for a plea bargain. The exact terms of Talhouët's proposals are not known, but the minister of finance and above all Dubois turned down the offers. In the meantime, d'Argenson stopped interrogating Féburier and turned to Gally, interrogating him four times without success. He arrested the broker Raymond and several other irrelevant characters who made money pretending to facilitate revisions through their alleged connections to clerks of the Visa; he followed leads into dead ends, including a door-to-door search for the fictitious Irishmen. By the end of June Dubois was growing impatient and telling Vatan to press the case. Finally on 2 July Féburier confessed and over the course of three days gave a detailed account and revealed where he had hidden his Indies shares.

There was now enough evidence to go after the commissioners: Talhouët was issued a writ on 7 July to the despair of his father-in-law who had spent weeks pulling all the strings he could and trying to arrange a plea-bargain. The same day Clément was arrested at his house, in the middle of a chemistry experiment that he enthusiastically tried to explain to the arresting officer. A search of his papers revealed that he was secretly married to the widow of his coachman who had born him several sons. Clément, racked by remorse, had thrown all his ill-gotten gains into the fire on the day of Talhouët's arrest. Now everything came crashing down around him: the revelation of his marriage meant the loss of his abbey and only revenue, and his grand hopes of a saltpeter factory in Paris were ruined. He spoke willingly, all the while imploring his relatives and friends to help him. Gally, to whom d'Argenson returned on 22 July also confessed swiftly. Daudé proved a tougher nut: interrogation started on 9 July but Daudé continued to deny until 5 August when he too spilled everything.[5]

The testimonies, all assorted with remorseful tears, were in agreement with each other and with the written evidence. A confrontation of the defendants produced only minor disagreements. Only Talhouët remained silent. From 12 July to 4 August he was interrogated four times, and each time he indignantly denied the special court's right to try him. Although the patents creating the court waived all privileges and exemptions, he insisted that, as member of the Parlement he could only be tried by his peers. It did not matter much: the evidence was now overwhelming, whether he spoke or not, and he was tried as a "muet volontaire" as the code of criminal procedure provided. Bosc pleaded with the Parlement to protect its privileges, and his colleagues called on the king to lay before him the privileges of its members to be tried by their peers. The king graciously replied that it would protect the Parliament's privileges in other matters, but that this was a matter of State. This was not a case on which Parliament was going to spend much political capital.

The investigative procedures ended on 14 August with the rather perfunctory interrogation of the last of the indicted, the cashier Sanson on whom none of the conspirators had anything to say. D'Argenson drafted his report and Vatan prepared the indictment. The court sat only one day, on 26 August. Talhouët rejected again the court's jurisdiction, and then haughtily announced that he had documents proving his innocence. D'Argenson asked permission to step out of his role as judged and patiently addressed him as a colleague to show the implausibility of such a claim. Talhouët fell silent again and d'Argenson reprised his stern role of judge, castigating him for his silence when all his accomplices had confessed and proof was overabundant.

[5]From late July d'Argenson handed over the interrogations to two maîtres des requêtes seconded to him: François de Baussan and Pierre Pajot de Nozeau.

3.4 *The Legal Issues*

The conclusions of the king's attorney are known from two drafts in d'Argenson's papers, and he probably contributed to their drafting.[6] We also have the lawyer Marais's comments: one of the commissioners sitting on the court's bench consulted him several times (Marais 2004: 672–679). Ultimately, three charges were retained: malfeasance, graft and forgery; but each one had its problems. Malfeasance, that is misconduct in an official capacity, was applicable even in the case of the temporary and ad hoc appointments of the commissioners and cashiers of the Visa, because the king's trust was no less betrayed in this important operation than in a permanent appointment. The king's attorney did not confront the fact that Talhouët and Clément's appointments had lapsed, which Marais thought was crucial.

Graft involved the misappropriation of public funds. The immediate objection was that the defendants appropriated shares in the Indies Company, and not public funds (a distinction that they bore in mind and which relieved their scruples). But the Company had been established by letters patent and was "an association common to all the king's subjects" on which the fortunes of many were dependent. Moreover, through the process of the Visa, the king had decided himself the total number of shares outstanding: hence the number of shares was a matter of public interest.

The third charge of forgery was seemingly straightforward: the accomplices had altered and destroyed official documents and generated new ones.[7] However the prescriptions of the code of criminal procedure that forgery be proved by experts had been ignored, for obvious reasons. The documents were authentic in their form as were the signatures of the cashiers and commissioners. The documents were not counterfeits made by unauthorised parties in the narrow sense of forgery. In the broader sense of acts or documents intended to deceive and harm others, which the king' attorney retained, forgery was proven by the testimonies of claimants who had never received supplementary shares issued in their names, and by the confessions of four of the five defendants.

[6] Bibliothèque de l'Arsenal, mss 2849, fol. 620–630.

[7] Daudé had not signed any document, but he had conspired with the others, come up with the scheme to forge claims under fictitious names, and generally betrayed his duties as comptroller.

There was hence no need to submit the documents to expert evaluation; again, Marais did not agree with this line of reasoning.

The king's attorney, based on the three charges, had a variety of sentences he could request, based on ancient statutes and practice. Since a statute of 1531 the death penalty for forgery had been extended to a broad variety of circumstances, most recently and appositely by a declaration of 4 May 1720 (at the height of Law's System), for forging or altering any royal or public bill or security ("tous papiers royaux ou publics"). The phrase "papier public" was vague and ambiguous, and all the examples given in the declaration were registers, receipts, or claims of public treasurers and receivers. Were shares of the Indies Company "public securities"? Assuredly, since they were bearer instruments. The death penalty was therefore appropriate.

3.5 *Motives and Self-Justification*

The public case against the defendants was not airtight. The lawyer Marais refused to see malfeasance and graft, only theft; he conceded that forgery carried the death penalty but did not think it properly proven. Yet in a deep sense, there was no doubt that a crime had been committed, but it was a strange one.

The accomplices had been cognizant of these ambiguities and they had played no small role in their motivations. All those who confessed explained that they had felt mistreated by the events of recent years: the Chamber of Justice of 1716 (for Féburier and especially Daudé), the losses during the System, and the Visa itself (for Gally in particular, who saw 80,000 francs reduced to four shares). Daudé complained that thirty years of honest toil, to which the Paris brothers could testify, had been in vain. It is true that Law's System had upset the social order by promoting rapid changes in wealth, both upward and downward. This was not an entirely new phenomenon: the financiers could also enjoy spectacular ascents, both before and after 1720, but in 1720 the speed at which fortunes were done or undone was unusual, thanks to a secondary market with highly volatile prices. This recent event may have weakened the standards by which to judge what were allowable means of enrichment.

In addition the whole Visa operation had been predicated on the concept of justice: impartial rules applied mechanically to all individuals, no matter what their social standing. The "suppléments de faveur" deviated from those principles, and did so secretly. The sight of the special treatment given to favoured persons at the government's discretion must have been galling for some observers. The sense of injustice may have grounded, in the perpetrators' view, the notion that they were merely righting a wrong done to them. Clément thought that he was merely doing justice to himself. Daudé claimed that he had consulted casuists who had assured him that it was ethical to compensate himself, as long as no individual was harmed and that the amounts gained did not exceed his past losses.

The scheme used by the perpetrators had the additional advantage that there was no apparent victim. They had carefully restricted their fraud to shares of the Indies Company, shunning anything to do with the King's debt. The accused thought that they were stealing from no one, since there was no victim (and indeed there were no plaintiffs at the trial). Of course the argument hinges on the nature of the Company and the economic effect of counterfeiting. As argued by the king's attorney, the Company was really quasi-public, or as we might say in today's language a government-sponsored enterprise. It had a royal charter, although that was of course necessary for any new corporation (before nineteenth century laws made incorporation a routine matter); but beyond that the King had always been more or less involved in the management, and its shares were widely held. In January 1721 the government had decided that the Company's survival was in the national interest, and since April 1721 the Company was in fact directly managed by the government. Hence the protection of the Company's shares was a matter of public interest.

Counterfeiting shares, like counterfeiting money, is stealing from all shareholders at once. No single individual was harmed, but all shareholders were. The extent of the harm might seem at first quantitatively limited. As the king's attorney conceded in his closing paragraph, less than a thousand illicit shares were issued against a total of over 55,000.[8] Quantities alone could not explain why the price of Indies Company shares, on which the wealth of so many families depended, had fallen by half since the affair had broken out.[9] The deeper reason was the blow to public trust.

[8]A total of 935 shares was identified. At market value of March 1723 this was around 1.5 million livres.

[9]Vatan was not exaggerating. The shares, which were below 1000 until October 1722, had peaked at 1600 in late March 1723, and fallen to 830 on 9 July. On 23 August they were at 890; three days after the verdict they reached 1300 and stayed at that level for the rest of the year.

Here the difference between the cashiers and the commissioners comes into play. Clément may have complained about his personal losses in the System, but his abbey (where he never needed to set foot) yielded him 5000 francs a years, the same income as 50 shares. As for Talhouët, he was considered one of the richest men in his class. Indeed Talhouët's motivations remain a mystery, largely because of his stubborn silence. His associates complained repeatedly of his greed: whereas Daudé, Gally, and Clément shared their profits equally, Talhouët took two-thirds from the profits with Féburier, and the first time Gally dealt with Talhouët he remarked what a tough bargain he drove. Féburier once complained directly to Talhouët, who responded that he wanted to "build his house".[10] He was known as a big spender, but he must also have been somewhat reckless. The most surprising is his attempt to extract a hundred shares from his accomplices under the pretext of bribing the minister of finance, even as the dragnet was closing in on him. Perhaps he truly believed that his high connections would save him no matter what, as he once asserted to his reluctant accomplices who, in his opinion, needed him more than he needed them. If so, he badly misjudged.

We saw that Bosc's attempts to save his son-in-law were vain. As the judgement day approached the duc d'Orléans advised Bosc and his daughter to leave Paris for a while. Likewise Clément's father did all he could, and even prevailed on the king of Spain to intervene, to no effect. In a society where station, rank, and connection meant so much, this failure is remarkable. But more was at play here than Cardinal Dubois' well-known intransigence. The deeper meaning is apparent in the closing sentence of Vatan's statement to the court: "Convinced as we must be of His Majesty's pure intentions in ordering the Visa, we believe that no punishment can be too prompt or too public against those who betrayed the King's trust and caused his subjects harm beyond their own fortunes' ability to repair." The harm done to public trust was not just reflected in the price of the Company's shares: it was a blow to the Visa itself. If the public ceased to believe in its fairness, then it had all been in vain. And to ensure fairness the Visa had been entrusted to the highest class of civil servants, the maîtres des requêtes. That one of them, out of sheer greed, would have jeopardised the whole enterprise, was intolerable.

[10] "Bâtir sa maison" could be litteral or figurative, in the sense of establishing his house or family.

Class and privilege meant nothing where the State's supreme interest had been injured.

3.6 *The Outcome*

As the court deliberated on 26 August a brief under the king's signet arrived to suspend judgment on Féburier, honoring the promise made to him. The other sentences were sent to Versailles first, and published in Paris the next morning. Talhouët and Clément were sentenced to death, but letters patent of the same day commuted the sentence to perpetual banishment and confiscation of estates. Gally and Daudé were sentenced to death by hanging but the sentences were suspended. The 935 illicit shares were to be taken out of their estates.[11] Sanson's trial was to continue. The others (the cashiers' clerks, the broker Raymond and other incidental figures) were acquitted.

The commutations and suspensions disappointed the public: the lawyer Barbier (1866, 1:300) complained that "here we will never have the pleasure of seeing knaves of importance hanged". Dubois' death on 10 August did leave the duc d'Orléans without the discipline that kept his weakness in check, and may have saved the necks of Talhouët and Clément. But if they escaped the scaffold, they did little better. Talhouët was sent a few weeks later to an island fortress off the coast of Provence; he remained there until he was sent in 1747 to a prison outside Lyon where he died in 1770, almost half a century after his crimes, hardly forgotten but with no hope of forgiveness. Clément, thanks to his purported saltpeter recipe, was sent to Saumur where he might be put to work, but nothing came of it. He was eventually set free and ended up back in Paris, where the parish priest of Saint-Roch complained that his charity scams were taking alms away from the poor. The government expelled him and he found a position working for the Indies Company up the Senegal river in western Africa; he and his wife died there of disease soon after their arrival in 1732.

The cashiers fared somewhat better. Féburier of course was let free immediately, and died in 1728 in Paris, leaving a son who eventually became a minor tax collector. The death sentences of Daudé and Gally were used to extract from them restitution of their gains, but Daudé's

[11] Presumably the market value of those shares would be seized from the estate and used to buy an equal amount on the market and cancel them.

wife having run off to Switzerland with the shares little could be hoped from him and he was banished from France. He settled in Brussels and died there in 1753. Gally was able to repay nearly all and was also banished from France but allowed to return discreetly in 1725; on the occasion of the king's marriage the following year he received a pardon. He started a successful career as a wood merchant and died in Paris in 1743. Sanson, the other cashier who had been arrested but turned out to have been unconnected to the conspiracy, was merely a thief: he was released and died a little while later, having never completely repaid his theft.

4 Conclusion

The Visa was an extraordinary operation, designed to handle an extraordinary situation. As the number of claimants makes clear, Law's System (particularly the fact that the Bank notes, issued in denominations as small as 10 L) had affected the fortunes of many households. Rather than default wholesale, the government under the advice of the Paris brothers tried to limit the damage done and mitigate the redistributional impact of the failed debt conversion and ensuing inflation. Clearly the goal was to restore confidence, as far as possible, in the national debt.

For this to succeed the Paris brothers set up an amazing machinery, a masterpiece of bureaucratic engineering. To staff it they resorted to the cadre of high civil servants, the councilors of State and the maîtres des requêtes, and to an army of clerks, many drawn from the multitude of financial operations that had served the State in debt collection and war provision in recent decades. This was a world the Paris brothers knew well, and they relied on their judgement to choose cashiers and clerks. The transparency of the process was crucial to the appearance of fairness, which was in turn crucial for the reestablishment of the government's credit.

The scandal was extremely serious and threatened to destroy that most fragile outcome, trust. Fortunately for the government, the bureaucratic machinery, which had failed to prevent the fraud, generated the documentation necessary to confound the accused. It nevertheless took an offer of immunity to turn one cashier, and the obstinate silence of Talhouët prevented a full account from emerging, but did not prevent justice. The government paid no heed to the interventions of the commissioners' relatives and friends, however high placed they were. The Regent reminded them that he had let the count of Horn, a relative of his, be executed for having murdered a brokerbroker to steal his securities in 1720. Even fifty years after the fact Talhouët found no pardon.

The legal difficulties of the case also point to the novel nature of freely traded bearer shares, and the ambiguous position of the Indies Company as a non-State entity nevertheless vital to the national interest. The legal apparatus was not well designed to handle this kind of insider fraud, and the lack of clear victim made it difficult to shoe-horn the case into established categories. Yet if anything, the public was only partly contented by the outcome. Yet, even if the counterfactual is hard to prove, it seems possible that the Visa, and the swift justice meted out to the perpetrators, saved France from greater political upheaval, and bought the monarchy several decades of respite. How it used this respite is another story altogether.

References

Barbier, E.J.F. 1866. *Chronique de la Régence et du règne de Louis XV (1718–63)*, vol. 1. Paris: Charpentier.

Combeau, Y. 1999. *Le comte d'Argenson, 1696–1764: Ministre de Louis XV*. Paris: École des Chartes.

Deschamps, F.-M.-C. 2015. *Lettres sur le Visa des dettes de l'État, ordonné en 1721. Edition critique by F.* Classiques Garnier: Velde.

Marais, M. 2004. *Journal de Paris*, ed. H. Duranton and R. Grande-Route. Saint-Étienne: Publications de l'université de Saint-Étienne.

CHAPTER 7

Tax Officials Stand Accused: Reform in Taxation and Public Morality in the Dutch Republic, 1748–1756

Toon Kerkhoff

In 1748, protest erupted throughout the Dutch Republic about abuses in the system of tax farming. Demands for change came from an angry population and reform-minded agitators. In an explosion of popular protest, interests from various hitherto non-aligned parties converged to strive for a different system of taxation. Largely driven by this protest, Stadholder William IV—who governed from 1747 to 1751—and the Provincial Estates of Holland decided to change the system in an attempt to eradicate abusive practices. Thinking on how "old" tax farming could be converted into "new" public tax collecting led to the implementation of many new bureaucratic elements. In turn, bureaucratisation (or: "going public") meant rethinking public and private and why certain practices could therefore no longer be tolerated. As such, the period

T. Kerkhoff (✉)
Institute of Public Administration,
Leiden University, Leiden, The Netherlands
e-mail: a.d.n.kerkhoff@fgga.leidenuniv.nl

J. Félix and A. Dubet (eds.), *The War Within*,
Palgrave Studies in the History of Finance,
https://doi.org/10.1007/978-3-319-98050-8_7

offers a view on remarkable changes in the foundations of early-modern Dutch public administration and public morality.

Discontent with the system of taxation was part of wider turbulence in Dutch politics and society at the time. While actual taxation was itself no longer fundamentally rejected (Ma 2003: 448), protest erupted because the system had become corrupted. It emerged in the context of socio-economic, military and political difficulties faced by the Republic at the time (Israel 1998: 1069–1078). In fact, a corrupted system of taxation had become indicative for a corrupted system of government. In a classical sense, it was a symptom of a decaying society at large (see Buchan and Hill 2014). Abuse of office by tax farmers, often in close alliance with ruling city regents, became emblematic for the abuses of the administrative elite. Tax farmers were considered to be in league with regent authorities and both were seen as part and parcel of a corrupted body politic. In addition, as part of the War of the Austrian Succession (1740–1748), French military threat in the Austrian Netherlands heightened fears that neither the newly instated Stadholder William IV nor—especially—the ruling regents could defend the Republic. Linked to tax riots were, therefore, calls to increase the power of the Stadholder and take it away from the regents. Finally, a declining economy added fuel to the fire. A general sense of economic decay made the wealth of tax farmers and regents intolerable (Israel 1998: 959–1121; Pfeil 1998: 44–49). Lavish living was proof that tax officials enriched themselves at the expense of others. Many public pamphlets of the time critiqued such "avarice, usury, greed, haughtiness and general lack of decency" (*Burgerlyke oplettendheid* 1748: 5–9).

1 A System of Tax Farming

The Dutch Republic of the eighteenth century had a relatively high number and large variety of taxes; something contemporaries had already noticed (De Mandeville 1988: 187; Smith 1981: 906). Taxes mostly consisted of indirect excises on popular consumer items such as bread or wine. Since 1583, the collection of these excises in the province of Holland was largely done by tax farmers in collaboration with public authorities. Tax farmers were private businessmen who bought the right to collect taxes, usually for half a year or a year (but sometimes for years in succession), during annual auctions organised by the local authorities in close consultation with general guidelines as set out by the Provincial

Estates. In order to acquire the farm, tax farmers had to pay a deposit and were obligated to hand over a part of their proceeds to the authorities in monthly payments. The amount to be paid was determined in advance of the auction and was based on expected returns.

Tax farming systems have been around since antiquity and were common in other early-modern European states such as France, Prussia, Britain or Spain. The system ensured the authorities of a steady flow of revenue without having to establish or operate an elaborate and expensive organisation for collection (Ma 2003: 9). At the same time, the system encouraged aggressive levying. After all, tax farmers had to collect enough to pay their monthly dues and had to recover their deposit. In addition, they were also allowed to keep the difference between the estimated amount (the money they paid to the authorities every month) and the money they actually collected (Dekker 1982: 134; Heringa 1983: 83). The authorities relied on the self-interest of entrepreneurs to acquire revenue; entrepreneurs willing to take risks (consider harvests or trade routes affected by bad weather or war) that government thus did not need to worry about.

While the system was beneficial for tax farmers and authorities alike, its basic set-up led to abuses, also in the Republic. While the Dutch tax farmers, together with the city and provincial regent elite were, in theory, tied to excise levels set by the authorities (Dekker 1982: 132), they did often abuse their powers to collect more than was allowed. Lack of supervision and complexity and variety of rules were part of the problem. There were also other—more fundamental—issues. Most importantly, the organisational arrangements of tax farming effectively facilitated fraud and abuse of power. Self-interest was a major catalyst of the system and ensured that tax farmers and public "law enforcement officials" (bailiffs, sheriffs, debt collectors and the like) were, for instance, awarded parts of people's fines to supplement their income. This could for instance lead to arrests on false charges to collect more pay. The variety of offences such as smuggling, bribery or price fixing was endless. People would change the prices of excises, deliberately over- or underestimated expected revenues, cheated with tax receipts, or bribed people who weighed goods at markets. Public officials in charge of supervision seemed unwilling or unable to end illegal practices (Engels 1862: 39–41). This too was partly institutional: local bailiffs and process servers would for instance be paid for their assistance in combating fraud or tracking down tax offenders. This made it interesting for them to apprehend people on false charges.

2 Riots and Protest

The system would lead to violent and large-scale popular protest across the Republic in June 1748. Riots occurred in the provinces of Groningen, Friesland and Holland. In the later—most important—province, cities such as The Hague, Leiden, Haarlem, Rotterdam and Amsterdam witnessed riots focused on the (moral) degeneration of the system. Furious mobs ransacked homes and possessions of hated tax farmers (De Vrankrijker and Elias 2005: 44). Pamphlets denounced fraudulent tax farmers and local officials alike. In the town of Leiden, the house of tax farmer Van der Kok was pillaged and destroyed. A pamphlet of the time read: "See here a crude image of Van der Kok, a tax farmer, renowned along the Rhine and Vecht for his extortion, the supreme Beelzebub, full of pride and vanity, so proud that even his house looks like the palace of some rich Venetian. His secret comforts alone have cost more than I have earned in all my life" (*Brief van een Zwitsers officier* 1748: 19–20).

In Holland, the protest had immediate administrative consequences. Initially, Stadholder William IV had been reluctant to act[1] but he finally squashed the riots on 25 June 1748 with a proposal to abolish tax farming (*Propositie van Syne Hoogheid* 1748). In his proposition he urged the Estates General to think of a new system of taxation. He seems to have grasped the root cause of the problem. According to the Prince, the citizens are not out to evade taxation in general. "It is", he wrote, "not their purpose or desire to avoid carrying the burdens that support the common cause". It was instead the way in which taxes were collected, which "hurts the common land". On 26 June 1748 the Estates of Holland decided to abolish tax farming because of the recent "grave disturbances" (*GPB* 1658–1796, Volume [vol.] VII, folio [f.] 1204–1205, dated [dd.] 26 June 1748). In Holland, tax farming was immediately abolished. However, to ensure that tax revenue would still come in, the Holland Estates announced a provisional arrangement on 26 July 1748 (*GPB* 1658–1796, vol. VII, f. 1204) whereby the indirect excises on consumer items were replaced with direct taxes to be paid by the cities in annual quota, based on the estimated use of goods by their citizens.

[1]A variety of official warnings is collected in the Groot Placaet Boeck [GPB], *Collection of Ordinances and Regulations by the Estates General and the Estates of Holland and West-Friesland (1658–1796)*, Volume VII, folio, 830–831, 832, 836.

For this, the cities were tasked to directly tax their citizens. In this way the Estates of Holland hoped to make fixed quotas out of the formerly farmed excises (Heringa 1983: 84; Wagenaar 1997: 93–94). However, due to a lack of cooperation from local functionaries as well as tax payers, revenues dropped significantly. The transitional arrangement did not work. As a result, the Holland Estates decided to return to indirect taxation through tax collecting in July and August of 1749. The main difference was that this new and permanent system of tax collecting was fully public. It was to remain intact until 1805 (*GPB* 1658–1796, vol. VII, f. 1360; Heringa 1983: 84).

In a motivation for introducing the new public system, the Holland Estates directly addressed the grievances of the populace. On 5 July 1749 they wrote that there "shall be introduced, tax levying on an equal footing for the whole of the province and the money collected in this way shall go into this countries' treasury, and our citizens will be freed from the vexations that so often occurred during the time of tax farming of the common means. In this way the reasons for all the displeasure that we have come to find against tax farming are all taken away and have ceased to exist". They also addressed the moral problems of the previous system of tax farming when they wrote how those tax farmers who had been inclined to do evil had caused much harm to the country (*GPB* 1658–1796, vol. VII, f. 1214–1215, dd. 4 July 1749). In the general ordinance of 28 August 1749 it was stated they wanted to "deter as much as we can all those who are looking for profit through fraud and stealing, and protect the good tax payer from being cheated and oppressed" (*GPB* 1658–1796, vol. VII, f. 1119). Of course, the Estates had less "noble" motives as well as they sought to end the riots and increase revenue. They vowed, for instance, to act against those who "willingly and knowingly, deliberately, profit from tax collecting and thereby extract revenues from the country" (*GPB* 1658–1796, vol. VII, f. 1360, art. Ix. See also GPB, vol. VII, f. 1005–1010, dd. 22 July 1749).

As things changed from 1748 onwards to meet the demands of both rioters and reformers, the design of a new public system of tax collecting became the most time-consuming responsibility of the daily administration of the province, the so-called *Gecommitteerde Raden* (Fockema Andreae 1961: 45; Israel 1998: 278–280). Among those mostly involved were Anthony van Wesele (1701–1757) and Jacob Vosmaer (1717–1781). Van Wesele became fiscal attorney and "attorney general" of the Gecommitteerde Raden (*GPB* 1658–1796, vol. VIII, f. 1022, dd. 5 May

1757 and GPB, vol. IX, f. 734, dd. 9 January 1762). Vosmaer was placed at the head of the new central provincial office of the common means. Together, they set up a new system from about 1750 onwards in which a new administrative structure of command was put in place and the tax farmers were replaced with public tax collectors. The new public tax collectors now had a legal position as public servants and became part of a chain of hierarchy and command. Main tax collectors would collect taxes in their area with the aid of some assistants (such as clerks, accountants or bookkeepers). The latter were all appointed and officially employed by the Provincial Estates, which was a big difference with before. In the case of large excises such as beer the main tax collector would be supported by subordinate tax collectors. The system had a strong emphasis on hierarchy, control and supervision. New public supervisors served as a link between the main tax collectors and Gecommitteerde Raden and the office of Vosmaer which served to implement and guide the reforms (Heringa 1983: 91; Wagenaar 2004: 558).

With tax collecting becoming public, a more bureaucratic organisation was created. Measures that were already there (most notable oaths of office and instructions) were revitalised. Many new measures were also introduced after 1748 (Kerkhoff 2011: 117–135). Tax officials now became public servants, i.e. protected by the provincial government, and control and supervision mechanisms were introduced. To increase hierarchy and ensure proper bookkeeping, guidelines were for instance established about the regularity and continuity of the work of public tax collectors. For example, every year tax collectors would receive two ledgers. One "rough book" or daily journal, the other an official ledger. These had to be updated every day and a balance sheet would have to be made at the end of each month. For every missing day, collectors would be fined ten guilders (*GPB* 1658–1796, vol. VIII, article [art.] ix, dd. September 1748; *Instructie voor de collecteurs* 1748). Van Wesele and Vosmaer also ordered the use of a specific type of book that was to be provided by the authorities. On the first page a clerk of Vosmaer's office wrote down the exact number of pages and sign off on them. The thread used to bind the book was then sealed at both ends with the coat of arms of the Province of Holland (*Instructie voor de collecteurs* 1748, art. viii, dd. 7 August 1748). With this, the Estates hoped to make it more difficult for tax collectors to take out pages, insert new ones or otherwise withhold or alter information. Many cases against "fraudulent" tax collectors after 1750 show just how serious the Estates were about proper bookkeeping.[2] Lower law enforcement officials in charge of stopping or preventing illegal activities after 1748 would, for instance, have to inspect the different tollbooths and weighing houses "at least once a day at irregular hours, to see or hear whether the people working there did so properly, in a sober and capable way" (*Instructie voor de hoofdchergers* 1760, art. iv, dd. 17 April 1760). "Policemen" would have to provide detailed accounts of their daily rounds every month (Idem, art. iv, art. xiv–xv).

Other measures included adding formal rules and procedures such as a mandatory oath of office to try and ensure neutrality of public officials vis-à-vis citizens. As a way of "purification", officials had to promise they had not obtained the office in return for certain favours. Also, the oath meant to stamp out personal feelings and use of discretion. A "good" administrator was to be pure and incorruptible by following instructions and oath and was not to mix personal finances with public office. Measures were taken to increase merit-based appointment and selection. Tax officials were also to be debt-free and frugal Calvinists, able to read, write and calculate properly. All public officials were also assumed to know at least the basics of different decrees and instructions regarding the common means. They were also expected to be "sober and capable men of honest behaviour and reputation" (*GPB* 1658–1796, vol. VIII, art. i, dd. 2 October 1748). The instruction drafted by Vosmaer after 1748 stated, for example, that a public tax collector "shall be an able and diligent person, of the true reformed religion, a born Dutchman, a legal scholar or skilled user of the law, especially experienced with the levying of excises on the common means" (*GPB* 1658–1796, vol. VIII, f. 1007, art. i, dd. 11 June 1750). Higher officials were often explicitly expected to have legal expertise as well. Sometimes a "service oriented" state of mind was encouraged among tax officials. For instance, it was stated how public inspectors of weights and measures at the weighing-house were to be "decent people, over twenty five years old who should treat everyone with kindness, help people as quickly as possible and, above all, make sure citizens would not be delayed any longer then strictly necessary" (*Instructie en eed voor de ykers van de zoutmaten* 1797, art. vii). Further requirements usually dealt with reducing possible conflicts of interest and

[2] For examples, see the archive of Gecommitteerde Raden, National Archives, The Hague, The Netherlands, *Gecommitteerde Raden van de Staten van Holland* en Westfriesland 1621–1795 [Archive of the Daily Administration of the Estates of Holland and West-Friesland], access number 3.01.05, inventory number 4077.

limiting large concentrations of power. Provincial inspectors should, for instance, not themselves be an interested party in any of the common means (*Instructie voor de inspecteurs* 1751, art. i–ii). Tax officials were also not allowed to simultaneously occupy the post of bailiff, sheriff or mayor. Nor could they be any other kind of legal magistrate (*GPB* 1658–1796, vol. VII, f. 1005, art. iv, dd. 22 July 1749 and GPB, vol. I, f. 1806; GPB, vol. IV, f. 728). At the same time knowledge of and experience with the local community was also considered a good asset for tax officials (Heringa 1983: 86).

Other bureaucratic elements were establishing non-ownership of office and providing tax officials with the means to do their job. It was stipulated how offices could not be sold or passed on to friends or family, in an attempt to rule out nepotism. Also, from 1748 onwards, there was a move towards supplying public tax officials with books and other materials, such as pens and ink and peat and candles (for heating and light). A decree in 1760, for instance, asked inspectors to provide such necessary equipment in order to properly separate public office from private means—and common good from private interest (*Instructie voor de hoofdchergers* 1760, art. iv, art. xiv–xv, dd. 17 April 1760). Local and provincial authorities increasingly acknowledged the importance of being rewarded with a regular salary. Tax farmers had been paid based on what they collected. Before 1748, higher public officials in the system—such as provincial inspectors—did sometimes get a salary but this was almost always supplemented with ad hoc emoluments. Furthermore, their salaries depended on the amount of revenue that was brought in (*GPB* 1658–1796, vol. IV, f. 1968, dd. 30 July 1711). After 1748, this changed as fixed salaries would slowly but surely became the norm. Although this did not happen overnight and mixed forms of salaries would still be around, the idea of a fixed salary started to gain ground and was a major shift in attitude. According to several instructions, for various officials the idea behind fixed salaries was most of all that it would keep officials from accepting gifts or bribes (*Instructie voor de opsienders* 1760, art. lxv, dd. 4 April 1760). Standard salaries were regarded as a means to curb corruption and bribery and keep officials in check. After 1748 the Estates of Holland wrote that "now everyone is rewarded based on their qualities in a reasonable fashion" and that "because the collectors are, in fact, to be considered receivers of money owed to the treasury of the common land [...] each shall have to be fairly rewarded based on his quality and condition by the common land

[...] which is of course more natural, fair and consistent with the nature of things than using parts of fines to that end" (*GPB* 1658–1796, vol. VII, f. 1020, art. xxii–xxiii). The Estates argued how a salary (instead of emoluments or premiums) was meant to end accepting any gifts (Idem, vol. VII, f. 1020, art. xlv).

3 Corruption in a Changed System: Tax Officials Stand Accused

Of course, change did not come about in one clean sweep and old and new could still be entwined. Similarly, what is written on paper is not always executed in practice. In the transition after 1748, many of the now public tax officials must have felt they needed to keep up. Some were invariably left behind. The bureaucratisation of the newly established public system of tax collecting aligned with new or at least re-emphasised public values, perceptions of corruption, and expectations with regard to the "proper" behaviour of public (tax) officials. If you did not adhere to the new morality, you would have a problem. This much becomes clear from looking in detail cases of "corruption" by tax collectors after 1748. In the following some cases are presented as examples where "old" behaviour had become wrong. First, there is the case of tax officials Pieter Reijers and Frederik Vaster in Amsterdam. Second, there is the case of tax officials Jacobus Cras and Jacob Nolla in the town of Leiden.

3.1 Pieter Reijers and Frederik Vaster

In June 1751 Pieter Reijers, main public tax collector of the wines, and Frederik Vaster, public supervisor of the tax collecting of the wines in Amsterdam, made a bad decision. Both men knocked on the Amsterdam town council's door to recover losses they had supposedly suffered at the hands of a certain aldermen of the local court. The alderman, they claimed, had not handed in a tax receipt provided by Reijers for the purchase of some wine and had, therefore, not paid his taxes. While the action of Reijers and Vaster was lawful and indeed fitted well with the new bureaucratic regulations regarding public tax taxation (*GPB* 1658–1796, vol. VII, f. 1005, art. I, dd. 22 July 1749), the authorities were not amused with such a brute and "insolent" treatment of regents by these lowly tax officials. With their complaint, Reijers and Vaster seem to have disregarded the unwritten rule that regents should be left alone if at all possible. On 26 June 1751 the Amsterdam aldermen-commissioners wrote a letter to Gecommitteerde Raden in which they spoke of the "indiscrete, indecent and disrespectful actions" of Reijers and Vaster.[3] They requested Gecommitteerde Raden to interrogate both men for their disloyalty and asked for a full account of these interrogations. These followed on 8 July 1751 during which Reijers and Vaster apologised in an elaborate way, and vowed to have been unaware of any indecent action.[4] Furthermore, they were prepared to state the same to the Amsterdam aldermen-commissioners and the specific alderman in question if they were only allowed to do so. They hoped that would be sufficient.

In their reply to Gecommitteerde Raden the aggrieved commissioners stated that this was not the case. They believed the response by Vaster and Reijers had been credible but simultaneously argued that Vaster and Reijers were too unequal to be judged in the same way. As a result they chose to accept the apology of Vaster (the higher ranked supervisor) but not that of Reijers (the lower ranked collector) and Gecommitteerde Raden agreed. Reijers was subsequently fired while Vaster would be allowed to stay in office until 1757.[5] Reijers then made a bold move. He fled Amsterdam with a supposedly large sum of collected tax money. As far as the available sources can tell us, he was never caught. Since he did not show up at his trial he was sentenced *in absentia* and banned for life from the province.[6] The verdict was minimal and does not speak of any stolen money. However, Reijers was ordered to pay the costs of his trial. Bicker Raye, an Amsterdam regent who kept a journal of events in Amsterdam during his lifetime, writes that with Reijers being on the run, his parents were forced to pay a certain amount to the Estates of Holland, which supposedly ruined them (Beerinck and De Boer 1963: 195).

Interestingly, the unequal treatment of Reijers and Vaster by Gecommitteerde Raden and the fact that Reijers' parent were held financially responsible for the actions of their son, point to a lingering

[3] National Archives [NL-HaNA], access number [an.], 3.01.05, inventory number [in.], 3103, f. 1388, dd. 26 June 1751.

[4] Idem, f. 1447, dd. 8 July 1751.

[5] Amsterdam City Archives [hereafter: NL-AsdSAA], an., 5031, *Archive of the Mayors, documents on offices 1413–1859*, in., 109, f. 1.

[6] NL-HaNA, an., 3.01.05, in., 4074, f. 124, dd. 29 July 1752.

of pre-bureaucratic characteristics. After all, having the parents pay denotes some sense of ownership of office or at least personal, individual ***and*** family responsibility for a public office. Still, many changes were also visible in the case against Reijers and Vaster. Various sources other than judicial ones condemn both men for specific transgressions. Various anonymous pamphlets showed outrage over so much disloyalty and thieving, committed by people who were responsible for collecting tax money. Images and short verses soon appeared in which both men were mocked and scolded, for instance calling Reijers a coward and a villain. In a satire directed at him and Vaster (and tax collectors in general), it is lamented that the high and mighty always protect each other and always get away with anything by means of bribery and use of connections to the detriment of the land and its citizens. The pamphlet complains that Reijers will probably soon get some high office again, perhaps even at court. It also marks the "obvious" futility of the oath taken by Reijers and other tax collectors. He also notes their hypocrisy as they continuously profiteer and line their pockets. He writes, for instance, "alright gentlemen, now swear your oath, swear you sweat, blood and bile, swear you will not steal a dime but all the while fill your skinny bellies" (*De Cerberus* 1751, 10 and Appendix).

Another pamphlet was an imaginary letter from Reijers to his mother, as he was supposedly running from the law (*Copye van een merkwaardige missive* 1751). As a new horse is saddled up at some roadside inn, Reijers is made to reflect. "Sometimes", the letter states, "I am overcome with thousands of thoughts due to my lies and false oaths, and then I think of the state of mankind which comforts me. While we are all more or less sinners, he who is less so is most happy; the secret crimes that I have committed against the heavens, press hardest on me". The letter has him saying that "stealing from the lands' cash register is the least of my crimes, it is my bad upbringing that has made me incapable to be honest". Then, the letter gets to the heart of the matter as it says how Reijers has never been fit to hold such an important office in the first place. Whereas everywhere in Europe, state servants are of such virtue and nobility, Reijers is—according to the pamphlet—only of low birth and lacks morals as well as education. And how could it be otherwise, with a mother who (apparently) sold cooked eel on the streets.

Reijers quickly became something of a symbol for the fraudulent, thieving and greedy tax official, also after the new system had taken effect. Importantly, he is also attributed a distinct role in the wider political quarrels of the time. For one, he appears in an image alongside Daniel Raap, a porcelain salesman and former Doelist leader in Amsterdam.[7] Raap had been a confidant of William IV at the height of the Doelist revolt of 1748. However, with the failure of the Doelist movement he had fallen from grace and had become the symbol of its failure instead. In the image, Reijers and some other unknown fraudulent tax collector are already at the gallows waiting for Raap to arrive (Breen 1934: 229). The link between Reijers (the symbol of fraudulent tax collectors) and Raap (the symbol of failed Doelist reform movement) is interesting and demonstrates how "discussions" of corruption by tax officials were explicitly tied to social-political events of the time. According to popular opinion, corruption by tax officials could still continue precisely because of the failed Doelist reforms. A pamphlet from 1751 tells us this much. Now, Vaster and Raap are presented as imposters pretending to serve the common good but only serving their own. They deceived the people and mocked all that is holy, forgot their oath and duty and even dared to claim that it was all the fault of William IV, they abused his name for their own profit. All their promises were only meant to deceive, to provide false hope and to keep up appearances (*Advertentie* 1751).

Other tax officials were soon caught up in the scandal. Henricus Wachloo, main collector of the excises on butter in Amsterdam, was accused of having acquired his office from Raap, in return for a handsome sum of money and his support for Raap and the Doelist movement. On 2 November 1751, Wachloo is sentenced *in absentia* to banishment for life from the province.[8] Although Gecommitteerde Raden again do not discuss the crimes in detail, here too there was no shortage of pamphlets. A letter supposedly written by Wachloo is circulated in which he admits that while he was a wine tradesman "he had always been able to lead a quiet and advantageous existence by means of smuggling" (*Brief van Henricus Wachloo* 1751). He also directs his own anger at Raap, who is cursed for having approached him. "If only the judge would know", Wachloo writes, "that you [Raap] and your

[7]The Doelists had been merchants arguing for more political representation, a strong Stadholder and restoration of old guild privileges. They were the enemies of the ruling regent elite which excluded them. On the Doelist movement in Dutch history see De Voogd, N.J.J., *De Doelistenbeweging te Amsterdam in 1748*. Utrecht, 1914.

[8]NL-HaNA, an., 3.01.05, in., 4074, f. 112, dd. 2 November 1751.

accomplices sold offices for money, your fate will surely be worse than mine". Reijers is mentioned as well as the pamphlet discusses how Reijers had been allowed to carry on his "corrupt ways" for a long time. It read: "why is my colleague Reijers, a.k.a. pretty Pete (known as such by all the whores and strumpets) so forcefully protected, when everyone knows how he manages to keep a family, a whole array of whores and a mistress [...] for everyone knows that he had lots of debts when he started collecting".

Andries Mallan, another former Doelist agitator—this time from Rotterdam—and afterwards main tax collector of the excises on peat and coal in The Hague. One pamphlet portrayed Mallan as a fraud and a thief. In a pamphlet dripping with sarcasm, Mallan supposedly writes: "I acquired through this and other dashing actions the title of Patriot and because of this my sober countenance and dress came to be regarded by some as half and by others as three quarters divine. So it was in that time that I finally came to acquire the honourable position of collector of peat and coal for The Hague [...] in which I was so competent that in the first year I managed to borrow two thousand guilders from the communal coffers (to somewhat improve my sober appearance). By providing false monthly statements I managed to get as far ahead in life that I was publicly sentenced for being perjurious, without honour and shameful" (*De Cerberus* 1751: 3–4). The accusations of this pamphleteers were at least partly true. Mallan was sentenced by Gecommitteerde Raden for breaking his oath and instruction and having stolen *f*2024 from the provincial coffers. At his trial—at which he appeared[9]—he confessed that he had in fact taken an oath and also did not deny having received a clear instruction. As such he acknowledged that he had promised to report all incoming revenues to the supervisor. To Gecommitteerde Raden this was enough for a guilty verdict. Since, upon checking his books, Mallan proved to be short the *f*2024, Gecommitteerde Raden concluded he must have taken this money "for his own use or that of his family". Mallan did not deny the charges but defended himself by saying that "necessity has led me to use some of the nations' money for myself and my family, but I always intended to give it back". Gecommitteerde Raden still blamed him for "severe negligence, together with perjury, falsity and thievery which cannot be tolerated in a land of justice but

[9] NL-HaNA, an., 3.01.05, in., 4076, f. 102.

should be punished if only to let it be an example for others". Mallan was banished from the province for the rest of his life. Interestingly, the cases of Reijers, Wachloo and others were explicitly linked in various pamphlets, denoting the general atmosphere of the day. Their "many sinister, base and villainous acts and foul deceit" and "godless behaviour of the three bandits or refugees" warranted "to arrange the collection of the countries' common means in a better way" and to do something against "the enormously villainous acts committed by these false patriots [the Doelists] to the detriment of the common good" (*De Cerberus* 1751: 3–4).

3.2 Jacobus Cras and Jacob Nolla

A second case that shows specific attention to and changes in public morality in the course of a changing system of taxation was that of Jacobus Cras and Jacob Nolla. Cras was a supervisor of the countries' sealed and unsealed tax receipts in Leiden from 4 December 1749 to 6 August 1756.[10] As such, he was one of the new high-ranking public officials put in place after the changes in the tax system of 1748. As supervisor in the new system Cras was responsible for the supervision and control of all main and subordinate tax collectors and local investigators in Leiden (at the time the third largest city of Holland). He was also responsible for handing out tax receipts to the main collectors. Officials such as Cras had an important role in the new public system of tax collecting. This also meant they were always in the thick of it once problems occurred. The latter was often the case in the early days of the new system. The new rules were vague, people were unsure what to do or expect and old ways still lingered on.

In 1756, a scandal erupted when Cras and other tax officials were formally convicted by Gecommitteerde Raden for offences in the execution of their duties. The conviction concerned events and actions since 1747. One of the collectors Cras was meant to supervise and inspect was Jacob Nolla, main collector of the taxes on quite a few common means such as cows, horses, servants (a tax based on the number of servants one had) and general wealth (an early form of property and income tax), tobacco, coffee, tea and ferry fares in Leiden and some surrounding

[10] NL-HaNA, an., 3.01.41, in., 1226, f. 1.

villages. Nolla had been in office since 1747 and was one of those former tax farmers who stayed on as public tax collector after the tax riots. He remained in office until his death in 1756 which revealed many discrepancies in his administration. Investigations by Gecommitteerde Raden into Nolla's books showed he had taken quite some "accountancy liberties". It appeared that by the time of his death Nolla had a deficit of *f*17,000. The investigation soon led to Cras as the latter was after all Nolla's supervisor. Cras' books showed Nolla only had a deficit of *f*4000. Gecommitteerde Raden found that Cras had violated the rules of his instructions that obligated him to "accurately supervise whether the main and other collectors kept their administration in proper order". Second, Cras had obviously made some grave "accounting mistakes" himself when dealing with Nolla's books and accounts after Nolla had died. How else, after all, did his books reflect a deficit of only *f*4000 instead of *f*17,000?

Nolla could, due to his death, of course no longer be punished or prosecuted (although his widow and children had to sell everything they owned to repay as much of his debt to the province as they could.[11] Cras, however, was accused of bad supervision and bad accounting; two offences against instruction and oath. In his response before Gecommitteerde Raden, Cras admitted he had not noticed the "liberties" taken by Nolla over the years.[12] He had not gone through the latter's books as he should have. He also admitted having written to Gecommitteerde Raden right after Nolla's death that all things were indeed in order—even though they had clearly not been!—and that the office had been run properly—which it had not. When Gecommitteerde Raden asked Cras during the trial to comment on these false statements and Nolla's deficit, Cras had to admit how "such had not been possible had he obeyed the proper order to prevent such disloyal acts". He also stated that his negligent behaviour as supervisor "is the cause of the great loss now suffered by the common land". Cras thus takes the blame for bad supervision and negligence but denies any criminal intent; a statement that is supported by the fact that the verdict of Gecommitteerde Raden does not mention Cras stealing money for himself (Heringa 1983: 98).

[11] See Regional Archives of Leiden [hereafter: NL-LdnRAL], *Schepenbank/Oud Rechterlijk Archief* [hereafter: ORA], an., 508, in., 50jj, f. 156, dd. 15 December 1757.

[12] NL-HaNA, an., 3.01.05, in., 4077, f. 33–35, dd. 25 August 1756.

During the course of the investigations yet other activities of Cras were brought to light. Cras had apparently been involved in earlier dealings with Nolla. Nolla had been a butcher before becoming a tax farmer of the excise on meat in 1747. In 1749 he became main tax collector. His son Jan Nolla then took over the butcher shop since collectors in the new system were not allowed to have any business links with the common means for which they collected excises.[13] Even though the shop was now officially owned by the son, father Jacob still had an indirect interest. As such he provided meat to Cras between 1751 and 1753. Cras seems not to have been too eager or quick about paying Nolla for the meat. He told Gecommitteerde Raden, however, that he eventually gave Nolla an "I owe you' worth *f*600, in which he promised to pay this amount in four instalments". Nolla died before the debt was paid and the obligation went "to a certain grocer in Leiden". Cras did not know whether the obligation had been transferred to this grocer before or after Nolla's death.[14]

In what appears to be a rare case of legal openness, Gecommitteerde Raden provide a basis for their verdict. They pointed to a resolution of the Holland Estates from 1749 (repeated on 31 October 1753) which stipulated that higher public officials are not allowed to borrow or provide money or credit to lower ranked (i.e. subordinate) officials.[15] In violating this resolution, Cras was guilty of having had a conflict of interest and of abusing his superior position for financial gain. The conclusion of Gecommitteerde Raden was that "all this is highly damaging and disadvantageous to the common land and its finances [...] such acts should be punished without connivance as an example to prevent such things in the future, especially when it concerns a supervisor".[16] Still, Gecommitteerde Raden seemed determined to make an example out of Cras, possibly also to boost people's confidence in the new system of public tax collecting. His job had been, after all, precisely to prevent or stop the kind of corruption he had hidden from view and participated in himself. Cras was declared "incompetent" and sentenced to "repay the damages inflicted upon the country". If he did not or could not comply he would be

[13] NL-HaNA, an., 3.01.05, in., 3099, f. 848, dd. 29 November 1749, art. 2.

[14] NL-HaNA, an., 3.01.05, in., 4077, f. 34, dd. 25 August 1756.

[15] NL-HaNA, an., 3.01.05, in., 3099, f. 861–867, dd. 1 December 1749.

[16] NL-HaNA, an., 3.01.05, in., 4077, f. 35, dd. 25 August 1756.

banished from the province for life. In the end, the records are unfortunately unclear about the actual punishment but it seems likely that Cras paid at least some amount of money. In addition, the aldermen-commissioners of Leiden again ordered Cras on 8 November 1756 to pay his creditors.[17] From a list of creditors that was eventually presented to Cras by the aldermen-commissioners on 12 July 1757 it can be seen that Cras at that time still had a debt of almost *f*2000, to be divided between no less than nineteen creditors. Among the creditors are also several tax collectors of various common means, the Bailiff Van Alkmade and a large number of grocers. Apparently, Cras had purchased more than just meat on credit.[18]

4 Changing Public Morality in a Changing System of Taxation

The cases presented offer an insight into the reasons why public (tax) official behaviour was condemned or condoned and provide a view on what was considered good or bad administrative practice. Crucial values and value statements included those linked to bureaucratisation, such as keeping one's books in good order, being neutral towards citizens, keeping one's oath and instruction and holding regular office hours. In fact, an interest in each characteristic of bureaucratisation was in itself often an implicit value statement and/or guide for proper behaviour. Behind many of the characteristics of bureaucratisation we find implicit but nonetheless fundamental "new" or re-emphasised public values such as having expertise (knowledge of the new rules), being neutral (avoid conflicts of interest, avoid having multiple jobs at the same time), act with legitimacy (with tax collecting now being a public affair) or accountability (towards the province or city instead of friends and/or family, in keeping oath and instruction). The demand for loyalty toward the authorities instead of one's colleagues was clearly going against the old and widespread collegial and shop floor way of doing things. Virtues such as caution and prudence were re-emphasised as were values such as continuity, regularity, uniformity, adhering to formal rules and procedures (oaths and instructions), hierarchical organisation (rank was

[17] NL-LdnRAL, ORA, an., 508, in., 50jj, f. 148, dd. 8 November 1756.

[18] NL-LdnRAL, ORA, an., 508, in. 52+4A, f. 169–172, dd. 2 July 1757.

important in sentencing), use of written documents (keeping a proper administration) and procedures of discipline and control (being vigilant, prosecute offenders).

Although formal legal codes were mostly absent in the cases provided, Gecommitteerde Raden did have a reasonably clear and certainly interesting view on matters. In the case of Reijers and Vaster their verdict adopted the line of argument held by the aldermen-commissioners. They seemed to "convert" what were essentially shop floor codes of conduct among offended aldermen into legal codes. Furthermore, instead of condemning Reijers and Vaster for their attempt to hold an alderman accountable for not paying his taxes on time, they fired Reijers and rebuked Vaster. Similarly they seemed to have interpreted the new laws rather interestingly when dealing with Reijers after he had stolen the money and fled the city of Amsterdam. They could of course do little else than give a guilty verdict. However, in making his family pay for his alleged crimes, they denied any bureaucratic separation between office and official. The punishment of the lower official Mallan provides yet more views on public morality as expressed in legal codes. Gecommitteerde Raden convicted him for breaking his oath and instruction and blamed him for having taken (public) money for his own (private) benefit. They also blamed him for neglecting his duties, perjuring himself, being false and thieving.

The legal codes in the cases of Cras and Nolla are more elaborate and offer a good view on bureaucratic characteristics. This is most likely due to the different nature of the case but can also be due to the new system having been in place for a little bit longer. In the roughly five years between the case of Reijers, Vaster and Mallan and the case of Cras and Nolla, people were likely to have become more accustomed to the new system. Although—it has to be said—one need not look for many sweeping statements or pleas from the court on how officials should behave, many assumptions of proper public behaviour can still be found. Judgement, verdict and punishment in the case of Cras seem to have been based firmly on legal sources and bureaucratic principles and arguments. Instructions, oaths of office and official proclamations regarding tax collecting (i.e. bureaucratic characteristics) provide the court with enough ammunition to convict and sentence corrupt tax officials. Often recurring is, for instance, the public value of loyalty, sometimes towards ones' superior official but mostly towards the Provincial Estates or the "common land".

We also see many other legal-bureaucratic ("Weberian") values such as upholding promises made in oath and instruction. Cras was condemned for violating oath and instruction in which he had promised to supervise well and keep the books in good order. His "corruption" also consisted of having had improper financial relations (a clear conflict of interest) with a subordinate (Nolla) and having therefore abused his office for personal gain. From his conviction it therefore becomes apparent that the Gecommitteerde Raden attributed much importance to accuracy and precision in administration and bookkeeping.

What was *not* mentioned, however, also provides interesting information. The legal codes hardly bothered with harm done by corrupt tax officials to individual citizens or even citizens as a group. While the reasons for changing the system were moral in nature and directly related to citizens being harmed by wrong behaviour, these reasons cannot be found in court files. For this, one has to look at public opinion material. Pamphlets paid more attention to the broader political, social and economic circumstances of the day. As such, we find long tirades against the immoral behaviour of public officials which is subsequently linked to our specific cases. We also see a mix of fact and fiction. This is not surprising as the general reading audience is likely to have been unaware of the actual course of events and legal affairs in general. Pamphleteers wanted to get their message across as best as possible in order to make some money on sales or to prove some point. Making things up or exaggerating obviously helped. However, in order to reach these goals their pamphlets had to connect to the ideas held by (the majority of) their reading audience. The message that was subsequently broadcast was that tax officials and the corrupted tax system were part and parcel of the wider failure of Doelists, Orangists and corrupt regents alike to bring about administrative and moral change. This meant that Reijers, Vaster and others seem to have been used mostly as scapegoats and examples regardless of what they were actually guilty of. It did not seem to matter, for instance, that Reijers and Vaster had initially acted correctly in dealing with the alderman.

From this point of view, it becomes clear why Reijers was automatically accused of using his connections to get out of trouble (nepotism was meant but the term itself was not used), of getting ahead in the world by means of bribery, of flaunting his wealth and of lining his pockets whenever he could. According to public opinion this was simply what people like him did. One rhyme from a pamphlet read: "little thieves are hung between heaven and earth, but the big thieves ride in carriages and on horses. While those who steal the most are given countries and cities to rule" (*Historisch verhaal van het tumult* 1748, 41). In popular perception, people like Reijers were imposters, only out to deceive others and enrich themselves by the taking from the common land. It is also why Reijers, Vaster and others were all accused of leading a comfortable life while others suffered, despite the fact that their cases had very little to do with each other. Hypocrisy turns out to be another negative value that often occurs in the pamphlets. Saying one thing but doing another seems to have been very much despised in public opinion. Other negative values that were mentioned were disloyalty (similar to legal codes but now regarding citizens as well), *sluykery* (used not as a verb for smuggling but as a value, i.e. being a *sluyker*), thievery, lacking nobility (being dishonest, not being of good disposition) or deceit (of people and civic duty). Acquiring your office by paying for it (for instance buying it from the *Doelist* Raap) was also on the whole considered wrong.

5 Concluding Remarks

The tax riots and subsequent reform of the system in these turbulent years of the Dutch Republic shows interaction between bureaucratic reform and changing perceptions of corruption and public morality. Most striking is, perhaps, that there seems to have been little real disagreement between tax officials, provincial authorities and even public opinion about what was right or wrong moral behaviour for tax officials in the new system after 1748. In other words: little evidence can be found that distinct value systems clashed. The examined tax officials did not as such dispute the basic values underlying the (new) system or brand them as nonsense. All parties essentially seemed to agree that the acts described in the previous were in fact corrupt or wrong. There was little value pluralism.

Of course, this is not to say that everyone was happy with the new system or was able to work within it. Had this been the case, the corruption would not have occurred.[19] In fact, implementation of the new

[19]For a large collection of fraud cases see NL-HaNA, an., 3.01.05, in., 4074–4075, *Sentencing in Criminal Affairs Regarding the Common Means Over the Period 1723–1766*. See also: NL-HaNA, an., 3.01.05, in., 4076–4080, *Registers of Sentences in Criminal Affairs Regarding the Common Means in the Period 1738–1807*.

system did not always go smoothly, changes did not occur overnight and old habits died hard. There were still, for instance, possibilities to form monopolies whereby groups of people acquired the exclusive right to trade or produce certain goods. Furthermore, a part of the salary of various officials could still be based on a percentage of the proceeds and/or fines, thereby still encouraging fraud and aggressive levying. Furthermore, local authorities would themselves sometimes still obstruct the introduction of public tax collecting after 1748 (Heringa 1983: 93–99). Also, William IV and the Holland Estates had initially gained much appreciation from the general public for abolishing tax farming, especially from small shopkeepers and artisans (Wagenaar 2004: 556), but this soon evaporated with the introduction of public tax collecting and the return of the indirect excises (Dekker 1982: 137; Wagenaar 2004: 551). Proof of the bad reputation tax officials and the system still had after 1748 was that upon introduction of the public collection some small riots erupted once more in several parts of Holland. Furthermore, the Estates of Holland had large difficulties recruiting public collectors after 1748 (Heringa 1983: 96, 99). Discontent therefore lingered and abuses did not end overnight. Still, this was not evidence of truly clashing value systems. Rather, it can best be seen as the result of normal difficulties when implementing a new system. Establishing proper uniformity in rules takes time, especially (perhaps) in people's minds, as the introduction of a new bureaucratic system requires an equally radical change in mindset. People simply had to get used to new procedures and its implicit assumptions of corruption and correct public official behaviour.

Institutional or organisational difficulties should also not mask a second conclusion from the cases that there was a visible change in moral attitude around 1748. A great number of bureaucratic characteristics was specifically designed to counter inappropriate conduct and to improve the morality of tax officials in particular and the new system in general. The cases show that bureaucratisation functioned as such in practice and that public official conduct was clearly an important issue for many from 1748 onwards. There seems to have been a sense that things needed to change. Reorganising Holland's tax system and "going public" provided a window of opportunity to tackle important societal moral issues. The fact that types of political corruption that had hitherto been accepted practice were either no longer supported or seem to have been more actively prosecuted after 1748, points to such change. The same can be said for the fact that rules and regulations that were meant to prevent and combat corruption became more elaborate and seem to have been, as it appears from the cases, quite actively enforced. We can say this, even though change was neither abrupt nor completely new. There had been instances before 1748 where tax farmers were held accountable to bureaucratic and/or legal rules and principles.

The aforementioned has established a link between societal and political unrest—in part driven by military threat and a sense of economic decay—and bureaucratic reform and changing public morality. Apart from a wide variety of public values (and virtues) there were also different interpretations or normative connotations of specific public values and/or behaviour among various sources. Punctuality and accuracy (in bookkeeping for instance) or vigilance (in locating offenders or supervising subordinates) were, for instance, very important to the provincial authorities. However, to the tax officials the same value would often mean cumbersome paperwork. Similarly, a value such as efficiency (denoting aggressive levying rather than anything else) was considered important by authorities and tax officials alike but thought too rigorous or extortive according to tax payers. Opinions on what was important for public officials also—naturally—varied depending on who was asked but some general lines were drawn in the sand. For example, the increased emphasis on being loyal to the province or to the citizens of a town rather than oneself or one's immediate environment is interesting. Although ideas of popular sovereignty or accountability were still far from the (tax) authorities' minds in the middle of the eighteenth century, a beginning of such ideas can still be seen (Kerkhoff 2014). The very fact that the Estates did heed some of the rioters' calls for reform is a sign for this. The common interest (i.e. something bigger than self-interest) that was so often invoked shows that public officials could no longer serve their own interests quite like before. This also meant that corruption or bad public behaviour came to be more defined in terms of private abuse of public money. With office and person and public and private becoming more disentangled, values such as accountability, loyalty and responsibility were re-emphasised and acquired new meaning.

The main reason for a change in moral attitude, finally, seems to have been the combination of protest fuelled by social-political and economic circumstances of failed reforms, military threat, a sense of economic decline and regent oligarchic abuses on the one hand and riots combined with efforts of a relatively small group of reform minded administrators on the other. Social-political and economic circumstances opened the door to achieve reforms in the tax system in 1748 as a limited group of reformers like Van Wesele and Vosmaer devised new and/or reinforced old regulations. It also enabled them to ensure that provincial and local courts based their prosecution on (normative) bureaucratic characteristics. Popular protest in 1748 triggered institutional reform and new public morality. As new administrative layers were designed, new officials were instated and new rules and regulations were announced, reformers tried to ensure a more moral system.

References

Archives

Erfgoed Leiden en omstreken [NL-LdnRAL], *Schepenbank (Oud Rechterlijk Archief)*. Nummer toegang 508 [Regional Archives of Leiden, Aldermen Assembly (Old Judicial Archive), Access Number 508].

Nationaal Archief, Den Haag Nederland [NL-HaNA], *Gecommitteerde Raden van de Staten van Holland en Westfriesland 1621–1795.* Nummer toegang 3.01.05 [National Archives, The Hague, The Netherlands, Archive of the Daily Administration of the Estates of Holland and West-Friesland 1621–1795].

Stadsarchief Amsterdam [NL-AsdSAA], *Archief van de Burgemeesters: stukken betreffende ambten en officiën 1413–1859.* Nummer toegang 5031 [Amsterdam City Archives, Archive of the Mayors, Documents on Offices, Access Number 5031].

Sources

Advertentie door de gezaamentlyke wyn-handelaars [...] aan de heere inqvisiteurs, F. Vaster, D. Raap en haar illustri gezeltschaap [...]. *Voornaame stookebranden van allei Onrust* [Advert by the Joint Wine Traders]. 1751.

Beerinck, F., and M.G. De Boer (eds.). 1963. *Het dagboek van Jacob Bicker Raye, merkwaardige notities over het dagelijks leven in de jaren 1732–1772.* Amsterdam: Paris.

Breen, J.C. 1934. *Uit Amsterdam's verleden: studien.* Amsterdam: De Bussy.

Brief van een Zwitsers Officier over de Beroertens in de Republiek der Vereenigde Nederlanden voorgevallen aan zyner Vrienden te Baden [Letter by a Swiss Officer on the Troubles in the Duch Republic]. 1748.

Brief van Henricus Wachloo, gewezen collecteur van de boter aan zyn vriend Daniel Raap. *verwaanden previlegie-zoeker* [Letter by Henricus Wachloo to Daniel Raap]. 1751.

Buchan, B., and L. Hill. 2014. *An Intellectual History of Political Corruption*, ed. P.M. Heywood and D. Hough. *Political Corrupion and Governance*. Basingstoke: Palgrave Macmillan.

Burgerlyke oplettendheid nopens de Vaderlyke Vermaaningen [Civil Attention to the Fatherly Admonitions]. 1748.

Copye van een merkwaardige missive schreeven door den vluchtende collecteur Pieter Reiersz uit het land van Onrust. *aan zyne Respectieve Mama Mi Pan-Aal* [Copy of a Remarkable Letter by the Fugitive Pieter Reijers]. 1751.

De Cerberus of drie koppige Helhond, verbeeld in een Samenspraak tusschen Andries Mallan, Gebannu. Henr. Wachloo, Gedaagden en Pieter Ryers, Bauqueroeterenden Collecteur; *Vervattende nevens de harlequin op de Beurs, het voornaamste Leven en Bedryf van dit Drietal Belials Gebroedzel* [The Cerberus or Three-Headed Hound of Hell]. 1751.

De Mandeville, B. 1988. *The Fable of the Bees or Private Vices, Public Benefits*, ed. F.B. Kaye. Indianapolis: Liberty Classics. Original Edition, 1714.

De Vrankrijker, A.C.J., and A.M. Elias. 2005. *De Vrankrijker's Geschiedenis van de Belastingen*. Amsterdam: De Bataafsche Leeuw.

Dekker, R. 1982. *Holland in beroering: oproeren in de 17de en 18de eeuw*. Baarn: Ambo.

Engels, P.H. 1862. *De belastingen en de geldmiddelen van den aanvang der Republiek tot op heden*. Utrecht: Kemink.

Fockema Andreae, S.J. 1961. *De Nederlandse staat onder de Republiek*. Amsterdam: Noord-Hollandsche Uitgevers Maatschappij.

Groot Placaet-Boeck. Collection of Ordinances and Regulations by the Estates General and the Estates of Holland and West-Friesland (*GPB*). 1658–1796. 9 vols., The Hague & Amsterdam.

Heringa, J.W. 1983. Van zelfstandig collecteur tot ambtenaar. Problemen rond de belastingdienst in Holland, 1750–1760. *Holland: Regionaal Historisch Tijdschrift* 15: 81–101.

Historisch verhaal van het tumult voorgevallen zo binnen als buiten Amsterdam op den 24 Juny en volgende dagen 1748. *Benevens een zeer nauwkeurig en oprecht verhaal van het plunderen van de huizen der pachters, en alle 't geen daar by voorgevallen is* [Historical Tale of the Uproar in Amsterdam on 24 June 1748]. 1748.

Instructie en eed voor de ykers van de zoutmaten [Instruction for the Inspectors on Weights and Measurers of Salt]. 1797.

Instructie voor de collecteurs in sommige steeden en op de dorpen [Instruction for the Collectors in Towns and Villages]. 1748.

Instructie voor de hoofdchergers of opzigers [Instruction for Chief Investigating Officials in Holland]. 1760.

Instructie voor de inspecteurs, van en over de comptoiren der 's lands middelen en regten dewelke by collecte werden geheeven in het zuider quartier [Instruction for the Inspectors of the Officies of the Nations' Means in the Southern Quarter]. 1751.

Instructie voor de opsienders van 's lands recht op de gezeegelde en ongezeegelde billietten, als meede over de leverantie van de boeken en schryfbehoeftens voor de gaarders binnen de provintie van Holland [Instruction for Inspectors on Delivery of Books and Writing Equipment for the Collectors in Holland]. 1760.

Israel, J.I. 1998. *The Dutch Republic: Its Rise, Greatness, and Fall, 1477–1806.* Oxford: Clarendon Press.

Kerkhoff, A.D.N. 2011. Organizational Reform and Changing Ethics in Public Administration: A Case Study on 18th Century Dutch Tax Collecting. *Journal of Public Administration Research and Theory* 21 (1): 117–135.

Kerkhoff, A.D.N. 2014. Early Modern Developments in Dutch Public Administration: Patriot and Batavian Authors on Public Morality (1770s–1813). *Administrative Theory & Praxis* 36 (1): 73–94.

Ma, J. 2003. New Public Management in the Early Modern Period: Lessons From Tax Farming History. *Administrative Theory and Praxis* 25 (4): 435–456.

Pfeil, T. 1998. *Tot redding van het vaderland. Het primaat van de Nederlandse overheidsfinanciën in de Bataafs-Franse Tijd, 1795–1810.* Amsterdam: NEHA.

Propositie van Syne Hoogheid aan de Heeren Staaten van Holland en Westvriesland dd 25 juny 1748 [Proposition of His Majesty]. 1748.

Smith, A. 1981. *An Inquiry into the Nature and Causes of the Wealth of Nations.* Indianapolis: Liberty Classics. Original Edition, 1776.

Wagenaar, F.P. 1997. 'Dat de regeringe niet en bestaet by het corpus van de magistraet van Den Hage alleen': de Societeit van 's-Gravenhage (1587–1802), een onderzoek naar bureaucratisering. PhD dissertation, Rijksuniversiteit Leiden, Leiden.

Wagenaar, F.P. 2004. Excises, Postal Services, Oaths of Office and Property Taxes. How Small Local Administrative Adjustments Led to Large Changes in Intergovernmental Relations. *Administrative Theory & Praxis* 26 (4): 545–565.

CHAPTER 8

Between Private and Public Interests: The *Moral Economy of Collaboration* in Eighteenth-Century Spain

Agustín González Enciso

The moral aspects implicit to public–private collaboration in the spheres of tax farming and military procurement have usually been cast in a negative light, on the basis of the alleged abuses of private individuals. It has been assumed that the financiers who negotiated with the state exploited government needs and took advantage of this situation to turn a huge profit from their business activities. Thus, armed conflict would give rise to another confrontation, in this case a "'war within' that pitted those who benefited from war expenditure against those who paid for the military effort".[1] This would account for the specific measures that successive governments would take against those who prospered from this state of affairs.

[1] I have borrowed this phrase from the proceeding of the conference "The War Within: Finance and Morality in Europe, 1630–1815", University of Reading, 3–4 December 2015, which has led to this book.

A. González Enciso (✉)
University of Navarra, Pamplona, Spain
e-mail: agenciso@unav.es

J. Félix and A. Dubet (eds.), *The War Within*,
Palgrave Studies in the History of Finance,
https://doi.org/10.1007/978-3-319-98050-8_8

That interpretation was based primarily on the controversy arising from the complaints of contemporaries, which focused on corruption as a habitual practice. Whether tax farmers and contractors, or whoever was involved, actually obtained substantial benefits is still an issue open to debate, since views were divided at the time. Nevertheless, it must be remembered that these entrepreneurs normally did an admirable job (Knight and Wilcox 2010; Torres Sánchez 2016: 29, 45); if this had not been the case, to our mind, it would have been impossible to wage war efficiently.

Furthermore, there is another aspect that also interests us here: the political attitude towards these practices and their consequences for economic life. From this perspective, the ethicality of such practices was understood not so much in terms of what some might have lost (the bane of corruption and abuses), but of what some might not have earned, insofar as they resulted in measures being taken against what we now call "equal opportunities", by establishing exclusionary forms of collaboration with the state.

The trend towards exclusivism was particularly evident in Spain. War expenditure created a lot of pressure, given the state's limited means. Throughout the eighteenth century, this led successive governments to adopt a defensive stance and increasingly more centralised organisational methods in which growing state intervention was seen as the best way of dealing with the challenges. In this climate, there was shift from a situation in which there were many contractors collaborating with the state to another in which there were only a few, controlling important monopolies granted by the monarchy. After tax farming was abolished in 1749, the pace of change accelerated.

1 Sovereign Entrepreneurship in Great Britain

The English model serves as a contrast here insofar as, in the eighteenth century, Great Britain becomes a "viable and successful example of the mercantilist state" (O'Brien 2007: 95). The policies implemented there with regard to tax farming and military procurement differed from the perspective of collaboration, or not, with private entrepreneurs. A specific moral sanction was applied to tax farming inasmuch as the system could damage the interests of the taxpayer (through the abuses of the collectors) and the state (whose revenues would fall and which would be incapable of controlling its tax revenues). In England, the proponents of state fiscal autonomy and of the king's right to manage his tax revenues won an early victory, since tax farming was abandoned between 1671 and 1684 (Wilson 1965: 212). Thus, a situation that was believed to be doubly immoral was brought to an end and the principle that direct administration was fairer and more efficient was established (Wilson 1965: 216). In Spain and France, different paths were taken. The former finally introduced direct administration in 1749, for similar reasons as in England; whereas the latter would not follow suit until 40 years later (Durand 1976: 16).

In England, however, the policy on military procurement, a task still performed by private concerns, did not vary, which in practice confirmed everyone's right to participate in the market. In this case, there was what has been called a "silent revolution" (Knight 2014: 349–350): the discrete success of private contractors, merchants, and financiers in state military procurement.

In Great Britain, therefore, what we could call the "sovereign entrepreneur" prospered. We use this expression as a counterpart to the "sovereign consumer" in a free market. This has been defined by modern economic theory as the right of the consumer to a natural market, the assertion that consumer preferences determine the production of goods and services (Hutt 1936), without regard to any monopoly. In consonance with that sovereign consumer, we should also speak of a sovereign entrepreneur, whose preferences may also influence the supply of some or other type of product. Can this approach be applied to military procurement?

In Great Britain, military procurement respected the sovereign entrepreneur approach to the extent that the state relied on the free market to cover its military requirements, with very few exceptions. Although these needs were those of a sole client—the state—any entrepreneur could attempt to secure an agreement with it (Bannerman 2008; Morris 2011). This had positive consequences: contractors profited from war expenditure, which increased the demand for their products and services (Bowen 1998: 64–65); the state was well served; and taxpayers, while always paying more, could do so because consumption increased (O'Brien 1989: 347), despite the fact that they bore the brunt of tax contribution through excise duty (O'Brien 1988). In any case, it was in Great Britain, as in the United Provinces, where there was a consumer revolution (De Vries 2008).

That the final outcome of the armed conflicts raging throughout the eighteenth century was a British victory, in both the military and commercial and financial spheres, undoubtedly had to do with the way in which issues pertaining to taxes and military procurement were handled. In this regard, the main characteristics of the policy governing these matters are clear: direct tax administration and military procurement by private individuals, two worlds in which the public/private dichotomy was resolved in a different manner. By pursuing this approach, Great Britain managed to triumph over its rivals at the end of the Long Eighteenth Century. It employed the most efficient method and applied the best mercantilism (O'Brien 2011).

2 Method or Efficiency? Spanish Policy as Regards Private Actors

What policy did Spain implement vis-à-vis two issues inherent to tax farming and military procurement? If we were to highlight one of its characteristics, that would be the progressive encroachment of the public on the private during the Long Eighteenth Century: the central government became increasingly more present in the financing and procurement mechanisms that war demanded, so we could say that war was a factor of nationalisation in Spain during that period. This did not involve state formation, which was the case everywhere, but nationalisation, viz. the predominance of state administrative structures over private management.

This was apparent in three aspects: firstly, the demise of tax farmers; secondly, the low number of contractors handling the most important aspects of procurement; and thirdly, the disappearance of contractors in some areas that were then administered directly. The first was also true in England, but not the other two. Thus, the conditions imposed by the state gradually narrowed the market as regards military procurement. The state asserted its status as a major buyer (in the case of some products, the only one, since third-party sales were not permitted), and therefore established the game rules on the margins of the market.

Before the eighteenth century, there had been no tradition of this type of organisation in Spain. Since an early stage, a framework of collaboration between the Spanish state and private concerns was established, as happened, for instance, during the reign of the Catholic Kings (1479–1504) (Ladero Quesada 1978: 107 1 ff.; Molas 2008: 23 and ff.). In the sixteenth century, the monarchy's territorial scope imposed such a disperse structure that the efficient mobilisation of military resources required a complex balance between the Crown and the diverse social groups and lands under its sway (Yun Casalilla 2004: 329, 333; Escribano Páez 2015). As a result, the military and naval administration, which was already very decentralised in the time of Charles V (1516–1556), would remain that way with the coming of the eighteenth century.

There was an exception to this general state of affairs during the reign of Philip II (1556–1598), whose ascension to the throne "brought an immediate reassertion of direct administrative control" (Thompson 1976: 5). The process would culminate around 1580. This control only affected the mobilisation of war resources, and not the contractors. At any rate, the direct administration of procurement did not reach all areas, and even declined as regards some products, for which it was necessary to resort to contractors in areas previously administered by the state (Jiménez Estrella 2010).

The trend towards direct administration did not last long at the time. As the number of challenges facing the monarchy multiplied, the situation began to change and, by the time of the reign of Philip IV (1621–1665), indirect administration methods were back in place (Thompson 1976: 7). Thompson claimed that a state which did not directly administer the mobilisation of its resources was a weak one. Philip II had flexed his muscles in this respect, while the process of decentralisation that occurred afterwards can be perceived as a decline. Handing military procurement back to private contractors also implied a political decentralisation, a shift from central to centrifugal government with respect to the different kingdom's provinces and regions, all of which fragmented the state's authority (Thompson 1976: 275).

Thompson's thesis is plausible if applied to seventeenth-century developments. Nonetheless, it cannot be generalised. State power was not bound to administrating directly the mobilisation of resources. Thompson himself noted that "contracting could on occasions be highly aggregative" (Thompson 1976: 275). In point of fact, the mobilisation of resources in Spain and in other countries always relied heavily on private participation (Bowen 2006), which went to show that the growth of state power and the participation of the private sector in procurement were not incompatible (Parrot 2012: 2–3). The state revealed its power not so much in the method as in its proven efficiency in obtaining supplies, which was what really counted when all was said and done (Torres Sánchez 2013: 162–163, 170).

Identifying a strong state with direct administration does involve paradoxes. In England the state abolished tax farming, but depended heavily on private contractors. In Spain, the weak reign of Charles II (1665–1700) gave rise to a trend towards centralising military recruitment. Despite the lack of planning, this policy would ultimately be implemented to obtain uniformed and equipped troops (Rodríguez Hernández 2012: 55–58). Moreover, the new Bourbon governments of the eighteenth century had no objection to maintaining a high level of collaboration with the private sector as regards tax issues until 1749 (Torres Sánchez 2013: 162; Torres Sánchez 2016: 5, 13), this being always the case in the area of military procurement, a stance that coexisted with a process of administrative centralisation and a new concept of power (Vázquez Gestal 2013).

3 The Principle of Efficiency According to the State

If it was not the method but efficiency that was decisive, success lay in choosing an efficient method. The Spanish governments of the eighteenth century began to accept that the most efficient way to obtain financing and supplies called for the administration's direct involvement in resource mobilisation mechanisms. This required the abolition of tax farming and more stringent controls on contractors. Changes in this direction gave rise to a new political approach that implied new moral assumptions with respect to the economic relationship between the private sector and the state. As a point of fact, the encroachment of the public on the private had a basis of justification. In the case of the abolition of tax farming, the same arguments as those employed in England were resorted to: the abuses of private individuals; lower state revenues; and its diminished tax administration capacity (Moya Torres 1992: 141, 304).

In the procurement area, there was a sharp drop in the number of contractors, which demonstrated the state's ability to implement its policies. The few remaining firms were granted huge concessions. With this policy, the Spanish state put excessive profits in the pockets of a handful of contractors, which contradicted the concern for the private gains of tax farmers. Why were these contractors allowed to turn a large profit, whereas tax farmers were not permitted to do so? The answer lay in the need to ensure state procurement. A weak contractor could offer no guarantees, so the only way open to the state was to bolster the position of a privileged few, thus creating a long-term de facto monopoly (Torres Sánchez 2016: 106). In those cases in which direct administration was established, the arguments made also had to do with efficiency and quality.

It does not seem that the state was at all concerned about private profit-seeking, provided that efficiency was ensured. The case of the contractors whose position had been greatly strengthened would apparently confirm this. Such a policy also had a moral sanction, what we could call the "moral economy of collaboration". This would require that all those private individuals capable of collaborating with the public sector should be allowed to do so. But it was not always the case. What happened in Spain was that collaboration was restricted and there was a biased perception of the role of the state, inasmuch as the powers that be understood morality in terms of government interests, which thus impinged on private activity, limiting the markets. Consequentially, this gave rise to a subtle moral dilemma, the creation of a legal framework through the granting of privileges, thus diminishing the possibilities of participation in specific business areas; in addition to the state's role as the sole guarantor of the commonweal in key economic issues.

4 Tax Farmers and Contractors Before 1749

The two collectives most involved in collaborating with the state were tax farmers and contractors. Until 1749, practically the same people participated in both financial services in Spain: they were two sides of the same coin. The coincidence between the most important tax farmers and contractors was a distinguishing feature in comparison with Great Britain and France. In Great Britain, tax farmers had disappeared; in France, the majority of the *fermiers généraux* were more closely associated with financial and administrative functions than with military procurement (Durand 1976: 52). Although any relationship between the two tasks cannot be excluded, this was not as clear-cut as it was in Spain.

One of the reasons behind combining the two tasks in one activity could have been the renewal of procurement contracts undertaken by the new dynasty, especially at the time of the War of the Spanish

Succession. Necessity encouraged newcomers to become involved in financial dealings with the state, most of whom were Spaniards (Torres Sánchez 2002a). In this climate of change and with the arrival of new blood, financiers had to win all the profitable business available. In this regard, it is important to bear in mind the relatively low military demand at the time which limited the profitability of procurement contracts, thus making it necessary to cast about for other sources of profit; moreover, the state's financial straits, which delayed payments, obliged contractors to secure income through a number of alternative channels.

The procurement business was not a simple matter, above all in the case of victualling. It was essential to have many contacts in Spain and even abroad to obtain the necessary grain at a given moment. If the franchise area was large—for instance, an army procurement contract covering many provinces—there were not only greater possibilities of gain, but also greater difficulties and risks. Financial rewards might have been obtained from the prices that the state was charged. Whether these were more or less profitable for contractors depended on their bargaining power, on the reliability of their businesses, or on their influence at court, though cutting them to outdo their competitors was always a good tactic. In practice, the price was a political one imposed by the administration (Torres Sánchez 2016: 23–24).

If, notwithstanding the challenges, contractors sought out these business openings, it was because doing business with the state was an excellent occasion to obtain successive procurement contracts or to gain access to the most profitable ones. Likewise, they could also expect political and social benefits, such as posts in the central administration, ennoblement, or other opportunities to climb the social ladder. In any case, the high financial risks that tax farmers and contractors ran made it highly advisable to diversify them with other enterprises.

Normally, tax farming was a safer, more lucrative activity, but also more difficult to obtain. The procurement business could be endangered by management challenges or low political prices. The state also benefited from this formula. It not only ensured the loyalty of a group of reliable men when honouring the procurement contracts, but the system was also well-adapted to the kingdom's new fiscal and military organisation: taxes were collected by province, military organisation was also province-based, so it was easy to collect taxes and provision the army in the same places.

5 Against Tax Farming

The balance was upset because tax farming was living on borrowed time in Spain. The doubts about its appropriateness were age-old, as elsewhere. In 1684, the same year the system had been abolished in England, the Castilian tobacco tax began to be administered directly for the lack of a farmer (Rodríguez Gordillo: 1984). At the time, however, there was no intention of maintaining this measure in force and the debate on the issue dragged on in Spain, as in France (Durand 1971: 432–437). Nonetheless, it does not seem that treasury officials in Spain were in favour of discontinuing the system before the 1720s (González Enciso 2015).

Tax farmers were the target of general criticism due to the abuses that they committed against the taxpayer, the biases that their schemes produced in the administration, and the high profits that they obtained, monies that never reached the royal coffers. It was all considered a fairly immoral social evil. But not everyone shared the same view and some defended the system's advantages: the king was guaranteed tax advances and administrative savings were made. It was also considered by some Spanish officials that farming methods could be improved, as in the 1714 reform when the collection of several taxes was unified by provinces and the control of the Tesorería Mayor improved so limiting fraud possibilities for tax farmers (Dubet 2015: 62 and ff.). Moreover, in the opinion of some persons, direct administration could be a way for the powerful to cover up abuses in the distribution of taxes among neighbours, therefore, tax farming was preferable (Delgado Barrado 2007: 134–135; Dubet 2012: 30). As a matter of fact, the system was retained in France, where in 1726 it was revised and strengthened (Félix 2011). That same year in Spain, as coincidence would have it, the post of Treasury Secretary was occupied by José Patiño, a pragmatic opponent of the tax farming system in the interests of "good governance".[2] The royal treasury needed to boost its income and tax farming was apparently an obstacle in this regard.

Patiño was able to rely on several precedents. In 1714, two taxes started to be administered directly; although they would be farmed out again in 1725 and 1730, respectively (Artola 1982: 254, 284–287).

[2] Escamilla (2011: 175–177). Spanish reformers repetitively used the idea of "buen gobierno", with moral, as well as administrative meaning. See, for instance, Dubet (2015).

In 1730, the Treasury Secretary won an initial victory with the direct administration of the tobacco tax. It was the first that would not be farmed out again, but also an isolated case. The positive effects took time in making themselves felt because the measure coincided with a rise in the price of tobacco (Rodríguez Gordillo 2000: 53–104), which led to many consumers resorting to the black market and to a drop in official consumption. In any event, both the benefits generated by the rise in prices and the savings made on the tax farmer's profits ultimately outweighed the disadvantages, and by the end of the 1730s the total tax revenues had increased (Rodríguez Gordillo 2007).

In the experiments of 1714 and 1730 alike, the administrators still did not realise that direct administration was more productive. As priority was given to efficiency and the need for income, over theoretical debates, the measures were not implemented across the board and tax farming was upheld. Significantly, nothing was done about the Castilian provincial taxes, the so called *rentas provinciales*, the most important source of revenue. It was enough to accept the arguments of Uztáriz, who claimed that if the number of tax farmers were reduced—as had been done before—and their activities adequately supervised, it would be unnecessary to administer the taxes directly (Uztáriz 1968: 390).

In was only in 1742, during José Campillo's ministerial term of office, when the process of bringing all the taxes, including the provincial ones, under direct administration was implemented, as the farming contracts began to expire. This does not necessarily mean the minister was convinced direct administration was best.[3] The process was continued by Ensenada, who really was in favour of administration, ended in 1749 during the reign of Ferdinand VI (1746–1759). There is in this process a strange coincidence with England, 80 years before. The measures introduced there to abolish tax farming coincided, or followed, the banking crisis of 1672 (Wilson 1965: 21, 215); in Spain, definitive measures were implemented after the financial crisis of 1739 (Dubet 2017b). So, in both cases, it seems that bankruptcy highlighted the need to dispense with tax farmers.

[3] Dubet (2017a). I thank Anne Dubet for this and other wise suggestions.

6 Farmers' Profits

The basic argument in favour of doing away with the system rested on farmers' profits. But were they really that huge? The matter still is not well-understood, but there is indeed some coherent evidence that can help us to approach the matter. This is the case of the opinion of José Rodrigo, a member of the Saragossa Court (Kamen 1974: 287, 377), who in 1716 calculated that if a tax farmer obtained 100,000 reales from the taxpayer, he would only hand over 30,000 to the king.[4] In spite of being only an estimate, Rodrigo was familiar with the problem; therefore, a 70% return was indeed possible. It should be noted, however, that returns are not profits, since farmers had to deduct administrative and other costs, which, although we have not a clue, must not have been inconsequential.

Another piece of information is also provided by Campillo, who in 1741 remarked that the wool tax was "deplorably farmed" (Ibáñez Molina 1994: 56), as Arizcun had farmed it out for 5.5 million reales when it was really worth 11 million. And Campillo was right, because when in 1749 this tax was finally administered directly, it generated the 11 million reales that he mentioned. That is, before 1741, Arizcun earned, in absolute terms, at least 50% of the monies collected from the taxpayer. This figure can be compared with the 70% that Rodrigo had suggested, in a less precise fashion, 30 years before. From the moral perspective that interests us here, it should be noted that Campillo did not deem that fraudulent practices were involved. He simply criticised a system that allowed a private individual to make disproportionate profits; it was a legal system that, in practice, reduced state income and led to inequality, and this was what made it unfair.

Another document allows us to reach a more accurate estimate. It compares the value of tax revenues for the period 1752–1757, after the consolidation of the system of direct administration, with the revenues that the king received from these same taxes in 1740,

[4] J. Rodrigo, "Instrucción presentada a S. M. ... por D. José Rodrigo... en el año de 1716". Ms. 18055, fols. 186–194, Biblioteca Nacional de España, Madrid.

Table 1 Tax farming profits (figures in millions of "reales de vellón")

Tax	*A* *1752/1757*	*B* *1740*	*C* *A – B*	*D* *% C/B*
Provincial	63.2	52.3	10.9	20.8
General	35.8	25.8	10	38.7
Salt mines	18.5	12.5	6	48
Wool	11.3	8	3.3	41.2

when they were still being farmed. They are net values in both cases (Table 1).[5]

What interests us here is, above all, Column C, which shows the difference between the net value collected by the state in the 1750s and that of 1740. It is assumed that this was the amount that farmers earned in absolute terms, around 1740. As can be seen, the difference varies depending on the amount of the tax collected. Column D expresses these figures as a percentage—ranging from 30–50%, approximately—with respect to the state's net income in 1740. Although these figures are generally lower than those that we have provided in the aforementioned examples—which surely mean an improvement in state administration between 1716 and 1740—they must have been discouraging for anyone familiar with the challenges facing the Treasury in the 1740s.

7 Shifting Scenarios

The implementation of direct administration had its advantages for the Treasury. On the one hand, it increased its income. On the other, it streamlined tax management, in view of the fact that, without other interests at stake, the government was free to modify, in due course, taxes or their collection (Solbes Ferri 2016: 117–126). This had already been experienced with the tobacco tax, directly administered since 1730. The change also led to a modification in the price of tobacco, which would not have been so easy with the intervention of a farmer.

In any case, the disappearance of tax farming brought with it other problems. The one that is of greatest interest to us at the moment is that it deprived contractors of that second activity which offset the Crown's payment defaults or arrears for military supplies. Without that to fall back

[5] Report prepared by Luis de Ibarra Larrea, 15 October 1759. Biblioteca Nacional, Madrid, Ms. 10695, fols. 301–359.

on, the risks increased for contractors, which led the authorities to propose a different set of rules for them. Another acute problem (which we will only touch on briefly here) was that, in the new scenario, the financial market in Spain dwindled significantly, which undoubtedly encouraged those with cash to invest in land. The shortage of currency in circulation would affect trade and become a serious headache later on, when the kingdom's financial problems escalated at the end of the century.

Those challenges were not immediately evident in 1749. The abolition of tax farming came after the Treaty of Aix-la-Chapelle of 1748. The years of peace that followed reduced the need for military procurement and the Treasury's pecuniary problems. In this situation, the pressure brought to bear on the contractors by the state also diminished. There were even opportunities for Ensenada to introduce changes, such as placing army victualling under direct administration. At the end of 1752, a directorate-general was created and placed under the authority of Francisco Mendinueta, hitherto a procurement contractor. The aim was to cut administrative costs, but this was not achieved and in 1755, with Ensenada now gone, the tendering and contracting system was reintroduced, the victualling contract again being awarded to Mendinueta (Torres Sánchez 2002b: 127–128).

Ensenada's policy was not consistent. It appears that, against all odds, efficiency and private interests prevailed. Ensenada had implemented the abolition of tax farming, initiated by Campillo, and also attempted to bring victualling under direct administration. However, he continued to employ other major contractors, including Arizcun in naval victualling, Olivares at the cannon foundry in Liérganes and Mendinueta at the munitions factory in Eugui (Torres Sánchez 2010; Alcalá-Zamora 2004; González Enciso 2011). Significantly, in the naval reconstruction programme Ensenada relied on Fernández de Isla, a prominent Santander merchant, who was granted many privileges (Maiso González 1990). Some of these cases represent what would become the modus operandi: the favouring of a sole contractor to bolster his position.

That tendency became evident as of 1759, the year marking the beginning of the reign of Charles III, when the policy of collaboration changed yet again. The new reign brought with it new ministers, above all Esquilache, an Italian with no links to Spain, and the kingdom's involvement in the Seven Years' War. The new situation was also characterised by a stronger centralist mentality, which would be revealed in new procurement policies.

8 The Procurement Policy of Charles III (1759–1788)

With the kingdom yet again at war, the new monarch had to face a dilemma that had been deferred during the 11 years of peace: on the one hand, the risks involved for those contractors without the support of a tax farm; and on the other, those involved for the state if contractors without support failed to deliver. It was a known fact that any contractor who did not have the wherewithal to fulfil his contractual obligations was a liability to the state, but how did the government cope with this situation? In Great Britain and, with respect to some areas, also in France, the state resorted to the market to find a larger number of contractors to cover military procurement needs together. The competition between them was a guarantee of quality.

On the contrary, the governments of Charles III decided against resorting to the market in favour of backing—at least in the most important contracts—one sole contractor, who would be given all the necessary support to succeed in his endeavours. As an incentive, contractors were granted generous privileges, though the state refused to negotiate contract prices. Since the privileges awarded to the winning contractors gave them a truly dominant market position, they would retain their franchises for many years. In point of fact, even though the contract was of a temporary nature, the contractor's weight made him practically indispensable, thus guaranteeing its renewal.

It cannot be said that this situation was completely new. In fact, some of the kingdom's contractors had been in the business for some time; but the system, instead of being liberalised, as was apparently required by the times, became reinforced and spread to other areas of procurement. The practice would remain in force until the 1790s, after the reign of Charles III. Another trend was to establish the direct administration of procurement in specific areas.

Those changes were not fortuitous or arbitrary; there was a dual objective and a seemingly adequate method behind them: that supplies reached the right place at the right time; and that products were good value for money (i.e. that the state paid the lowest possible price, while guaranteeing quality). The method employed to achieve these objectives varied depending on the product or service (Torres Sánchez 2016: 16), but efforts were always made to ensure that the administration controlled the process. Particularly in the case of victuals, it was deemed best to back a sole businessman with influence and the capacity to handle large quantities over extensive areas. The state could not be omnipresent, but an important entrepreneur could indeed through his contacts. Thus, in this sector it was thought that the best course of action was to favour a major company and legally empower it to deliver supplies, even imported, at the best price. It was the task of the rulers to weigh up the situation and choose, in each case, the sole businessman regarded as the fittest for the task in hand. Among them were companies such as the "Five Great Guilds" of Madrid and the Bank of San Carlos (Torres Sánchez 2014; Pérez Sarrión 2016). If they changed it was because they were not always capable of fulfilling their obligations, in spite of their privileges.

In that context of administrative intervention, the procurement system followed the path of centralisation. Given the quantitative importance of military procurement, the granting of exclusive privileges to a limited number of firms determined market development and prevented many merchants from participating in this area, which was as lucrative as it was exclusive. As has already been noted, even without addressing corruption, what was involved was a policy restricting markets at the expense of the commonweal in an attempt to ensure service to the state.

The policy of procurement comes in contradiction with other "liberal" measures taken during the reign of Charles III. Since 1760, the previous trend towards lowering taxes or to expanding the scope for participation in commercial trade was reinforced. Worthy of mention is the far-reaching freedom of trade decree of 1778, which put an end to the Cadiz monopoly with Spanish America by permitting many other ports in the peninsula to participate in the transatlantic trade with the colonies. The decree multiplied the possibilities for trade, if only for a few years (Fisher 1985).

In spite of the possibilities opened up by the decree of 1778, there were no contractors with an imperial approach. Contracts were distributed between mainland Spaniards and Americans, both groups working within a regional perspective, and neither group benefiting from the freedom of trade. More warships were built in Havana, to the detriment of the peninsula shipyards, and iron and bronze cannons, including shot, were manufactured in the Peninsula, without this industry developing in the colonies. As to the transport of arms, a distinction was drawn between transport within metropolitan Spain and the shipment of cannons to the colonies (González Enciso 2016).

Table 2 The shrinking procurement contract market

Contract	*Period*	*Number of companies*	*Average duration (years)*
Victualling the army	1700–1730	8	3.7
	1730–1739	Direct admin.	9
	1739–1799	4	15
Victualling the navy	1722–1790s	1 family	70
Transport of arms	1715–1795	1 family	80

9 Fewer Contractors, Longer Contacts: An Overview

In the long run there was a gradual reduction in the number of contractors throughout the century. This decline went hand in hand with an increase in contract length or with numerous contract extension agreements, as can be seen in Table 2, relating to the most important contracts.[6]

The most important contract was for victualling the Army. During the War of the Spanish Succession, this was a complicated matter and it was necessary to resort to several contractors, since some failed to deliver (Dedieu 2011). After the conflict had ended, the number of contractors fell, while their areas of influence were extended. In 1730, the government decided to bring procurement under direct administration. The experiment lasted nine years. Following this there were only 4 consecutive contractors who enjoyed their franchises for an average period of 15 years. All of them benefited from *general* procurement, that is, a sole contractor for the whole of Spain (Torres Sánchez 2016: 55 and ff.). In other areas of procurement, the choice of one contractor and the renewal of his contracts in his own benefit or that of his heirs had been a normal practice since the first decades of the century, as was the case of victualling the Navy, monopolised by the Arizcun family for 70 years, or the transport of arms within the Peninsula, in the hands of the family of Mendinueta for 80 (Torres Sánchez 2010; González Enciso 2012).

True enough, none of these contractors-monopolists worked alone. Even though a company handled *general* procurement, the purchase of grain had to be done locally and, therefore, the general contractor had to cooperate with local merchants within extensive networks. But whoever

[6]Sources: Torres Sánchez (2002a, b, 2010); Dedieu (2011); González Enciso (2012).

organised the network received the lion's share of the profits, as he had all the key contacts, so the most lucrative contracts were soon in the hands of few. As the number of contractors was restricted as the century advanced, the market became very exclusive.

In addition to market restraints, this policy had the modified attitude and mentality of entrepreneurs, insofar as what was important for them was not to discover or create markets, but to negotiate with the government to obtain good terms and conditions for the same contract or non-monetary benefits. In other words, rather than business acumen, what prevailed was political negotiating power and weight of influence. While it is true that contractors had to manage their affairs like a business, once they had won their contracts they actually managed a monopoly, without competition, and with privileges that allowed them to prevail over their fellow merchants, smaller producers, and other market actors—for instance, local institutions—whenever necessary, and with the advantage of always being able to use their position as servants of the Crown to their own benefits.

10 The Nationalisation of Cannon Foundries and Munitions Factories

A more radical aspect of state interventionism and the limitation of markets was the nationalisation of cannon and munitions factories. During the 1760s, the state purchased the Liérganes-La Cavada iron cannon foundries, followed by the Eugui munitions factory. Thenceforth, the public administration would directly manage these companies. The bronze cannon foundries in Seville and Barcelona already belonged to the state, but they were managed with the help of the master smelters who acted as factors and performed under a state contract. In the 1760s, however, there was also a higher level of interventionism in these companies, to the extent that the smelters-factors directly managed the manufacturing of bronze cannons.

Table 3 summarises the evolution towards the nationalisation of Spain's bronze and iron cannon foundries.[7]

The munitions factory in Eugui was also a private concern that performed under a state contract, until it was nationalised in 1766

[7] Sources: Alcalá-Zamora (2004); Aguilar Escobar (2010); González Enciso (2018).

Table 3 From the private sector to nationalisation: cannon foundries

Foundry	*Period*	*Ownership*	*Management*	*Funding*
Seville, bronze guns				
	1565–1634	Private	Private	Private
	1634–1717	**State**	Factor	Contract
	1717–1767	**State**	Factor	Mixed
	1767–1808	**State**	**State**	**State**
Barcelona, bronze guns				
	1717–1767	**State**	Factor	Mixed
	1767–1808	**State**	**State**	**State**
Liérganes, iron guns				
	1622–1763	Private	Private	Private
	1763–1834	**State**	**State**	**State**

(González Enciso 2011: 301). Later on, the Crown would create new munitions companies, such as that in Orbaiceta, all owned and managed by the state (Alcalá-Zamora 1974: 178–179; Alcalá-Zamora 1999: 360 and ff.). This was also the case with the arsenals and their reverberatory furnaces, and others such as the anchor, nail, and soft iron factory in Marrón (Alcalá-Zamora 1974: 179; Alcalá-Zamora 2004: 40). Hence, we could say that in these branches of industry there was a shift from a "contractor" to a "factory state" (González Enciso 2013: 475–476; González Enciso 2018: 95 and ff.); the state stopped resorting to contractors and began to manage directly the factories it owned through its specialists from War and Navy corps.

The main argument employed to justify these nationalisation of arms factories was quality. Apparently, by the 1760s, the quality of cannons and munitions was behind the times (Helguera Quijada 2012). Even so, the problem could have been resolved differently: for example, by paying contractors more to enable them to make the necessary investments; or by opening up the market to competition. With the companies under its control, the state invested more money than it had earmarked for private contracts, which proved that it was not only concerned about quality, but also about placing production under its direct control.

The nationalisation policy is also in contradiction with the "liberal" approach of the period. If other tax and trade measures tended to contribute to there being "more market" (Pérez Sarrión 2011), the market disappeared in the case of arms production. All of which points, yet again, to the pragmatism of the time (González Enciso 2009). In some cases, pragmatism reinforced the idea of a greater freedom of action for subjects; in others, however, the intention was to guarantee some objectives through direct state intervention, as it was in particular the case of arms procurement.

11 Conclusions

For different reasons, the Spanish state abolished tax farming and implemented a conservative policy as regards procurement contracting, dealing only with a small and privileged number of contractors. Moral presuppositions were behind both solutions: firstly, the aim was to stamp out the abuses of private individuals; and secondly, to safeguard the interests of an under-budgeted state. In reality, state interests prevailed in both cases.

The joint effect of these actions had a negative impact on business by reducing business opportunities, leading to a reduction in the number of financial groups. The few that remained stood as one with the state, thanks to the efficiency of their monopolies: a handful of reliable men; a privileged elite dependent on the state. The situation was taken to an extreme when the state nationalised ordnance and munitions companies for quality reasons and political interest.

This shows that the morality of collaboration was defined mainly by ideology and pragmatism. The state distrusted private individuals and restricted the right of businessmen to participate in those markets that it considered strategic, granting scope of action to a privileged few at the expense of others. A morality based on the ideological assumption that the state was the best administrator and should therefore retain control over the most sensitive economic sectors, was behind nationalisation. All this goes to show that the state identified its interests with the commonweal, also in economic spheres. This resulted in an exclusivist and monopolist mentality, changing the *moral economy of collaboration* into a *dis-economy* which harmed the sovereign entrepreneur by closing the market.

All this was occurring in an international context in which the financial world was gradually expanding; also at a moment of growth for the Spanish economy and of the Army and Navy's greater procurement requirements. The situation would have called for a greater number of large businesses to cover those needs. Instead, the followed policy was in the opposite direction. The worst consequences of this will appear later when in the late 1790s the Spanish state, due to a lack of a real financial system, found itself unable to face the increased demands of war.

References

Aguilar Escobar, A. 2010. *Cañones de bronce para el ejército. Historia de la Real Fundición de Sevilla en el siglo XVIII.* Madrid: Ministerio de Defensa.

Alcalá-Zamora, J. 1974. Producción de hierro y altos hornos en la España anterior a 1850. *Moneda y Crédito* 128: 117–228.

Alcalá-Zamora, J. 1999. *Altos hornos y poder naval en la España de la Edad Moderna.* Madrid: Real Academia de la Historia.

Alcalá-Zamora, J. 2004. *Liérganes y La Cavada. Historia de los primeros altos hornos españoles (1622–1834).* Santander: Estudio.

Artola, M. 1982. *La Hacienda del Antiguo Régimen.* Madrid: Alianza.

Bannerman, G.E. 2008. *Merchants and the Military in Eighteenth-Century Britain.* London: Pickering and Chato.

Bowen, H.V. 1998. *War and British Society, 1688–1815.* Cambridge: Cambridge University Press.

Bowen, H.V. 2006. Introduction. In *Mobilising Resources for War: Britain and Spain at Work during the Early Modern Period*, ed. H.V. Bowen and A. González Enciso, 15–24. Pamplona: EUNSA.

Dedieu, J.-P. 2011. Les groupes financiers et industriels au service du roi. Espagne, fin XVIIe-début XVIIIe siècle. In *Les financiers et la construction de l'Etat en France et en Espagne (milieu du XVIIe siècle-milieu du XIXe siècle)*, ed. A. Dubet and J.-P. Luis, 87–104. Rennes: Presses Universitaires de Rennes.

Delgado Barrado, J. M. 2007. *Aquiles y Teseos. Bosquejos del reformismo borbónico (1701–1759).* Jaén: Universidad de Jaén.

de Uztáriz, G. 1968. *Teórica y práctica de comercio y de marina [1724]*, ed. G. Franco. Madrid: Aguilar.

De Vries, J. 2008. *The Industrious Revolution.* Cambridge and New York: Cambridge University Press.

Dubet, A. 2012. Comprender las reformas de la hacienda a principios del siglo XVIII. La buena administración según el marqués de Campoflorido. *Revista HMiC: Història moderna i contemporània* X: 20–52.

Dubet, A. 2015. *La Hacienda Real de la Nueva Planta (1713–1726), entre fraude y buen gobierno.* Madrid: Fondo de Cultura Económica.

Dubet, A. 2017a. José Campillo y las secuelas de la suspensión de 1739: un proyecto político para la Hacienda real. *Cuadernos de Historia Moderna* 42 (2): 629–652.

Dubet, A. 2017b. La suspensión de pagos de 1739: ¿una medida de "buen gobierno" de la Hacienda? *Espacio, Tiempo y Forma* 30: 19–56.

Durand, Y. 1971. *Les Fermiers généraux au XVIIIe siècle*. Paris: Presses Universitaires de France.

Durand, Y. 1976. *Finance et mécénat. Les fermiers généraux au XVIIIe siècle*. Paris: Hachette.

Escamilla, I. 2011. *Los intereses malentendidos*. México: UNAM.

Escribano Páez, J.M. 2015. *El coste de la defensa. Administración y financiación militar en Navarra durante la primera mitad del siglo XVI*. Pamplona: Gobierno de Navarra.

Félix, J. 2011. Modèles, Traditions, Innovations. Le Peletier des Forts et la renaissance de la finance sous le règne de Louis XV. In *Les financiers et la construction de l'État. France, Espagne (XVII–XIX siècle)*, ed. A. Dubet, and J.P. Luis, 125–154. Rennes: Presses Universitaires de Rennes.

Fisher, J. 1985. *Commercial Relations Between Spain and Spanish America in the Era of Free Trade, 1778–1796*. Liverpool: TBC.

González Enciso, A. 2009. Libertad, privilegio y monopolio en la política económica de Floridablanca: la Renta del Tabaco. *Res Publica* 22: 257–268.

González Enciso, A. 2011. Military Expenditure and Entrepreneurial Promotion in Modern Spain: An Unsuccessful Expedient. In *The Spending of the States*, ed. S. Conway and R. Torres Sánchez, 285–312. Saarbrücken: VDM.

González Enciso, A. 2012. La renovación del asiento de transporte de municiones y armas en 1793 y el protagonismo de una familia navarra. *Memoria y Civilización* 15: 51–69.

González Enciso, A. 2013. Del *Contractor state* al estado fabricante. El cambio de propiedad en la fábrica de municiones de Eugui en 1766. *Revista de Historia de la Economía y de la Empresa* VII: 455–480.

González Enciso, A. 2015. La supresión de los arrendamientos de impuestos en la España del siglo XVIII. *Tiempos Modernos*, 30–31.

González Enciso, A. 2016. La provisión de artillería en el imperio español en la primera mitad del siglo XVIII. In *Jesús Longares Alonso: el maestro que sabía escuchar*, ed. F.J. Caspistegui and I. Peiró, 127–144. Pamplona: EUNSA.

González Enciso, A. 2018. War Contracting and Artillery Production in Spain. *Business History* 60 (1): 87–104.

Helguera Quijada, J. 2012. De La Cavada a Trubia. Intervencionismo estatal y cambio tecnológico en las fundiciones de artillería del norte de España (1760–1800). In *Empresa y empresarios en el norte de España (siglo XVIII)*, ed. J. Ocampo, 153–182. Oviedo: Trea.

Hutt, W.H. 1936. *Economists and the Public*. London: Jonathan Cape.

Ibáñez Molina, M. 1994. D. José del Campillo ante los problemas fiscales a principios de 1741. *Cuadernos de Investigación Histórica* 15: 47–68.

Jiménez Estrella, A. 2010. Asentistas militares y fraude en torno al abastecimiento de pólvora en el reino de Granada (siglo XVI). *Investigaciones Históricas* 30: 11–30.

Kamen, H. 1974. *La Guerra de Sucesión en España*. Barcelona: Grijalbo.
Knight, R. 2014. *Britain Against Napoleon: The Organization of Victory, 1793–1815*. London: Penguin.
Knight, R., and M. Wilcox. 2010. *Sustaining the Fleet, 1793–1815: War, the British Navy and the Contractor State*. Woodbridge: The Boydell Press.
Ladero Quesada, M.A. 1978. *España en 1492*. Madrid: Hernando.
Maiso González, J. 1990. *La difícil modernización de Cantabria en el siglo XVIII*. Santander: Ayuntamiento de Santander.
Molas, P. 2008. *Los gobernantes de la España Moderna*. Madrid: Actas.
Morris, R. 2011. *The Foundations of British Maritime Ascendancy: Resources, Logistics and the State, 1755–1815*. Cambridge: Cambridge University Press.
Moya Torres y Velasco, F.M. 1992. *Manifiesto universal de los males envejecidos que España padece* [1730], ed. A. Domínguez Ortiz. Madrid: Instituto de Cooperación Iberoamericana.
O'Brien, P. 1988. The Political Economy of British Taxation, 1688–1815. *Economic History Review*, Second series 41: 1–32.
O'Brien, P. 1989. The Impact of the Revolutionary and Napoleonic War, 1793–1815, on the Long Run Growth of the British Economy. *Fernand Braudel Center Review* 12 (1989): 335–395.
O'Brien, P. 2007. Taxation for British Mercantilism from the Treaty of Utrecht (1713) to the Peace of Paris (1783). In *War, State and Development. Fiscal-Military States in the Eighteenth Century*, ed. R. Torres Sánchez, 295–356. Pamplona: EUNSA.
O'Brien, P. 2011. The Nature and Historical Evolution of an Exceptional Fiscal State and its Possible Significance for the Precocious Commercialization and Industrialization of the British Economy from Cromwell to Nelson. *The Economic History Review* 64: 408–446.
Parrot, D. 2012. *The Business of War: Military Entrepreneurs and Military Revolution in Early Modern Europe*. Cambridge: Cambridge University Press.
Pérez Sarrión, G. (ed.). 2011. *Más Estado y más mercado. Absolutismo y economía en la España del siglo XVIII*. Madrid: Silex.
Pérez Sarrión, G. 2016. Gremios, Gremios Mayores, Cinco Gremios Mayores de Madrid: Madrid, 1680–1790. In *Recuperando el Norte*, ed. A. Angulo and A. Aragón, 19–62. Bilbao: Universidad del País Vasco.
Rodríguez Gordillo, J.M. 1984. *Un archivo para la historia del tabaco*. Madrid: Tabacalera.
Rodríguez Gordillo, J.M. 2000. Las estadísticas de la Renta del Tabaco en el siglo XVIII: nuevas aportaciones. In *El mercado de tabaco en España durante el siglo XVIII*, ed. S. de Luxán, S. Solbes Ferri, and J.J. Laforet, 53–103. Las Palmas de Gran Canaria: Universidad de Las Palmas.
Rodríguez Gordillo, J.M. 2007. La Renta del Tabaco en el primer tercio del siglo XVIII. In *El monopolio español de tabacos en el siglo XVIII. consumos y valores*,

ed. M. Rodríguez Gordillo and M. Gárate Ojanguren, 25–106. Madrid: Fundación Altadis.

Rodríguez Hernández, A.J. 2012. Los primeros ejércitos peninsulares y su influencia en la formación del Estado Moderno durante el siglo XVII". In *Un Estado Militar. España, 1650–1820*, ed. A. González Enciso, 19–64. Madrid: Actas.

Solbes Ferri, S. 2016. Privilegios territoriales en la España borbónica del siglo XVIII. *Mélanges de la Casa de Velázquez* 46 (1): 117–126.

Thompson, I.A.A. 1976. *War and Government in Habsburg Spain, 1560–1620*. London: The Athlone Press.

Torres Sánchez, R. 2002a. Cuando las reglas del juego cambian. Mercados y privilegio en el abastecimiento del ejército español en el siglo XVIII. *Revista de Historia Moderna. Anales de la Universidad de Alicante* 20: 487–511.

Torres Sánchez, R. 2002b. El gran negocio de la época, la provisión de víveres al ejército por Francisco Mendinueta (1744–1763). In *Francisco Mendinueta: finanzas y mecenazgo en la España del siglo XVIII*, ed. S. Aquerreta, 101–134. Pamplona: EUNSA.

Torres Sánchez, R. 2010. Los navarros en la provisión de víveres a la Armada española durante el siglo XVIII. In *Volver a la "hora Navarra". La contribución navarra a la construcción de la Monarquía española en el siglo XVIII*, ed. R. Torres Sánchez, 213–263. Pamplona: EUNSA.

Torres Sánchez, R. 2013. Administración o asiento. La política estatal de suministros militares en la Monarquía española del siglo XVIII. *Studia Historica. Historia Moderna* 35: 159–199.

Torres Sánchez, R. 2014. In the shadow of Power: Monopolist entrepreneurs, the state and Spanish Military Victualling in the Eighteenth Century. In *War, Entrepreneurs and the State in Europe and the Mediterranean, 1300–1800*, ed. J. Fynn-Paul, 260–283. Brill: Leiden.

Torres Sánchez, R. 2016. *Military Entrepreneurs and the Spanish Contractor State in the Eighteenth Century*. Oxford: Oxford University Press.

Vázquez Gestal, P. 2013. *Una nueva majestad: Felipe V, Isabel de Farnesio y la identidad de la monarquía (1700–1729)*. Madrid: Marcial Pons.

Wilson, Ch. 1965. *England's Apprenticeship, 1603–1763*. London: Longman.

Yun Casalilla, B. 2004. *Marte contra Minerva*. Barcelona: Crítica.

CHAPTER 9

Why Did *Chambres de Justice* Disappear in Eighteenth-Century France? Fiscal Profit and Institutional Change, 1688–1788

Joël Félix

> I cannot lend you more than fifty Thousand Dariques of Gold, for really the Customs of the Empire have brought me in but three Hundred Thousand this Year. Babouc enquired who the Man was, that complained of getting so little. Voltaire (1754: 17)

> It is a matter of fact, that we cannot exclaim with Babouc, in one of Voltaire's tales, *that there are in Persepolis, forty plebeian kings, who hold the empire of Persia under lease, and who give a trifle for the monarch.* Necker (1787: i, 98)

Criticism of excessive fiscal profit, in particular of benefits gained in the management of government finances, was a leitmotiv in early-modern Europe. This was especially the case in France, and was the result of two main factors. First, with the accession of the Bourbons, the kingdom of France became the foremost tax state until 1789, in volume if

J. Félix (✉)
University of Reading, Reading, UK
e-mail: j.m.felix@reading.ac.uk

J. Félix and A. Dubet (eds.), *The War Within*,
Palgrave Studies in the History of Finance,
https://doi.org/10.1007/978-3-319-98050-8_9

not per capita (Félix 2012a). Second, as *financier* Joseph Marquet de Bourgade reckoned in 1768, the very existence of the *corps de la finance*, i.e. a corporate body of financiers who managed the king's finance, was a distinctive French phenomenon and, according to him, a constitutive element of the Bourbon system of government. Indeed, by that time, leading Europe countries, like England post-Civil War, followed by Spain and the Netherlands in the 1740s, were progressively substituting a system of direct administration of fiscal revenue for the older habit of privatising tax collection (Coffman 2013).[1]

Paradoxically, while fiscal needs promoted structural reforms in Europe, the existence of substantial resources in France seems to have strengthened the monopoly of individual financiers or private companies to harvest the wealth of the kingdom on behalf of the king. In this respect, Marquet de Bourgade did not consider his comrades as predators. On the contrary, he regarded the *corps de la finance* as forming an intermediary body between the Crown and the king's subjects. To him, financial intermediation was essentially beneficial to the kingdom because financiers were able to inspire (or deter) confidence in the public when the government was looking for money. In other words, Bourgade saw in the financiers a fourth power, sitting next alongside the executive, legislative and judiciary powers, the role of which was to act as a check upon the relationship between the king, his creditors and the taxpayers.[2]

Attributing such moral qualities to Old Regime finance and financiers may seem like an oxymoron. After all, Marquet de Bourgade, who was very wealthy, did not hesitate to ask for the government's help to rescue the affairs of his profligate brother, Marquet de Grèves, a *fermier général* (tax farmer) who managed to ruin himself by erecting lavish buildings. In the same family, his nephew Marquet de Peyre, whose Bourgade supervised the training in Amsterdam and for whom he bought an office of tax collector, was one of the *receveurs généraux des finances* who went bankrupt in 1788. Others, like Antoine de Lavoisier, the famous chemist who also happened to be a tax farmer, were no less ruthless when it came to defending their financial profit. Under Louis XVI, Lavoisier was deeply critical of the government policy of

[1] See the relevant chapters in this volume by Agustin Gonzales-Enciso and Toon Kerkhoff.

[2] Archives nationales [AN], 144AP 102, pièce 106, *Mémoire* (juin 1769).

cutting down on administrative costs tax farmers were allowed to retain on payment of their lease to the king. While an ordinary family of peasants and a well-established craftsman would earn about 500 and 5000 *livres tournois* (lt.) per year respectively, Lavoisier found that 50,020 lt. was 'not excessive for the maintenance of his house, the payment of his secretaries and clerks, the education and the subsistence of his family', notwithstanding the eventual distribution of 1,200,000 lt. in benefits (de Lavoisier 1893: vi, 158).

Arguably, the needs and lifestyles of the financiers were remote from those at of the king's ordinary subjects. Their conspicuous display of wealth impacted on society in many ways. In the eighteenth century, it generated a lively dispute among French intellectuals who argued whether luxury contributed to the progress of civilisation or its corruption, thereby paving the way for economic reflections about the accumulation of wealth (Shovlin 2006). In general, however, financiers' wealth raised bitter debates about what was wrong in the social fabric. The average value of the financiers' estate at death ranged between 1.5 and 3 million in the 1750s. This was about 1% of the king's annual tax revenue. Even if the fortunes of the most powerful aristocrats and successful financiers and bankers were even larger, Old Regime financiers were probably, and in proportion to the 2016 budget, as affluent as today's 500 richest French tycoons (Clayes 2011; Broch 2015).

True, there was a qualitative difference in the wealth of these magnates. Although it is very difficult to assess the origins and evolution of their respective estates, in the main the fortune of the financiers came less from economic investment than from handling of the king's monies, or both (Chaussinand-Nogaret 1970; Ozanam 1969). When it occurred, merging of economic with fiscal activities usually led to the creation of financial dynasties. Such a perspective was profoundly disturbing to Jean-Joseph de Laborde, an international merchant who prided himself for arming dozens of ships full of goods which navigated the oceans. During the Seven Years' War, Laborde's credit and international network of correspondents naturally made him the ideal candidate to take over from the older Jean Paris de Montmartel, keeper of the Royal treasury, the role of *banquier de la cour* (court banker) for remitting money abroad and cutting down on foreign exchange costs. Yet the merchant's arm had to be seriously twisted before he succumbed to Choiseul's later demand that he also become one of the king's tax farmers (Durand 1971a, b). This unease shows the extent to which the enduring image of the financiers as parasites who fed on the very blood of the kingdom was further reinforced in an age of growth which went in tandem with the development of a new political economy, namely economic liberalism.

Up until the early-eighteenth century, public opinion and pamphlets regularly petitioned the king to set up extraordinary courts, known as *Chambres de Justice*, to try the financiers and press those leeches and sponges who were accused of sucking the blood out of his subjects. Historians have shown that these jurisdictions served various purposes which were moral and financial as well as political. In wartime or as peace came, the call for *Chambres de Justice* answered public outcry for social justice; more pragmatically, they were used by governments to help balance the budget by recouping money paid to financiers during the war; finally trials against moneylenders were an opportunity for the king to assert his authority as a judge and to promote his image as a father for his people. Whether *Chambres de Justice* were just or not, they were tools which helped the kingdom come to terms with the impact of warfare on the body politic, both by settling accounts with the financiers and also by whitewashing their remaining profits. In this process, however, the indictment of a few financiers convicted of fraud and embezzlement, together with the restitutions demanded from almost all of them, reinforced the popular view that, one way or another, they were public thieves (Bayard 1974; Goldner 2008, 2013; Pitts 2015).

A vexing problem, which has been identified by historians but not fully explored, is how to account for the disappearance of *Chambres de Justice* after 1716 (Bosher 1973; Dessert 1984). Since the practice of blaming financial profit does not seem to have receded thereafter, one is tempted to evoke the impact of institutional change, in particular the development of a financial market in bonds, including the creation of the Paris Bourse in 1723, and increasing reliance on public loans underwritten by bankers rather than by the sale of offices (venality) by *traitants* and short-term loans managed and sold by the financiers. Such views, however, are at odds with the general interpretation of the fiscal crisis of 1787 and the collapse of the Absolute Monarchy in 1789 which is generally attributed to failure to reform royal institutions, notably to curb financial profit by effective administrative controls (Bosher 1970; Legay 2011). One way of resolving this apparent conundrum might be to identify qualitative and quantitative changes, which did not radically transform the fiscal system but altered the ways in which the king dealt with his financiers in response to specific pressures. In other words, the *Chambres de Justice* might be considered as one among the various tools monarchs used or devised, according to circumstances, to address financial and political constraints.

To test this hypothesis, this chapter proposes to examine the extent to which contractual agreements between the government and the financiers impacted on their profits under the Old Regime. Inasmuch as the term financiers was generic, i.e. applicable to all the individuals involved in the handling of the king's monies, the scope of this enquiry has to be limited. Focus will be on the *Ferme générale*, i.e. the main fiscal agency with responsibility for the collection of indirect taxes (excise duties and consumption taxes) on behalf of the French king. One reason for this choice is availability of primary sources. As is well known, the fiscal archives of the French monarchy have been almost totally destroyed, along with the papers of individual financiers and private companies which handled the king's revenue and expenditure. By chance, accidental and systematic destruction of fiscal data have spared some copies of crucial documents which, when pieced together, help us to revisit the secondary literature and allow new insights into the broad question of the role of the financiers in the last century of Bourbon power. This chapter is divided into four parts. The first part will briefly introduce the reader to the French system of tax collection. The second part will examine the impact of war on the relationship between ministers and financiers under Louis XIV. The third part will focus on the profits of the tax farmers under Louis XV and the final part will survey the reforms introduced from the 1750s onwards to maximise tax revenue and monitor fiscal profit.

1 The System of Indirect Tax Collection

Throughout the eighteenth century, a debate raged about the advantages and disadvantages of the two possible methods available to the government for collection of indirect taxes: namely the *ferme* or the *régie*. In the *régie* system (direct administration), the collection of taxes was handed out to *régisseurs* who received a salary for their services, and also might be incentivised via bonuses for meeting targets (*régie intéressée*). In the *ferme* system (tax farm), the king leased out the collection of taxes for a number of years (normally six) and for a set annual price. In this structure, the tax farmers received a salary for their services to the king. But their main incentive was the clause which allowed them to retain (and distribute among themselves) the difference between the lease price to be paid to the king and the actual taxes levied on the taxpayers. In this type of contract, the perspective of profits was offset by the risk of losses, especially in an economic downturn. For this reason, the lease agreed between the king and the tax farmers normally included two prices, one for peacetime and another in case of war, to take into account the impact of embargoes and higher tax rates.

A few years before Montesquieu put the blame on tax farms in his famous *De L'Esprit des Lois* (1749), a sieur Malezieu had already composed a quite impressive history of the *fermes du roi* (1746), in which he argued that the state, i.e. the king and his subjects, was always on the losing side when government leased taxes. For, Malezieu wrote, either the tax farmers creamed off the benefits of economic growth, or they asked for, and obtained, compensations from the king when tax yield did not match expectations of profit. To resolve this problem, Malezieu proposed two solutions: increase the duration of the lease to 12 years (to hedge against risk) or suppress the *ferme* and replace it with a *régie*. The first proposition was clearly unworkable. This is not so much because the evolution of the economy could make things unbearable for any of the parties but simply because tax farmers would not invest in a company for such a long period of time as they would not be able to finalise accounts and distribute profits for many years. Also the likelihood of deaths among them would be greater and the cause of all sorts of legal issues with their heirs. In any case, Malezieu favoured pure and simple abolition of tax farms (Félix 2012b).[3]

As was usually the case with eighteenth-century reformers, the discussions of the fiscal dilemmas of the monarchy were often presented in a very abrupt manner. In this respect, cardinal de Fleury's public statement, made in 1726, that tax farmers were the pillars of the state elevated the rather technical topic of tax collection to a question of principles, which broached the institutions of the monarchy. Since cardinal de Fleury was the effective ruler of France for almost two decades, mostly peaceful years and devoid of the series of defaults which had tarnished the end of Louis XIV's reign and the following Regency, his claim about the *fermes* carried quite some weight. In 1775, the wording was still resonating in a publication by Richard des Glanières (1774: 15–16) calling for fiscal reform: his ideas about reducing financial profit were

[3]On these points see Marquet de Bourgade's papers at the Bibliothèque nationale de France, Ms. Fr. 8013–8018.

illustrated by two pillars or columns, one old and barren, representing the current system, and the other solid with ivy twining up it.

At a time when Spain and the Netherlands were abandoning tax farming, the French system of tax collection was clearly becoming a major societal issue, although it should be noted that the French tax farmers enjoyed a reputation for fiscal efficiency and, as such, they were invited by foreign monarchs to run their tax system, for example in the case of Prussia or Tuscany (Waquet 1977; Schui 2013). Three main reasons explain the rise of conflicts and hostile discourses about tax farming. First, indirect taxes accounted for a little over half of the king's revenue. Second, unlike taxes on agricultural revenue, which were essentially managed by local parishes, the daily collection of indirect taxes was built upon an agency which, in the eighteenth century, employed tens of thousands of employees, and whose activities were anything but frictionless. The fight against fraud was a permanent source of tensions between tax agents and the population (Nicolas 2002; Kwass 2014). The policing of this workforce, often compared to an army, the costs of maintaining the necessary infrastructure (barriers and collection posts), and the profits to be made through its management were weighty matters of state. For these reasons, the system of tax collection was more complex than one might surmise from the crude debates over *ferme* and *régie*, especially as a group of reformers among the financiers promoted institutional change in the 1750s (Clayes 2011). Above all, the return of international warfare, the impact of increased taxation, which rose by 80% between 1740 and 1774, French defeats in the Seven Years' War and a succession of defaults on the debt between 1769 and 1770 paved the way to discussions about the shortcomings of the French fiscal system and ways of reforming it, both within and outside government. Before looking at the situation under Louis XV and Louis XVI, it is essential, however, to examine the system of tax collection in operation under Louis XIV.

2 A Fiscal Oddity? A *Régie* in the Name of a *Ferme*

When the revolutionaries abolished the Old Regime system of tax farming they put an end to an institution which was well over a century old. Although the system of tax farming was as old as the first taxes on consumption and trade introduced in the late Middle Ages, the constitution of a powerful fiscal agency was a much later development. The rationale behind Colbert's setting up of this unique body had been a determination to increase fiscal revenue by means of economies of scale through accretion of a number of small tax farms. As a result, the so-called *Fermes générales unies* (1681) became the largest private company and financial institution in the kingdom (Clamageran 1867–1876; Marion 1914; Roux 1916; Durand 1971a, b; Johnson 2006). To be allowed to collect taxes from the king's subjects and pay their lease to the Treasury, the tax farmers had to raise working capital (*fonds d'avance*) to operate the daily management of the infrastructure and keep cash flows running smoothly in the Treasury. In addition to paying the lease, the tax farm might be asked to lend money to the government, normally through the sale of promissory notes. By and large, the *Ferme générale* acted as a bank for the king. While the revenue from indirect taxes, in particular the salt tax (gabelle), was mortgaged to servicing the interests of long-term public loans (rentes perpétuelles and rentes viagères), the tax farmers' profits guaranteed their cash advances to the king. This role as credit provider was extended and officialised by Colbert during the Dutch War (1672–1678) when the tax farm was given responsibility over a *Caisse des Emprunts* which took deposits and issued *promesses des gabelles* on behalf of the king. Lenders in these short-term assets, which matured after six months, had the revenue from taxes as collateral plus the king's guarantee. As it turned out, this model of circulating credit instruments and helping liquidity at the Treasury was adapted according to needs and circumstances. After Colbert's death the *Caisse des Emprunts* was suppressed (1683), then reinstated (1702) and finally abolished (1715) (Félix 2018). Yet supply of short-term cash advances to the government remained a permanent feature of tax-farming throughout the period.

As a matter of fact, contractual arrangements with tax farmers were modified according to needs and circumstances under Louis XIV. In 1687, for instance, the collection of indirect taxes, which Colbert had united into a single tax farm, was split again between two companies (Domergue and Charrière). In 1691, two years before their leases expired, the two companies were merged into a new one operated under the name (lease) Pointeau. At first glance, such changes might seem purely cosmetic. In fact, this move was the response to a crisis of the system of tax farming in the Nine Years' War and a cover-up for its transformation into a *régie*. The reason for this is simple. Negotiations of the terms of the two leases had started in 1687, in peacetime, under finance minister Claude Le Peletier (1683–1689). According to Malezieu, the

Table 1 Losses on lease Domergue, 1688–1691[a]

Lease Domergue	*1688*	*1689*	*1690*	*1691*
Lease price	36,000,000	36,500,000	38,000,000	38,000,000
Expenditure	47,015,896	48,084,705	51,162,748	54,266,743
Revenue	48,278,130	45,312,252	45,953,223	48,435,513
Difference	1,262,234	−2,772,452	−5,209,521	−5,831,230
Combined surpluses/losses	1,262,234	−1,510,218	−6,719,739	−12,550,970

[a]Bibliothèque Nationale de France (BNF), manuscrit français 7725, Grandes opérations de Monsieur le Chancelier de Pontchartrain, Pièce 1, Table générale des produits et dépenses des fermes unies du Roy pendant les quatre années de jouissance du bail de Domergue fini au dernier décembre 1691

two lease prices had been inflated on purpose, with the view to exaggerating France's fiscal power in the eyes of its potential enemies. When the war broke out, however, the tax farmers quickly found themselves in a dire situation. From the second year of its lease (1689), which coincided with the beginning of the Nine Years' War (1688–1697), the Domergue company saw profits suddenly plummet. The tax farmers recorded a collapse in the revenue from taxes levied on internal trade. Tax hikes on the sale of salt and tobacco did not compensate rising costs to fight tax fraud. In 1689, the lease to be paid to the king exceeded the fiscal revenue actually collected. As shown in Table 1, things got worse. At the end of 1691, the combined losses since the start of the lease Domergue were 12.5 million, or about a third of the annual lease price.

This situation was unsustainable and the tax farmers started borrowing on the market to honour payment of the lease. After much discussion, newly appointed finance minister Pontchartrain (1689–1699) decided to abolish the two ongoing tax leases and negotiated a single lease with both companies under the name of Pointeau, and for the same annual price of 61 million. Once again the lease was a fake: as a memorandum explained, Pontchartrain enforced a lease for the price 'which he judged suitable to the needs of the service'. Although 'the *cautions* [i.e. tax farmers acting as guarantors] did all they could to prevent this', the minister 'told them that this was for the service of the state, that all the risks would be for the king, and that their work would be rewarded'. In other words, the *tax farm* was converted into a *régie*.[4] Meanwhile,

[4]Id., fos. 1–2.

Table 2 Results of lease Pointeau, 1692–1697[a]

Lease Pointeau 61 million pa	*Losses*
1692, 1693	7,642,674
1694, 1695	18,515,894
1696	7,266,787
1697	17,258,141
	50,683,496
Non valeurs (non-recoverable)	1,040,205
Total 1	**51,723,701**
Diminutions on the lease	
Passports	8,146,515
Interests	10,550,950
Total 2	**18,697,465**
Real losses	**33,026,238**
Annual average losses	5,804,372

[a]Id

Table 3 Loans of lease Pointeau[a]

Loans	
1st account	10,530,000
2nd account	16,066,000
3rd account	23,111,972
4th account	29,611,001
5th account	18,809,405
6th account	19,591,119
7th account	26,169,226
8th account	31,448,530
Total	**175,337,253**
Refunded	156,129,446
Interests paid	9,590,562
Outstanding	19,207,807

[a]Id., fos. 2–3

as shown in Table 2, the revenue from indirect taxes continued to fall, although losses varied from year to year. Unsurprisingly, a nadir was attained in 1694 and 1695, years which saw France experience one of its worst famine in history and lose 2 million people, ca. 10% of its population. Yet the worst results came in 1697, in the final year of the war, when tax yield fell 28% short of the expected lease of 61 million.

To compensate for these losses and still pay the lease, the tax farmers were invited to issue short-term bonds, the so-called *promesses des gabelles*, via their cashier in Paris. Table 3 lists the volume of the tax farmers's loans, probably between 1692 (1st account) and 1699 (8th account). The figures are hard to interpret because each account is for the total of bonds sold in a fiscal year. We do not know how many of the existing bills were refunded, renewed or added in each fiscal year and, consequently, how much of these sums were meant to either redeem capital and/or pay interests. It would certainly be wrong to infer from the figures that the rate of interest paid to the purchasers of *promesses* was about 5% (interests/total). Other archival evidence indicates that the tax farmers offered 10% interest per year to their notes, 2% of which it seems reasonable to believe they retained as the remuneration for their intermediation.

If one posits that the loans in *year n* were used to refund all of the bills issued in *year n-1* when they reached maturity, and to raise additional cash, then the actual value of new loans issued between 1692 and 1697 would total 65 million, a result broadly in line with the total losses incurred for the duration of the *bail* (lease) Pointeau. The same method applied to the net volume of bills sold during the years 1692–1699, to include loans also issued by Pointeau during the two years of peace, would come to 97 million, which, at 10% interest, would bring the costs for their service to 9.6 million in interest, and leave 18 million of outstanding bills in 1699. These results largely tally with the loans in 1699, the very moment when Pontchartrain handed over the finance portfolio to Michel Chamillart (1699–1708).

These accounts make it clear that the main purposes for secretly operating the tax farm as a *régie* were twofold. First, intermediation by the tax farmers was essential because they were able to attract lenders and supply the Treasury with cash. In his discussions with Pontchartrain, Domergue initially proposed to agree on a new increased lease that was to leave annual profits of 2 million to the tax farmers because, as he argued, '2 millions worth of profit between them will provide 20 millions in credit'. The proposal did not satisfy Pontchartrain who simply agreed on the principle of a compensation for their services by the king. The tax farmers involved in lease Pointeau were bitterly disappointed when they learnt that their reward would be 500,000 livres to be distributed among the 40 of them. They complained, arguing that the guarantors of Domergue and Charrière had received 500,000 livres in compensation for their lack of profit during the 4 years of their leases. A text from Lavoisier suggests that Pontchartrain took the remonstrance on board and finalised the deal with a bonus worth 800,000 livres, or 3333 lt. per tax farmer per year (Lavoisier: 131).

The tax farmers' harsh diet was softened by the perspective of rosier days. By chance, the expiry of the lease Pointeau coincided with the peace of Ryswick (1697). Pontchartrain agreed a new lease under the name of Templier and with *cautions* who were the same as in Pointeau's. The prorogation of the same company to exploit the new lease was probably regarded as an additional form of compensation. It was also a convenient method to avoid the complications and costs associated with the setting up of a new company, in particular the operations for raising new capital and refunding the previous tax farmers for their investments and cash advances. A system of shares would have certainly eased such transitions. But then shares would have had to be valued, an impossible task given the total lack of transparency on tax farmers' returns, a situation which reflected the legal basis of their partnership, which will be discussed later.

Now that peacetime had resumed, the tax farmers were probably planning to make up for the time lost. Unfortunately, the first year of the new lease Templier (1697–1703) suffered from the impact of frost on wine production, and, in general, a sluggish post-war recovery hampered by poor harvests and new international trade tariffs. Moreover, in 1700, the death of childless Charles II of Spain renewed hostilities between France and the Allies over the Spanish succession. In these conditions, the tax farmers became very nervous about their expected profits. They tried to obtain some favours which the tough Chamillart resisted until their recriminations were interpreted as the main cause behind a credit crunch in December 1701. In the end, however, worries proved far-fetched. The gloomy forecast had been based on partial accounts transmitted by the various local tax receivers employed by the *Ferme générale*. When the accounts were finalised, the net profit for the six years of lease Templier amounted to 11,607,000 lt., or a distribution of 290,175 lt. per tax farmer per year. In real terms, taking into account the monetary adjustment of 1726, this result would have been higher than the largest benefits made by the tax farmers under Louis XV and Louis XVI (see below).[5] The overall net profit on lease Templier was quite substantial, equivalent to almost 10% of the annual gross tax revenue for the year 1703. Struggling to find money and fund the new war, there was no way Chamillart would agree to such distribution to the tax farmers. In 1700, while he was trying to balance the peacetime budget, the new minister had levied a 50% windfall tax, worth 19 million, on the net profits earned by the *traitants* on the sale of offices during the Nine Years' War (Félix 2017). After much thought, the finance minister decided to fix the distribution of profit to 2 million, so recouping more than 9 million from lease Templier.

Under Pontchartrain and Chamillart the system of tax farms was nothing but a name. Ministers revised contractual arrangements as they saw fit, either in the course of the lease or retrospectively, and according to the needs of the Treasury. Apart from budgetary problems linked to funding the war and refinancing the war debts, one main reason for this was the difficulty of forecasting tax revenue and, therefore, agreeing on a reasonable sharing out between the king and the financiers. In this respect, the model of 'debt as contingent claim' used by Johnson and Koyama (2014) to describe the relation between the Crown and the tax farmers in the mid-eighteenth century seems to have worked only for leases Pointeau and Templier.[6] When war resumed, lessons from the recent past were factored into the preparatory discussions of the next lease. On the expiry of lease Templier, in the second year of the War of the Spanish Succession (1702/1713), the tax farmers refused to include revenue from customs in their lease. They still lent the king their administrative know-how and infrastructure to collect these very same taxes but procured their reward under a system of direct administration. The renewal of the lease, which coincided with a major fiscal crisis (1708) and the Great Winter (1709), could not find any takers at all, and the collection of all indirect taxes had to be placed under direct administration until Louis XIV's death in 1715.

[5] Following 25 years of alterations of its value, the French currency was stabilized in 1726 and, as a result, the *livre tournois* was ca. 40% lower than during the period 1689–1715.

[6] They rightly argue that the tax farmers and their lenders were able to distinguish between defaults buy the borrower due to unavoidable shocks from nature and true defaults due to lack of credibility. In the War of the Spanish Succession, however, these two aspects seem to have compounded.

3 Financial Profit and the Moralisation of Royal Finance

The primary sources we have used so far suggest that the profits made by tax farmer s on the collection of indirect taxes were severely revised under Louis XIV, at least between 1688 and 1715. Yet the few remaining declarations of revenue demanded by the last *chambre de justice*, established in 1716, show that the tax farmers were the richest financiers in the kingdom.[7] This is essentially because they were cherry-picked from very experienced and well-established individuals who had their fingers in many pies. For instance, half of the 40 *cautions* interested in lease Pointeau were fine d by Chamillart for the profits they made as *traitants* in the business of selling royal offices, of which 8 had to pay a tax of 200,000 lt. and above. Since the rate of Chamillart's windfall tax on *traitants* was 50% of their net profits, Luillier's fine of 403,301 lt. indicates he had earned as much from his investment in the sale of royal offices as the compensation paid by Pontchartrain to the cautions of Pointeau's lease, or 4000 times the average annual revenue of a peasant family. And this is not taking on-board the many opportunities for speculation on discredited bonds offered to monied men in wartime.

Although dealing in offices could be risky and a troublesome venture at times, the potential benefits were quite substantial as we will see later. Under Louis XIII and Louis XIV, much of the anger against the financiers was specifically directed at the *traitants*. The rapid growth of their wealth was not the only reason for public hatred. In general, royal taxes spared privileged groups while the sale of offices and forced loans on office holders also targeted the nobles and the well-off. If some bargaining with potential buyers did occur, pressure and bullying was exercised by the *traitants* and, above all, by their clerks who, on many occasions, behaved more like debt-collectors than salesmen offering opportunities to invest in financial products and tax evasion. As the government stopped selling offices in the eighteenth century and the economic trend was upwards, the financiers sought to dissociate themselves from the *traitants* who became a figure of the past and the symbol of the excesses of the flaws of Louis XIV's fiscal system at the end of his reign.

[7] BNF, manuscrit français 7584, Déclarations des personnes sujettes à la Chambre de justice (1716). Accessible on-line on gallica.

Yet for all the duc d'Orléans' efforts at reforming the fiscal system during the Regency (1715–1723), the volume of debts, the failure of John Law's system and the ensuing chaos left the government in want of regular revenue and a line of credit to smooth out cash-flows. Some started to consider that Louis XIV's financiers had not done such a bad job after all, in many dire circumstances. In 1726, the system of *régie*, which had been introduced by John Law as part of his reforms, and maintained by the famous financiers the Paris brothers, was abolished and the *Ferme générale* was restored, in its ever purest form. This decision by cardinal de Fleury and newly appointed finance minister Le Peletier des Forts (1726–1730) was the real driving force behind the denunciations of the profits of the tax farmers from the late 1720s, which led to their eventual beheading during the Terror in 1794 (Félix 2011). Almost immediately, rival groups lobbied the government and gathered data to prove that the new arrangements allowed the tax farmers to pocket about 100 million in the space of 6 years while France's gross annual tax revenue was 200 million.

As it turned out, the claims against the financiers' excessive profit fell onto deaf ears. Cardinal de Fleury's stubbornness was motivated by a willingness to restore some form of stability to the fiscal system which had been seriously shaken for about a decade. Evidence shows that, on occasion, Louis XV's Mentor relied on external criticisms to pressurise the tax farmers and exact from them some additional services in the course of their lease. But he did not succumb to the pressure of those, like Malezieu, who claimed that all the Bourbon monarchs, since Henri IV, and even Louis XV during his minority, had terminated the leases as they saw fit:

> 'If someone', Malezieu argued, 'was obstinate in the face of the strength of examples, at least he should surrender to that of reason, which dictates to anyone who is willing to hear that the interest of the state, which is the interest of the ruler united with that of his subjects, is the supreme law under which all particular interests, whichever they may be, must bend and vanish'.[8]

Writing in the wake of Fleury's death (1743) and just after the sacking of finance minister Orry, whose 16 years of tenure was regarded as a

[8]BNF, Nouv. Acq. Fr. 2565, Addition à l'histoire des Fermes du Roi depuis l'année 987, 1746, f. 1.

replay of Colbert's mercantile policy, Malezieu pleaded for a revolution based on what he considered an accurate interpretation of French fiscal policy: to him, the many examples of past cancellations of tax farms' leases were 'the just application which has been made at all times of a true and universal principle in all the states'.[9] This quote suggests that the issue with the moralisation of finance had moved from a mere question of profit under Louis XIV to a broader discussion about the king's right to renegotiate agreements with the financiers. As we will see, with the return of international warfare in the second half of the eighteenth century and the problem of refunding war debts, subsequent ministers were keen again to revisit the contracts with the financiers. But even the toughest or most resolute remained rather cautious. Under Louis XVI, only the newly appointed and rather inexperienced d'Ormesson (1783) felt sufficiently principled—and pressed for money—not to foresee the commotion to be caused by the king's agreement that the ongoing lease Salzard (1780–1786) be terminated before its expiry date. Issued on 24 October 1783, the decision was repealed on 9 November with a statement from 'His Majesty' to manifest 'on all occasion that any commitment agreed or recognised by him and which had become the pledge of public faith, will always be inviolable in his eyes'. As we know, the French Revolution was partly a rebellion of the elites against ministerial despotism and demanded that property, alongside liberty and equality, be the cornerstone of the new regime and its constitution.

Of course, one may ask whether expectations by financiers that the government stick to its agreements with them were realistic. It is now to time to examine the profits tax farmers made from 1726 onwards. This is possible thanks to a manuscript summary of the tax farmers' accounts—or *Comptes de société*—for each of the five successive leases for the period 1726–1756.[10] Calculations indicate that, on average, the benefits per lease were 61 million. As shown in Table 3, this sum was quite considerable, equal to 8% of the taxes collected. Moreover, as the sums managed were considerable (132 million per year) and since there were only 40 tax farmers at this time, each of them made 1.5 million worth of profit per lease or 250,000 lt. per year. This was more than the revenue of the highest paid

[9] Id.

[10] Archives nationales, 144 AP 113, *Résultat des Comptes de société des Fermes générales depuis le 1er octobre 1726*, 245 ff. The information was probably assembled for the attention of the finance minister in preparation for a new lease in 1767.

ministers at the time and close to that of the richest bishops and abbots in the kingdom. Data reveal that the profits of tax farming, together with the administrative costs to run the *Ferme générale*, made the whole tax collection system very expensive: between 1726 and 1756, when the king's subjects paid 100 lt., the government received on average 75 lt. (23%), 15 lt. going to administrative costs and 8 lt. to the tax farmers. If one takes into consideration the sums included in the administrative costs which funded the profits also paid to the 215 *sous-fermiers* (sub tax farmers), the system of tax farming allowed the financiers to pocket up to ca. 9.3% of the sums they collected on the lease Bocquillon (1750–1756).[11]

Still, this figure seems to be a long way away from what the public reckoned to be the costs of the tax system. In 1768, for instance, a reformer devoted many pages to justifying a lengthy proposal for a radical institutional shake-up based on the assumption that the financiers, as a whole, collected annually 530 million in taxes (both direct and indirect), out of which the king received only 280 million, therefore establishing the costs of the fiscal system at 250 million (47%).[12] This looks a lot like the figures proposed by marquis de Mirabeau in his *Théorie de l'Impôt* (1760), although they still looked very optimistic when compared to other pamphlets, in particular Darigrand's *Anti-Financier* (1763) which evaluated the total costs of tax farming to four times the revenue paid to the Treasury. In his more accurate *Administration des finances de France* (1784), Necker concluded that, on the whole, the cost of collecting taxes was 10.66% but rose to ca. 14% for the *Ferme générale*, so broadly in line with our data. Yet Necker did not include the benefits of the tax farmers, which, we reckon, would probably raise the whole figure to 20%, more or less, by that time.

Contemporary estimates of fiscal profit were clearly exaggerated, especially as the collection of direct taxes was much cheaper than farmed revenue. These numbers are nonetheless helpful: they suggest that denunciation of profit under the Old Regime may be disentangled from broader criticism of the system of taxes. For, on the one hand, the profit the financiers made on tax collection was essentially the expression of a contractual relationship between the king and his agents, which could

[11] According to Lavoisier, 137, at the moment of their suppression in 1756, the *sous-fermiers* numbered 215 individuals, divided into 27 companies, who were paid in excess of 3 million per year.

[12] BNF, manuscrit français 14102, *Mémoire sur les finances*, f. 6 vo.

be altered. On the other hand, however, the administrative costs of tax farming challenged the very nature of the taxes collected—such as the salt tax which generated various burdens on society, most notably the fight against fraud but also the impact on breeding cattle and agricultural growth. In this case, the golden bullet was a reform of indirect taxes or, as the famous *physiocrat s* argued from the 1760s, their replacement with a single and more efficient levy on the revenue from landownership. The question about the type of contract between government and fiscal agents still remained an issue because taxes would have to be collected nonetheless. So too was the question of identifying the most efficient tax to tap wealth, which implied a correct theory to understand the processes behind the formation of fortunes and the incidence of taxes, and to devise techniques, like a land survey, to assess taxable revenue. In practice, however, as we will see, and given the demands on the Treasury resulting from war, reducing financial profits was the easiest solution, for two main reasons: firstly, ministers knew that such policy would meet with popular support; secondly, they were keen to avoid the risks, to revenue and to domestic order, associated with any sudden and substantial reform of the tax system.

There is no doubt whatsoever that the system of tax farming under Louis XV generated enormous benefits to those who enjoyed the privilege of collecting revenue for the king. On average, each of the 40 tax farmers made 252,725 lt. per year between 1726 and 1756, with an all-time high reached in lease Prevost (1762–1768) worth 332,000 lt. An alternative way of assessing benefits—and their evolution over time—is to calculate a rate of profit on capital invested to run fiscal ventures. At this stage, it should be remembered that the *Ferme générale* was operated as a private company run by *cautions*, i.e. the tax farmers, who made an equal contribution to the working capital and were entitled to an equal share in the benefits of the *Ferme générale*. In his study of French financiers in the eighteenth century, T. Clayes also used the *Comptes de société* and calculated that the return on working capital was about 44–45% for this period. In an earlier and important article on French tax farmers, E. White (2004) had expressed doubts about such high returns which some in the eighteenth century estimated to have been as high as 49%. We also consider such a figure far too gigantic to be credible. Incidentally, a fall to 33% on return in lease Forceville (1736–1744), while benefits paid to tax farmers rose by 7%, casts doubts on the interpretation by Clayes (2011) of the data.

In his article, E. White observed that tax farmers did not only raise working capital to operate their fiscal business. They also had to pay to the Treasury a *cautionnement*, or surety bond, worth 8 million per annum, for which the government allowed a 5% interest. This surety bond, however, does not appear in the *Comptes de société* which, it is true, are a much abridged summary. Although figures in this manuscript are not always easy to interpret—and the end pages are missing—the reason for absence of information about the surety bond can be deduced from one of Lavoisier's memoranda on the *Ferme générale*. According to him, the *sous-fermiers* (sub-tax farmers), to whom the tax farmers sub-contracted part of their lease until 1756, were asked to pay a cash advance to the *Caisse des Fermes* worth just under 8 million, which replaced, as it were, the 8 million surety bond or advance supplied by the tax farmers to the Treasury. In short, the *cautionnement* should not be added to the working capital invested by the tax farmers.

This said, close analysis of the *Comptes de société* shows that various sums of money were paid out (expenditure) and refunded (revenue) to the tax farmers such as, for instance, the value of *effets*, i.e. capital assets received from the previous lease and handed over to the next one.[13] Accounts of the leases Forceville and La Rue also recorded *ordonnances*, i.e. orders of payment, on the tobacco farm worth 24 and 48 million respectively, which look like advances to purchase tobacco, an expenditure which was naturally passed over to the taxpayers. In the case of lease La Rue data reveal that 30 million were lent to the guarantors of next lease, Bocquillon. For all these details, the absence of a breakdown of revenue and expenditure of the *Caisse des Fermes* in Paris makes it impossible to identify whether the tax farmers were rewarded for paying these sums and how they mobilised the resources in the first instance.

What is for sure, however, is that on top of the working capital paid by the tax farmers to the *Caisse des Fermes*, they supplied additional *prêts* or loans to the government. Here again, the *Comptes de société* are insufficiently detailed to find out the origins of these funds. In the case of lease Desboves, however, the breakdown of benefits mentions interests of 2,057,625 lt. paid to the tax farmers for a loan of 39,815,000 lt. to the *Caisse des Fermes*. It is important to notice that the rate of interest,

[13]They were initially recorded as 12 million, a sum reduced to 8.9 million from lease La Rue onwards.

which can be calculated at 5.17%, was much lower than what tax farmers were paid for their working capital (*fonds d'avances*). Making sense of this difference was perplexing, until an observation by Necker helped us realise the obvious: the working capital was invested for the duration of the lease, whereas loans were short-term, probably in the form of *billets des fermes*, which replaced the earlier *promesses des gabelles* and also matured after six months. The question remains, however, as to whether the interests rewarded sums the tax farmers paid out of their own pocket or they borrowed. For historians are aware that a number of financiers, if not all of them, were de facto CEOs who invested their own money but also managed a venture partly financed by investors, backers or so-called *amis*, i.e. friends.

Whatever the origins of the funds, loans to the *Caisse* affect calculation of return on capital. Once loans are included, return on the sums actually supplied to the *Caisse* still remains high. But they are reduced to 35, 34 and 29% in the first three leases, respectively. This slight reduction (in percentage but not in volume) is more in line with the evolution of the product (tax collected minus expenditure and lease) and funds invested (working capital). Unfortunately, calculating a return on the fourth lease (La Rue) seems a long shot: our document indicates that in the course of those six years the loans to the *Caisse* rose to the enormous sum of 164.2 million. Even though such a change might be explained by the fact that lease La Rue coincided with the entry of Britain and the Netherlands against France in the War of the Austrian Succession (1741–1748), this huge figure remains problematic, especially as the working capital was reduced by 8 million in the course of this lease, the product (tax collection minus payment of lease) increased by 17 million and the benefits were the highest since 1726. Also such a huge loan would have to be repaid or, at least, renewed, and this would leave traces. So, one is bound to consider that the figure for the loan might be a clerical mistake which confused the working capital with the loan to the *Caisse*, and multiplied it by the number of years of the lease.[14] If that were to be the case, then the return on capital would rise slightly to 38%, which is also consistent with a rise in benefits during this lease, although it coincided with wartime. Similarly, if one includes a 30 million advance made by

[14] The purpose of the summary of the *Comptes de société* was to calculate how much money would be saved for the king if the interests the tax farmers paid themselves for their working capital were reduced to 5 per cent.

Table 4 Leases: Revenue collected, collection costs and tax farmers' profits, 1726–1756

		A	B	C		D		E
Dates	*Lease*	*Revenue*	*To the king*	*Collection costs*		*To the tax farmers*		*Total costs*
		Million lt.	*Million lt.*	*Million lt.*	*C/A (%)*	*Million lt.*	*D/A (%)*	*E/A (%)*
1726–1732	Carlier	620	505	77	12	43	7	19
1732–1738	Desboves	729	551	125	17	56	8	25
1738–1744	Forceville	760	567	113	15	61	8	23
1744–1750	La Rue	863	576	122	15	78	9	24
1750–1756	Bocquillon	844	682	130	16	65	8	24
1726–1756	*Average*	*763*	*576*	*113*	*15*	*61*	*8*	*23*

lease Larue to lease Boquillon, then the return on this latter lease can be calculated at 35%, also in line with a 14 million drop in benefits when peace returned (Table 4).

Whether our adjustments to calculate profits are correct or not, tax farmers drew very substantial benefits from the business of collecting taxes for the king. One method of comparison is to examine the profits made by the much hatred *traitants* as a result of the *traités*, i.e. contracts, they agreed with the king to sell royal offices, which was the main source of war finance under Louis XIV. The objective would be an impossible task, were it not for a few documents which have survived from Chamillart's paperwork produced to determine the windfall tax to be paid by the *traitants* in 1700. An account submitted by the *traitants* who contracted the sale of royal offices to supervise trade in cattle and poultry during the Nine Years War (1688–1697) shows that their company made a net profit of 437,841 lt. over a 3-year period, or 23.6% return on working capital. The comparison is quite stunning: it suggests that the profits of Louis XIV's infamous *traitants* were quite substantial but still lower than those made by the tax farmers under Louis XV, notwithstanding Chamillart's fine which recouped half of their benefits.[15] The traitants' sumptuous—and at times extravagant—lifestyles help us to better understand why enemies of the financiers in the eighteenth

[15]AN, G7 1566, *Traité des veaux et volailles*. Chamillart recalculated the net profit at 550,441 lt. and imposed a 270,000 lt. fine on the *traitants*.

century, and apologists of the direct administration system, systematically used the emotionally charged word *traitants* when they talked about the tax farmers. Yet, there were three main differences between these two types of financiers. First, in the seventeenth century the *traitants* were regularly subjected to *Chambres de Justice*—while tax farmers were usually protected—or had to pay windfall taxes. Second, the *traitants* were not merely tax collectors. They tapped the wealth of the kingdom by selling offices, i.e. they devised and sold financial products which were de facto long-term loans (Bien 1988). Third, *traités* were often contracted with financiers active in supplying the troops and used to raise cash for purchase of goods at the best rate or, simply, to refund cash advances or government debts (Félix 2017).

The benefits enjoyed by Louis XV's tax farmers can be broken down into three principal categories. First, the sums paid for their salaries, which made the smallest part of their profits: they averaged 7.2 million (12%) in the five leases, or 30,000 lt. per year and per tax farmer. It is worth noting that part of this *honorarium* was assigned to defray real administrative costs.[16] In the bail La Rue, for instance, the slight increase in the salaries was to cover costs towards additional visitations (*tournées*) to those normally carried out by the tax farmers (490,350 lt.). In contrast, the interests paid on the *avances* were quite substantial: they averaged a quarter of all profits received between 1726 and 1756. Only in the lease La Rue did the interests paid for cash advances record a significant drop (minus 18%) and so too, but to a lesser extent, the salaries (10%). Yet as Table 5 shows, lease La Rue stands out as the most profitable of the five leases, even though it started in the middle of the War of the Austrian Succession (1741–1748). In stark contrast to Louis XIV's difficult years, this conflict did not seem to have any impact on tax farmers' profits. Quite the contrary: the gap between revenue collected and the lease, which had been growing since 1726, reached a peak under La Rue. This may be the main cause behind the substantial fall in the interests paid for the working capital. In the leases Carlier and Desboves, cash advances were allowed 11.54 and 12.02% respectively. Thereafter, the interest fell by almost 4 points, to 8.19 (Forceville) and 8.24 (La Rue) before rising to 10%. Arguably, this evolution reflected an improvement in the cost of money in general, and the monarchy's creditworthiness in particular, which improved under Fleury and Orry.

[16] For this reason, Necker increased it to 50,000 lt.

Table 5 Tax farmers' profits and return on capital

	Lease	*Per tax farmer per year (lt.)*	*A Profits (m. lt.)*	*Salaries*	*Interests*	*Distribution*	*B Advances*	*Return A/B (%)*	*C Loans*	*Adjusted return A/(B+C)*
1726–1732	Carlier	178,422	43	3	11	25	98	45	26	35
1732–1738	Desboves	235,377	56	6	15	32	128	44	40	34
1738–1744	Forceville	253,651	61	7	16	38	184	33	28	29
1744–1750	La Rue	324,979	78	7	14	56	176	44	[27]	38
1750–1756	Bocquillon	271,197	65	8	16	41	155	42	30	[35]
1726–56	**Average**	**252,725**	**12**	**6**	**14**	**38**	**25**	**42**	**[30]**	**[34%]**
1756–1762	Henriet	240,000[a]								?
1762–1768	Prevost	332,000[a]								?
1774–1780	David	269,667[a]	97	7	22	68	94			22%

[a]Lavoisier: 138–139

4 From *Fermes* to *Régies* Again

The problems associated with the funding of the War of the Austrian Succession—the first serious international conflict since the reign of Louis XIV—and the refinancing of war debts soon raised questions about the efficiency of the tax farming system which had been firmly supported by Fleury and Orry, at least as long as they had held onto power. Neither the reforming minister Machault d'Arnouville (1745–1754), who took over the finance portfolio from Orry, nor any of his successors, were able to substitute *régies* for *fermes*. But, all, like Machault, who may well have commissioned Malezieu's work on the king's tax farms and who obtained insider's knowledge from Bouret, one of the tax farmers, were keen to maximise the system so as to raise more revenue for the king (Clément and Lemoine 1872). From 1750, renewal of the leases was seized upon as an opportunity to revisit the relationship between a government under duress and the financiers. Various methods were used successively or simultaneously.

Machault's goal was essentially to increase the volume of taxes paid to the king so as to get the extra resources that would help balance the budget and reduce the cost of debt service with help of a sinking fund (*caisse d'amortissement*). Since his policy met with staunch resistance from taxpayers, his successor, Moreau de Séchelles (1754–1756), changed tack: he saw renewal of the lease in 1756 as an opportunity for the king to build upon the tax farmers' creditworthiness and increase short-term borrowing to help with the financing of the Seven Years' War (1756–1763). To this effect lease Henriet (1756–1762) was contracted with the tax farmers on condition that they would advance 60 million lt. (ca. £2.5 million) to the Treasury, in lieu of the 8-million surety bond normally paid by the sub-tax farmers but who were now to be suppressed. The measure was facilitated by adding to the 40 tax farmers, who had broadly remained the same people since 1726, 20 new posts, making up the total of 60 *cautions*, or guarantors, who had to contribute 1 million each. This decision had a profound impact on the relationship between government and the financiers, and the stability of the fiscal system. Replacement of the tax farm by a *régie* was now dependent on the Treasury's ability to refund the cash advances, which increased with each new lease. Moreover, as Lavoisier explained, there was no way the 60 *cautions* could individually supply such a large sum (equivalent to a quarter of French gross annual tax revenue) and, on top of that, finance the weekly payments of the *Ferme générale* to the Treasury, regardless of the actual sums paid by taxpayers. For this reason, they decided to raise the working capital, another 60 million, by calling upon the public and selling *billets des fermes.*

It was not long before the French government abused the tax farmer's creditworthiness: a clause in lease Henriet allowing the tax farmers to recoup part of their 60 million advances by retaining 6 million per year on payment of their lease did not materialise. Quite the contrary: in 1759, in the aftermath of a major military defeat and deficit of the budget, the recently appointed controller general Silhouette (1758–1759) decided to renegotiate the terms of lease Henriet by appropriating half the tax farmers' expected benefits for the king, the product of which was immediately capitalised by issuing a much needed royal loan worth 72 million. This *anti-financier* measure did not help remedy the crisis: in November 1759, government ordered that payment of all the bills issued by the tax collectors, including the *billets des fermes*, be suspended, a decision which amounted to a default on the part of the tax farmers, although it was imposed by the king who took de facto control of the fiscal system. Silhouette's decisions were not merely ad hoc responses to urgent needs. They were part and parcel of the reforming views put forward by the new minister who sought to raise revenue through new taxes coupled with savings on financial costs, a policy which was pursued by his successors. More importantly, Silhouette's measures set a precedent whereby the king decided to take a share of the benefits of tax farming. As Lavoisier judged it, this principle was institutionalised by new appointed finance minister L'Averdy (1763–1768): widely expected to reform the king's finances, in 1764 he introduced a 10% tax on the salaries, interests and benefits paid to all the financiers, including the tax farmers. This *dixième d'amortissement* was destined to help fund an improved sinking fund to redeem French debts (Félix 1999).

These decisions were just the start of a more systematic attack on the benefits of the tax farms. Even though the government contracted the lease Prevost (1762–1768) on the basis of an even higher cash advance—worth 72 million, of which 60 million was intended to repay Henriet—the financiers managed to reap the benefits of peacetime on economic activity. As it turned out, they were becoming richer while the kingdom was getting deeper into financial trouble. In lease Prevost, each tax farmer was paid 332.000 lt. per year, or altogether 86 million over 6 years, a sum equal to the deficit of the Treasury in 1768.[17] For all their efforts, three successive finance ministers found themselves unable to put forward any workable solution to remove the likelihood of eventual default. In February 1770, abbé Terray (1770–1774) crossed the Rubicon: once again, the new finance minister decided to suspend payment of financiers' short-term advances, including 9753 *billets des fermes* worth 48.7 million and due to mature over the coming 12 months. Curiously, the defaults of 1759 and 1770 did not curb the appetite of the (rich) public for these short-term credit instruments. During the American War (1778–1783), for instance, the new *billets des fermes* traded at a premium. The main reason for this apparent incoherence is simple: the suspension of the bills was less a default than a rescheduling of capital repayment which was met with regularity, alongside servicing of interest. In short, current and future tax revenue was freed from its *anticipations* in the form of *billets des fermes* and new ones could be issued to supply the Treasury. Of course, the decision hit a number of financiers, like Laborde who held vast amounts of the financiers' bills in his portfolio. But they managed to weather the storm while those who had the right connections obtained government help. An emergency measure, Terray's default had been preceded by harsher conditions in the negotiation of the lease Alaterre (1768–1774): the tax farmers now had to share their benefits with the king, the rate of these benefits: the rate of these benefits varied according to complex calculations so as to ensure that they would continue working towards the reduction of administrative costs (White 2004).

As Lavoisier's complaints reveal, the ministers of the king were now closely monitoring the benefits tax farmers would be earning out of the fiscal system. Salaries were frozen and the interest rate on their advances was cut. In his memoirs, count Mollien, who started his career as a clerk in the finance ministry, estimated that the tax farmers in the lease David (1774–1780) were paid 5.66% for their individual advances of 1,560,000 lt., a figure which does not seem accurate. According to Lavoisier, the government allowed tax farmers to pay 10% on the first million and 6% on the remainder, or 8.56% in total, a figure which is in line with the interest offered to investors in life annuities during the American War

[17] According to Lavoisier, they only needed to raise 45 million in working capital in this lease.

(Mollien 1845: i, 67). This rate, noticeably higher than under La Rue, indicates a worsening of the cost of borrowing money which is consistent with the recent default. If this reading is correct, then new constraints imposed by the government on cash advances were essentially meant to keep interest as low as possible. Given the importance of the sums involved, there was a link between the cost of borrowing money, in general, and the interest paid on working capital, in particular.

Yet cutting the interest was not without a broader impact. As Necker and Lavoisier both observed, those among the tax farmers who had to borrow part of their advances did so at a higher cost than the interests they received each year to pay their creditors, a disparity which was only compensated for when the distribution of benefits was finalised at the end of the lease. In short, liquidity was a growing concern among financiers. This situation further increased discrepancies in the profitability of each post of tax farmer. The annual revenue of tax farmers was unequally burdened with pensions to the royal favourites or *croupes* (sleeping partnerships). This ad hoc method of targeting fiscal profit to pay debts or reward clients seem to have been counterproductive. These additional deductions, which were imposed from lease Carlier onwards on the tax farmers and increased substantially in the 1750s and 1760s, were the cause of resentment against the Court. *Croupes* generated tensions within the company: they complicated arrangements to fund advances, saw information about returns leaked-to the public and added layers of risk which affected profitability. For instance, Lavoisier mentions that delays in raising working capital in the lease David (1774–1780) were penalised by a 1.8 million loss on purchase of tobacco due to a sudden rise in price (Lavoisier: 158–160).

The results obtained by the successive actions of ministers during the 1760s and 1770s were not insignificant meaningless. Mollien estimated that in the course of lease David (1774–1780), the tax farmers made an annual profit of 300,000 livres, whereas Lavoisier mentioned only 270,000 lt., or a 22% return on their cash advances (Lavoisier 1893; Mollien 1845). This was a ca. 7–16% improvement on the returns paid in Louis XV's five first leases; also, the total benefits were 20% below the record level reached for lease Prevost. At the same time, however, a series of tax hikes ensured that the 60 *cautions* made the highest benefit so far, 97 million, or twice the sums they had gained in lease Carlier. In other words, the new arrangements ensured that more money entered the Treasury. Even though the relationship with the government generated some anger, which were partly justified and unjustified, being a tax farmer was still a very profitable activity and a costly one for the king.

To achieve even better results, the government needed to address the system of tax collection itself. Combined work by finance ministers Terray, Turgot and, above all, Necker (1776–1781), progressively limited the volume of indirect taxes leased out to tax farmers. At the time of Colbert's death, in 1683, the *Ferme générale* collected 66 million in taxes for the king, or just over half the fiscal revenue (120 million). A century later, in 1789, this share had dropped to 35% (165 million). With lease Salzard (1780–1786), Necker detached 120 million in indirect taxes which were to be managed under direct administration (*régie intéressée*). On the eve of the French Revolution, the new *Régie des aides et droits réunis* and the *Régie des domaines et bois* were responsible for collecting 50 million each per year. As Necker boasted, the *Ferme générale* was just a name. If the brand had been maintained, it was because the tax agency was able to inspire confidence among lenders, in spite of the two suspensions, and offered short-term credit resources to sustain the liquidity of the Treasury (Necker 1787). For some radical reformers, like economist and administrator Dupont de Nemours, the tax farm had become a hollow fortress which seemed urgent to topple in order to implement a comprehensive reform of the tax system by suppression of excise and customs duties. But as Louis XVI reckoned after the failure of d'Ormesson's attack against the tax farm of 1783, Necker himself had not felt strong enough to engage in a battle with a powerful group of financiers who supervised the largest fiscal organisation in the kingdom and offered reliable services to the Crown (Félix 2006).

5 Conclusion

To come back to our initial question about the reason(s) why *Chambres de Justice* disappear after 1716, one is tempted to argue that there is apparently no clear relationship between the actual rate of profit made by the financiers and the setting up of special courts to try them. On the contrary, study of the tax farmers under Louis XV indicates that profits from collecting indirect taxes on behalf of the king were higher, or at least equivalent, to those of Louis XIV's much despised *traitants,* and with almost no risk. A solution to this apparent paradox may lie in the fact that the main purpose of the *Chambres de Justice* was after all less a financial than political one. Although it may seem hard to separate finance from politics, it is worth noting that the two main *chambres* were set up in 1661 and 1716. Both were politically challenging years, following cardinal Mazarin's and then Louis XIV's deaths, combined with fiscal crises. In such contexts, a *chambre de justice* had been an ideal method, for both Louis XIV and the Regent, to assert their authority and take control of the purse strings. These conditions did not recur again after Louis XV's majority (1723), a king who on the contrary called back the financiers in 1726, nor at Louis XVI's accession in 1774. The new king could hardly target financiers after Terray's recent default, which many considered as a stain on the kingdom, and the measures introduced to cut down on financial profit. Arguably, the accusation, arrests and beheading of 35 tax farmers in Spring of 1794, at the height of the Terror, seem to confirm the political dimension of judicial indictment against financiers and their profits.

Maybe there are even more simple reasons for the end to *Chambres de Justice*. While praising Colbert's legacy, finance minister Desmaretz (1708–1715) was critical of his uncle's decision to try the financiers in 1661, essentially for its impact on the king's credit and public confidence. Desmaretz warned his own successor, maréchal de Noailles (1715–1717), against the latter's decision to set up another *chambre de justice* in 1716, which did bring some financial benefit but was broadly considered a failure. When Fleury called upon the financiers to access cheaper credit, the deal included a protective clause: all the leases contracted from 1726 onwards included an article that the tax farmers would be exempt from a *chambre de justice*. Yet the question of the financiers and their profits remained one of the most enduring subject of societal debate. As Marquet de Bourgade rightly commented they became a constitutive part of the Absolute Monarchy, a fourth power which had the capacity to support the king, but at a cost which was increasingly seen as unsustainable in a competitive European environment.

There was only ever so much that a minister could do to adapt a fiscal system which had evolved and revolved around the tax farm. Whether the reforms carried forward from the mid-1750s could eventually have tipped the balance once and for all towards direct administration is hard to tell (White 1989). Pressed for cash, Calonne restablished the *Ferme des postes* in 1786, which Necker had managed to suppress six years before by refunding the small cash advances of this minor tax farm.[18] As Mollien noted in his memoirs, finding 93 million lt. (a sum equivalent to the quarter of the English budget at the time) to pay off the advances of the main *Ferme générale* was quite a long shot for a government faced with a growing peacetime deficit, which was funded by a mix of public loans underwritten by bankers and a good dose of short-term advances provided by tax farmers, and still committed to funding its naval arm race against Britain. Altogether, fiscal pressure, criticism of fiscal profit, economic debates, administrative reforms and international relations eroded confidence in the pillars on which the tax system had rested since 1726. In such a context, the wealth of the financiers who benefited so much from the fiscal system was a permanent thorn in the side of the government. For all their skills at collecting taxes and raising short-term loans, the sums to be paid for the services of the tax farmers were bound to raise questions about value for money and, as such, call into question the position of financial dynasties which 'believed themselves to be in *possession of state*, like the nobility and the parlements' (Mollien 1845: 68–69). In the absence of an efficient system of public credit and effective checks upon government, in other words for lack of credible commitment, it is hard to see how, in the context of renewed international competition and the development of financial markets, administrative reforms might have prevented the repetition of fiscal crises and defaults, and resolve the political shortcomings of a polity which both united and opposed the king's dynastic aims, the financiers' private interests and the public good.

References

Bayard, F. 1974. Les Chambres de Justice de la première moitié du XVIIe siècle. *Cahiers d'Histoire* 19 (2): 121–140.

Bien, D. 1988. Offices, Corps and the System of State Credit. The Uses of Privilege Under the Ancien Regime. *Annales Economies Sociétés Civilisations* 43 (2): 379–404.

Bosher, J.-F. 1970. *French Finances, 1770–1795: From Business to Bureaucracy.* Cambridge: Cambridge University Press.

[18] Its annual lease was ca. 11.5 million lt.

Bosher, J.F. 1973. Chambres de Justice in the French Monarchy. In *French Government and Society 1500–1850: Essays in Memory of Alfred Cobban*, ed. J.-F. Bosher, 19–40. London: Athlone Press.

Broch, J. 2015. La moralisation de la vie publique sous l'ancien régime. La difficile lutte contre le péculat et la concussion aux XVIe, XVIIe et XVIIIe siècles. *Revue historique de droit français et étranger* 93 (1): 65–101.

Chaussinand-Nogaret, G. 1970. *Les financiers de Languedoc au XVIIIe siècle*. Paris: Colin.

Clamageran, J.-J. 1867–1876. *Histoire de l'impôt en France depuis l'époque romaine jusqu'à 1774*, 3 vols. Paris: Champion, Paris.

Clayes, T. 2011. *Dictionnaire biographique des financiers en France au XVIIIe siècle*, Paris, éditions SPM, 3e édition complétée, 2 vols.

Clément, P., and A. Lemoine. 1872. *M. de Silhouette, Bouret: Les derniers fermiers généraux; études sur les financiers du XVIIIe siècle*. Paris: Didier.

Coffman, D. 2013. *Excise Taxation and the Origins of the Public Debt*. London: Palgrave Macmillan.

Darigran, E.F. 1763. *L'Antifiancier, u Relevé de quelques unes des malversatiins dont se redent journellement coupables les fermiers généraux*... Amsterdam, Paris.

de Lavoisier, A. 1893. Calculs des produits de différents baux de la Ferme générale avec des détails très particuliers sur les frais de régie du bail de Laurent David (1774). In *Œuvres de Lavoisier*, vol. 6, ed. J.B. Dumas, E. Grimaux, and F.A. Fouquet, 125–185. Paris: Imprimerie nationale.

de Mirabeau, Marquis. 1760. *Théorie de l'impôt*. N.p, n.p.

des Glanières, R. 1774. *Plan d'imposition économique et d'administration des finances*... Paris: P.G. Simon.

Dessert, D. 1984. *Argent, pouvoir et société au Grand Siècle*. Paris: Fayard.

Durand, Y. 1971a. Mémoires de Jean-Joseph de Laborde, fermier général et banquier de la cour, *Annuaire-Bulletin de la Société de l'Histoire de France, Années 1968–1969*, 75–162.

Durand, Y. 1971b. *Les fermiers généraux au XVIIIe siècle*. Paris: Presses Universitaires de France.

Félix, J. 1999. *Finances et politique au siècle des Lumières. Le ministère L'Averdy, 1763–1768*. Paris: Comité pour l'Histoire économique et financière de la France.

Félix, J. 2006. *Louis XVI et Marie-Antoinette. Un couple en politique*. Paris: Payot.

Félix, J. 2011. Modèles, Traditions, Innovations. Le Peletier des Forts et la renaissance de la finance sous le règne de Louis XV. In *Les financiers et la construction de l'Etat. France, Espagne (XVIIe-XIXe siècle)*, ed. A. Dubet and J.P. Luis, 125–154. Rennes: Presses Universitaires de Rennes.

Félix, J. 2012a. Finances. In *The Oxford Handbook of the Old Regime*, ed. W. Doyle, 75–92. Oxford: Oxford University Press.

Félix, J. 2012b. Victualling Louis XV's armies. The Munitionnaire des Vivres de Flandres et d'Allemagne and the Military Supply System. In *The Contractor State and Its Implications, 1659–1815*, ed. R. Harding and S. Solbes Ferri, 103–129. Las Palmas: Universidad de Las Palmas de Gran Canaria.

Félix, J. 2017. Profits, Malversations, Restitutions. Les bénéfices des financiers durant la guerre de la Ligue d'Augsbourg et la taxe de Chamillart. *Revue Historique* 676 (4): 831–874.

Félix, J. 2018. 'The Most Difficult Financial Matter that Has Ever Presented Itself': Paper Money and the Financing of Warfare Under Louis XIV. *Financial History Review* 25 (1): 43–70.

Goldner, E.-H. 2008. *Public Thieves: French Financiers, Corruption, and the Public in the Chamber of Justice of 1716*. PhD dissertation, Columbia University, Columbia.

Goldner, E.-H. 2013. Corruption on Trial. Money, Power, and Punishment in France's Chambre de Justice of 1716. *Crime, Histoire & Sociétés/Crime, History & Societies* 17 (1): 5–28.

Johnson, N.D. 2006. Banking on the King: The Evolution of the Royal Revenue Farms in Old Regime France. *The Journal of Economic History* 66 (4): 963–991.

Johnson, N.D., and M. Koyama. 2014. Tax Farming and the Origins of State Capacity in England and France. *Explorations in Economic History* 51: 1–20.

Kwass, M. 2014. *Contraband*. Harvard: Harvard University Press.

Legay, M.-L. 2011. *La Banqueroute de l'Etat royal: La gestion des finances publiques de Colbert à la Révolution*. Paris: Editions de l'EHESS.

Marion, M. 1914. *Histoire financière de la France depuis 1715*, vol. 1. Paris: Arthur Rousseau.

Mollien. F.-N. 1845, *Mémoires d'un ministre du Trésor public, 1780–1815*, H. Fournier, Paris, 1845, 4 vols.

Necker, J. 1787. *A treatise on the administration of the finances of France*. London.

Nicolas, J. 2002. *La Rébellion française. Mouvements populaires et conscience sociale (1661–1789)*. Paris: Editions du Seuil.

Ozanam, D. 1969. *Claude Baudard de Saint-James: Trésorier général de la marine et brasseur d'affaires (1738–1787)*. Genève: Librairie Droz.

Pitts, V.J. 2015. *Embezzlement and High Treason in Louis XIV's France. The Trial of Nicolas Fouquet*. Baltimore: Johns Hopkins University Press.

Roux, P. 1916. *Les Fermes d'impôts sous l'Ancien Régime*. Paris: Librairie Arthur Rousseau.

Schui, F. 2013. *Rebellious Prussians: Urban Political Culture Under Frederick the Great and His Successors*. Oxford: Oxford University Press.

Shovlin, J. 2006. *The Political Economy of Virtue. Luxury, Patriotism, and the Origins of the French Revolution*. Ithaca, NY and London: Cornell University Press.

Voltaire, F.A. 1754. *Babouc, or the World as It Goes*. Dublin: H. Saunders.

Waquet, J.-C. 1977. Les fermes générales dans l'Europe des Lumières: Le cas toscan'. *Mélanges de l'école française de Rome* 89 (2): 983–1027.

White, E.N. 1989. Was There a Solution to the Ancien Régime's Financial Dilemma? *The Journal of Economic History* 49 (3): 545–568.

White, E.N. 2004. From Privatized to Government Administered Tax Collection: Tax Farming in Eighteenth-Century France. *The Economic History Review* 57 (4): 636–663.

CHAPTER 10

War, Resources and Morality: Sweden 1740–1770

Patrik Winton

1 Introduction

In February 1741, the cathedral dean in the diocese of Linköping Andreas Rhyzelius held a sermon at the royal court in Stockholm. In the audience were members of the royal family, councillors of the realm, representatives of the four estates, as well as many government officials. The sermon focused on the devastating effects of disunity in countries, and on how disunity led to war and destruction. In particular, the sermon identified persons who were supporting war as evil since they were malevolent both in their minds and in their actions, and since they were creating division. Anyone who was supporting war was therefore following the desires of the devil and his ambitions in society. Instead of military conflict, every true Christian believer should seek peace and concord both within societies and between states.[1]

[1] Andreas Rhyzelius's sermon 22 February 1741, Biskop A. O. Rhyzelii predikningar, vol. T211:3, Linköpings stifts- och landsbibliotek, Linköping.

P. Winton (✉)
Department of History, University of Uppsala, Uppsala, Sweden
e-mail: Patrik.Winton@hist.uu.se

J. Félix and A. Dubet (eds.), *The War Within*,
Palgrave Studies in the History of Finance,
https://doi.org/10.1007/978-3-319-98050-8_10

Rhyzelius held his sermon at a time when the relationship between Sweden and Russia was being hotly debated both in the formal halls of power and in Stockholm's informal political arenas such as taverns, gardens and squares. His words therefore became politically explosive (Carlsson 1966; Sennefelt 2008a; Bodensten 2016: 213–242). The main driver behind the rise in opinions for and against war was the government's desire to take advantage of growing opportunities in the European state system following the deaths of Czar Anna in Russia and Emperor Charles VI in Austria. The subsequent wars, commonly known as the Austrian War of Succession and the Anglo-Spanish War, saw hostilities on several fronts and they involved most major European powers. Although Russia was not an active participant in the conflicts, it was important for France to keep Russian forces from intervening on the Austrian side by occupying them elsewhere. The French therefore incited its ally Sweden to initiate a military campaign against Russia. Many in Stockholm hoped that such hostilities, with the financial and political support of France, as well as the backing of the Ottoman Empire, would lead to a successful outcome. By manifesting the realm's military capability against Russia, many also hoped that the government in Versailles would view Sweden as an active and trustworthy ally and that it would reward the Swedish state for its commitment to the French policies at the end of an efficacious campaign (Anderson 1995; Winton 2012a: 49–50).

However, it was not given that the government would receive the necessary political support for the military plans. There were many individuals, like Rhyzelius, who questioned the idea of a military campaign against Russia. Many of these critics held influential positions in the military and in the civil administration, and many were also participating in the meeting of the estates. Since Sweden had a parliamentary political system, which was, dominated by the Diet and its four estates, it was essential that a majority of the estates approved the war plans and supplied the armed forces with the necessary resources before a military campaign could start. No campaign would start if a majority opposed the war. Thus, there was no strong monarch who, like in 1630 before Sweden's entry into the Thirty Years War, could sway the opinion of the estates in one clear direction. Consequently, both sides of the issue mobilised support for their cause by spreading different descriptions of Sweden's position in the European state system. These competing claims constituted a war within where the different actors were not only negotiating the terms of the interactions between Sweden and the major European powers, but also struggling over the relationship between those who were benefiting from war expenditure and an active foreign policy, and those who were advocating less spending on military campaigns. These wars of words also continued after the military campaigns had ended when the government had to deal with the accumulated debts, and the members of estates evaluated the performance of the military and political leaderships, as well as articulated demands for accountability.

In this chapter, the Swedish state's war efforts in 1741–1743 will be compared with Sweden's participation in the anti-Prussian alliance during the Seven Years' War (1757–1762). More specifically, the chapter will analyse the political discussions before the wars were initiated, but also the actions of the procurement commissions which were set up to oversee the mobilisation of resources before and during the wars. Moreover, the chapter will analyse how the members of the Diet assessed the actions of leading officers, as well as the activities of the political leadership and key administrators during and after the military campaigns. How did members of the procurement commissions and the politicians who scrutinised the actions of the military and political leadership handle issues of accountability? By examining these issues we will not only gain a better understanding of how war was financed by a European middle-ranking power, but also how discourses about the relationships between private and public interests affected how resources were mobilised in such a state.

Previous research on Swedish developments in the eighteenth century has primarily focused on the shift from the era of great power ambitions in the seventeenth century to the realities of a middle-ranking power with much more limited foreign policy goals and a stronger concentration on internal economic cultivation during the eighteenth century. The change in 1719 from royal absolutism to parliamentary rule and the subsequent peace with Russia in 1721, when the Swedish Baltic provinces were lost, have been seen as pivotal events which signalled this transformation of political status and state capacity. In other words, scholars have described the eighteenth century as a period of military and political decline, caused by a lack of resources and unwillingness on part of the elite to commit to long drawn out warfare. Scholars have also emphasised that the major powers exploited this weakness. Thus, that states such as France and Russia were able to sway leading Swedish politicians by offering them bribes and by financing their political activities. The French government also used subsidies to influence the direction of Sweden's foreign policy (Melkersson 1997: 48–50; Nordin 2000: 182–184; Glete 2007; Lindström and Norrhem 2013).

Another popular topic of analyses has been the internal political developments during the period of parliamentary rule (1719–1772), especially the rise of organised factions or parties. Historians have seen these attempts at coordinating the mobilisation efforts before and during the meetings of the Diet as crucial for the structure of political life and the conflicts that existed during the period. Thus, almost all actions and utterances have been interpreted as expressions of the political affiliation of a member of the Diet to a specific political group. Furthermore, scholars have viewed the issues of foreign policy as driving the conflicts between the parties, mainly because different foreign powers financed their activities. This means that one group, usually termed the Hats, promoted the interests of France, while the other group, usually termed the Caps, supported the interests of Britain and Russia. In this perspective, the wars that Sweden was involved in during the period was a product of the French party winning influence at the Diet.[2]

A much less studied field has been the issue of how the financing of the wars against Russia and Prussia were organised.[3] Most historians have emphasised that the ruling elite planned the military campaigns very poorly and that the army lacked sufficient means to pursue the ambitious goals that some of the leading politicians in Stockholm had set for the campaigns. Some historians have therefore argued that unrealistic assessments of Sweden's military capacity and of the capabilities of the enemy states drove the wars.[4] Undoubtedly, the unsuccessful outcome of the campaigns have influenced the historians' interpretations. The first led to further loss of territory to Russia, and the second resulted in the preservation of the existing borders.

Instead of focusing on the party affiliations of the elite or the perceptions of the Swedish military capacity, it is necessary to examine what type of resources the state used for warfare, and how the state organised these resources during the military campaigns. Furthermore, we need to

[2] See for example Metcalf (1977); Roberts (1986); Ihalainen (2010). For a critical discussion of this perspective, see Winton (2006); Sennefelt (2010).

[3] The only major study is Åmark (1961), esp. pp. 832–844. See also Winton (2012b).

[4] See, for example, Roberts (1986): 19–24; Sjöström (2008).

examine how these fiscal measures affected domestic politics, and how the political system handled issues of accountability. The analyses will show that the state depended on the cooperation of merchants in order to gain access to the necessary military supplies during the two campaigns. Many questioned the merchants' role and their capacity to promote the common good, but it was only after Sweden's participation in the Seven Years' War that these criticisms led to a renegotiation of the link between the state and the merchants.

The chapter proceeds as follows. First, we will analyse the discussions and organisational efforts during the 1740s, and then we will focus on the 1750s and 1760s and the deliberations about the Swedish participation in the Seven Years' War. The chapter ends with a conclusion where we will compare the two wars and explore the connections between war finance and accountability.

2 The War Against Russia and the Persistence of the State-Merchant Link

The desire of the political elite to avoid the system of royal absolutism that had existed prior to 1719 structured the political system that was in place in 1741. Many leading actors viewed especially the last years of Charles XII's rule as disastrous. The king's stubborn way of leading the country and mobilising resources without regard for estate privileges during the long drawn out Great Northern War were seen as the primary reason behind the precarious situation the realm was in, and it had to be avoided in the future by dramatically reducing the influence of the monarchy. Controlling the sovereign's maneuverability was therefore the main concern in 1719 when the leading civil servants and military officers created the new political system. Consequently, the ruling king, Frederick I from Hesse, had mainly a symbolic role. He could participate in the meetings of the Council of the Realm where he had two votes, but it was impossible for him to pursue a policy that went against the majority of the council. The king appointed the members of the council, which consisted of 16 noblemen, but he had to choose from a list of individuals nominated by the Diet. The councillors also had to give account for their actions when the Diet convened, and the members of the Diet could dismiss councillors deemed to have made mistakes. Thus, instead of being dependent on the support of the king, like in Denmark or France, the councillors needed to seek the backing of the Diet. This in turn meant that it was difficult for the council to pursue policies that went against the wishes of the Diet (Roberts 1986: 1–13; Nordin 2011).

The Diet's four estates met on a regular basis in Stockholm and decided on such matters as foreign policy, taxation, government borrowing, legislation and military affairs. Each estate convened separately and for a decision to take effect three estates had to agree on a motion. The estate of the nobility consisted of representatives from the noble families of the realm who had the right to send representatives to Stockholm. The clerical estate consisted of both non-elected and elected representatives since the country's bishops had guaranteed seats at the Diet, while their peers in the dioceses selected the vicars who came to the capital. The burgher estate comprised elected representatives from the country's towns, and the peasant estate consisted of elected representatives from the rural counties (Roberts 1986: 69–70).

Although many politically active individuals argued that the four estates were equal, hierarchies existed between the estates. The estate of the nobility was the most powerful, while the peasant estate faced the greatest challenges in influencing policy. The Secret Committee, which consisted of 100 members from the nobility, the clergy and the burghers, took many crucial decisions. The peasants did not have the right to send representatives to this committee. Since the committee discussed issues such as foreign policy, the allocation of government resources and the governing of the Bank of Sweden, the peasants had a hard time swaying key resolutions. The informal side of politics, where especially leading noblemen organised open tables for members of the Diet and other visitors to Stockholm, also strengthened these hierarchies. The hosts offered food and drink at these events in order to persuade the visitors to be loyal when key political issues were decided. Leading noblemen could also influence political decisions by distributing patronage, such as positions in the state apparatus, to loyal supporters. By these measures, it was possible for a councillor to strengthen his position in the system, and to circumvent some of the political limits set by the constitution (Sennefelt 2008b; Winton 2010).

In the period after the Great Northern War, Swedish foreign policy focused primarily on maintaining peaceful relations with all powers around the Baltic. This was also in line with developments in the rest of Europe where most powers were reorganising their fiscal affairs after the War of Spanish Succession. When tensions between the major powers again rose in the 1730s, especially France and Russia tried to get Sweden on their side. The Swedish leadership under the auspices of the councillor Arvid Horn tried to take advantage of this interest by negotiating with them without clearly choosing a side. Consequently, Sweden did not join an alliance. Opponents to Arvid Horn in the Council of the Realm and at the Diet argued that it was better and more honorable to commit more clearly to one power, namely France, instead of shamefully and passively trying to adapt to the wishes of several powers. During the meeting of the Diet in 1738/1739, this faction pressured Arvid Horn into resigning from his position and it managed to persuade a majority of the representatives to dismiss five councillors for pursuing a defective foreign policy. Horn's opponents thereby took control of the government, which led to an alliance with France and the payment of French subsidies to the Swedish state. Starting in 1739 the French government transferred around 300,000 silver dalers per year in financial support (Åmark 1961: 162, 835; Roberts 1986: 113–115). The French subsidy payments meant that Sweden became part of the French alliance system, which also included the Republic of Genoa, the Ottoman Empire and Hesse (Dickson 1987: 394).

When the Austrian War of Succession started in 1740, France promised further subsidies if Sweden got more actively involved in the conflict. The government in Versailles was primarily interested in a Swedish military campaign to keep Russian forces occupied in the north. The French framed it as an opportunity for Sweden to retake territory that had been lost at the end of the Great Northern War (Jägerskiöld 1957: 132–143). This is also how the government presented it at the meeting of the Diet in 1740/1741. The supporters of the war—mostly noblemen and burghers—argued that it was necessary to be active militarily in order to promote the country's honor and reliability on the international stage. By taking active steps against the Russian government, Sweden would restore its virtue and its rightful place among the European states while counteracting the malicious plans of Russia. These views, which focused much more on the overarching need for action than the resources available for taking such steps, were articulated in the Secret Committee and other formal political arenas in Stockholm, but they were also presented in several handwritten squibs and pamphlets distributed throughout the capital.[5]

[5] Sekreta utskottets protokoll 1740/41, vol. R2737, 10 and 11 February 1741, Swedish National Archives, Stockholm (SNA); Carlsson (1966: 182–271); Bodensten (2016: 196–205).

The opponents to the war plans viewed the rhetoric about the need for activity as dangerous incitement and as a threat against the existing order. Many opponents, especially among the peasants and the clergy, but also from the nobility, argued that seeking peace and concord both within the realm and in relation to other states was better than mobilising for war. Many opponents also questioned if the available resources were sufficient for carrying out a successful military campaign in Finland. They argued that it was necessary first to make sure that the means were in place before any active steps against Russia could take place. Just like the supporters of war, the opponents mobilised through their actions in the Secret Committee and on other political arenas and by the distribution of handwritten pamphlets.[6]

The supporters of the war plans got the upper hand in the Secret Committee where there was a majority for mobilising the troops. When the authorities arrested the nobleman Gustaf Johan Gyllenstierna outside the lodgings of the Russian envoy in Stockholm Michail Bestucheff, it became more difficult for opponents of the war to act. Many accused Gyllenstierna, who was opposed to the war plans and who functioned as the Secret Committee's secretary, of passing on secret information to the Russian government's representative. A commission was quickly set up to investigate the activities of Gyllenstierna and his allies. This new political situation made it very difficult for anyone to criticise the war since the supporters could easily characterise the opponents' opinions as acts of treason. Consequently, the opposition could not prevent the Diet from sending troops to Finland and later declare war on Russia (Carlsson 1966: 349–351; Ryman 1978: 99).

A procurement commission, which administered the war effort, was set up in March 1741. Its role was to administer the specific resources that the commission received from the Diet and to handle all expenditure relating to the war effort. In other words, the commission was to provide the army and the navy with the necessary supplies and to organize the transportation of these supplies to the army in Finland. It acted independently from the ordinary administrative apparatus such as the Admiralty and the War Collegium. The main reason for this arrangement was a wish to reduce administrative hurdles and to expedite shipments

[6]Sekreta utskottets protokoll 1740/41, vol. R2737, 10 and 11 February 1741, SNA; Carlsson (1966: 193–271); Bodensten (2016: 272–314).

of army units and supplies as quickly as possible.[7] Using commissions as an administrative tool was an established practice in the Swedish realm during the seventeenth century, especially as a way for the central government to investigate irregularities in the local administration and to deal with complaints from local residents about the actions of government officials. By using leading public servants, such as councillors of the realm, as members in the commissions, it was believed that they would be able to override any bureaucratic resistance put up by local officials and to strengthen the legitimacy of the commission's work (Lennersand 1999: 58–75). Additionally, similar commissions had been set up in 1719–1721 and in 1739 to procure resources for the army and navy.[8]

One of the first issues that had to be decided on, after it was agreed that it was necessary to set up a commission, was who should serve on it. Following the established practice, the Diet selected a number of leading civil servants and military officers representing different areas of expertise. The head of the commission was the councillor of the realm Gustaf Fredrik von Rosen, who before he became a councillor in 1739 had been a colonel and general in the army. Another member was the admiral Teodor Ankarcrona, who was head of the navy squadron based in Stockholm. He was also knowledgeable in issues relating to trade since he had been a supercargo in the Dutch East India Company. Other members were Gustaf Palmfelt, who was the head of the Chamber Collegium (*Kammarkollegium*), Peter Drufva, who served in the same collegium as Palmfelt, and Gabriel von Seth who worked in the War Collegium. All of these five men were nobles and were supportive of the war plans, but no one questioned their expertise as administrators. However, several members of the committee challenged another suggestion made by the burgher estate. Many burghers expressed the opinion that it was necessary to include a merchant in the commission because of the commission's many purchases. Such transactions required knowledge about prices and various market conditions, which only active traders could provide. Opponents to this idea stressed that the commission should only include civil servants in order for the commission not to

[7] Sekreta utskottets protokoll 1740/41, vol. R2737, 10 March 1741, SNA. See also Åmark (1961: 164).

[8] Utredningskommissionen 1719, Protokoll 1719, Swedish Military Archives, Stockholm (SMA); Åmark (1961: 832–833).

become a political committee. Although no one stated it explicitly, it is clear that these opponents viewed the noblemen as serving the interest of the state, while the merchants' motives were murkier in character. Despite these reservations from many members of the Secret Committee, a majority decided that the merchant from Stockholm, Thomas Plomgren should be included in the commission.[9]

In the discussions, many emphasised that the procurement commission should arrange contracts with a number of merchants who agreed to provide supplies to the army and navy for a specific pre-determined price per soldier and sailor. However, Thomas Plomgren pointed out that it could be difficult to get merchants interested in such contracts, because many merchants who had agreed to similar arrangements in the past had not received payment on time and had fallen into royal disfavour after providing the requested resources. The commission should therefore stress that the merchants would receive swift payment and that they would obtain a full discharge as soon as they had fulfilled their commitment to the state.[10]

The representatives in the Secret Committee agreed with Plomgren, but when the commission offered a number of leading merchants to sign contracts with the state, the merchants hesitated. For example, the merchant Johan Clason argued that he had had trouble during the last war and that he had lost money from the arrangements. However, if he received information about the requested quantities he was willing to provide resources to the army and navy. The other merchants also gave similar answers. Although the members of the commission tried to persuade the merchants that the current political system was more trustworthy than the previous one and that they would receive payment on time, they did not manage to sign any broad long-term contracts with a few key merchants.[11] Instead, the commission had to rely on purchasing the necessary resources from a wider array of suppliers than originally planned. Such arrangements reduced the risk for the individual merchant since he or she only had to commit to one transaction with the Crown at

[9] Sekreta utskottets protokoll 1740/41, vol. R2737, 10 March 1741, SNA; Utredningskommissionen 1741, Protokoll 1741, 19 March, SMA. On the members of the commission and their political affiliations, see Carlsson (1981: 187, 196, 219, 247–248, 277).

[10] Sekreta utskottets protokoll 1740/41, vol. R2737, 10 March 1741, SNA.

[11] Utredningskommissionen 1741, Protokoll 1741, 19 and 21 March, SMA.

a time, but it made the commission's work more complex, both in terms of accounting and in relation to the number of negotiations it had to conduct.[12] Compared with Spain for example, where the Crown mostly negotiated with a single agent, the Swedish system opened up for competition between different suppliers (Torres Sánchez 2014: 281–283, 2016: 97–112).

After the failure of the commission to sign more long-term contracts, the negotiations to purchase foodstuffs and transport capacity from various merchants and other suppliers started and resulted in the signing of several contracts. For example, the merchant Christian Hebbe agreed to 18 contracts in 1741 valued at 236,000 silver dalers, while the merchant Jean Lefebvre signed four contracts valued at 8000 silver dalers. In total around 3.3 million silver dalers were used in 1741 to procure supplies and transport capacity.[13]

One big challenge for the commission as well as the military campaign as a whole was the problem of getting the necessary supplies to the army in Finland. Normally, an army used local resources during the early modern period because of the difficulties in transporting large quantities of food over long distances. This meant that most military campaigns were located in agriculturally rich regions, such as Flanders or Saxony (Parker 1975: 118–156). Finland on the other hand was a relatively poor region with limited grain production and with greater focus on animal husbandry. Consequently, grain had to be imported to cover the demand of the population. It was therefore impossible for the army to depend on local resources (Morell 2013: 71). Instead, it became necessary to ship supplies from Stockholm and other parts of the Baltic region to Finland. Thus, the commission purchased dried peas from Swedish Pomerania, salted beef and pork from Courland and rye from Riga and Wismar.[14]

Although goods did arrive in Finland, it was a challenge to get the supplies to the army, which was inland. The difficult supply lines contributed greatly to the quite passive behaviour of the army, and the army's retreat to Helsinki, where it subsequently surrendered to the Russians, was in large part driven by the need to move where food was available.[15]

[12] Utredningskommissionen 1741, Protokoll 1741, 21 March; Huvudbok 1741, SMA.

[13] Utredningskommissionen 1741, Protokoll 1741, 19 March and 21 March; Huvudbok 1741, SMA.

[14] Utredningskommissionen 1741, Huvudbok 1741, SMA.

[15] On the performance of the army, see Jägerskiöld (1957: 152).

Table 1 Sources of revenue for the procurement commission, 1741–1748

Source	*Sums in silver dalers*	*Percentage*
Loans and gifts from the Bank of Sweden	5,512,000	35.7
French subsidies	3,238,545	21.0
Advances from the government	2,499,792	16.2
Indirect taxes	2,469,912	16.0
Various other sources of revenue	1,731,216	11.1
Total	15,451,465	100.0

Source Karl Åmark, *Sveriges statsfinanser 1719–1809* (Stockholm 1961), p. 838

The resources that the commission utilised to purchase supplies originated from inside and outside the country. As can be seen in Table 1, the largest share of revenue came from loans from the Bank of Sweden. The bank, which had started its operations in 1668, was under the control of the Diet. The nobility, the clergy and the burghers elected the bank's directors, and the directors received instructions from the Secret Committee. The directors were also accountable to the Diet for their actions and the Diet could dismiss directors if they had oversighted their responsibilities. Although the bank's finances were not part of the state's coffers, it was difficult for the bank's directors to decline requests for loans from the state. Thus, in 1741, the bank had agreed to provide credit, and in 1742, when the procurement commission needed more resources, the directors agreed to further loans. The fact that Thomas Plomgren was both a director and a member of the commission simplified these negotiations (Hallendorff 1919: 6–86, 156–164).

The bank's finances were structured around deposits and lending to individuals and institutions. The recipients of loans received notes, which were negotiable and became accepted as equivalent to coin. The bank's metal reserves backed up the notes, but this relationship between notes in circulation and reserves became under pressure due to the war and the bank's involvement in the financing of it. In 1740, the total number of notes in circulation amounted to around 5.5 million silver dalers, while at the end of 1743 the volume had increased by 80% to around 9.9 million. This expansion of liquidity had a negative effect on the exchange rate, since the cost of 100 marks Hamburg banco went up from 103 silver dalers on average in 1740 to 121.78 silver dalers on average in 1744. Because of these pressures, the bank abandoned the convertibility of its notes and introduced a paper money system in 1745 (Hallendorff 1919: 95–219, 386; Denzel 2010: 344).

Another important source of revenue was subsidies from the French government. The French sent the payments as bills of exchange, and two merchants, Gustaf Kierman and Thomas Plomgren, exchanged them into Swedish currency. This inflow of capital helped to offset some of the negative effects of the expansion of liquidity by the issuing of bank notes. Many argued that the transactions had to be secret and the merchants, who were members of the Secret Committee, were well suited because of their patriotic zeal and their ability to keep secrets. However, it was controversial that Kierman and Plomgren should handle the transactions. According to one critic, the noble officer Lars Åkerhielm, it was difficult to understand why it was important to keep the transactions under wraps because in his mind it was necessary to interact with other actors on the open market in order to get the best exchange rates. Thus, secrecy threatened to make the transactions more complicated and costly.[16]

Two other sources of revenue for the commission were advances from the government (future revenue paid in advance) and a number of extraordinary taxes that the Diet decided on during the meeting in 1741. The peasants were part of the negotiations about these taxes, but the fact that only around 30% of the revenue came from taxes meant that the peasants, who contributed most to this revenue, had a limited influence on the war plans. In other words the loans and the subsidies, which were largely outside the control of the peasants since the Secret Committee and the procurement commission handled them, meant that the elite could command the fiscal process in a more autonomous way.

However, the poor performance of the army in Finland created a new political situation in which critics of the war could voice their disapproval of the handling of the war. It also made it difficult for the elite to keep vital information and key decisions within a limited group of decision-makers. The military situation, as well as the death of the Queen Ulrica Eleonora, meant that the Diet had to convene. In the local elections, it was clear that many peasants were very angry about the war and the elected representatives received clear instructions to promote the peasants' views in Stockholm. The peasants demanded peace and that the generals who had been in command should be held responsible

[16] Sekreta utskottets protokoll 1740/41, vol. R2738, 4 August 1741, SNA.

for the outcome of the war and brought to trial. They were also angry with the division of the costs of recruiting and equipping soldiers. They questioned why the peasants should bear a large share of this burden, while the nobility and the clergy paid very little. In order to appease the peasants, the other estates agreed to let the peasants into the Secret Committee when the Diet convened in 1742 (Sennefelt 2004: 189).

Although the military situation was in focus, the procurement commission's activities also attracted some attention. One of the opponents to the war, the vicar Jacob Serenius, argued in the Secret Committee that the commission had too many members and that their remuneration constituted a waste of resources. This thinly vailed critique of the commission's efficiency led to a response from one of its members, the admiral Teodor Ankarcrona. He pointed out that he had not sought the position in the commission and that he was willing to step down. In other words, he stressed that he was not sitting on the commission for personal gain. He then continued by praising the diligence of the members and the troublesome efforts they had made to amass 296 ships and numerous supplies in only 9 weeks' time. He wished that all administrative measures could be so quick and efficient and said that no one could have done a better job.[17]

The issue of the merchants' role in the commission also resurfaced in the discussions. According to the merchant Gustaf Kierman, it was good to include traders in the commission because they had detailed knowledge about prices and market conditions. They could also more easily ensure that the Crown did not receive any poor goods. He also pointed out that the participation of Plomgren in the commission had made it possible to purchase grain at a discount. At the same time it was important for Kierman, just as it had been for Ankarcrona, to stress that he did not wish to become a member of the commission, or that he had profited from selling goods to the commission. A peasant from the county of Östergötland disputed Kierman's claims. The anonymous peasant said that he had been in Stockholm when the supplies were loaded on to the ships and he asserted that they had had such a bad smell, that despite his ability as a peasant to withstand such scents, he had to walk another way.[18]

[17] Sekreta utskottets protokoll 1742/43, vol. R2810, 18 November 1742, SNA.

[18] Sekreta utskottets protokoll 1742/43, vol. R2811, 20 April 1743, SNA.

All of the claims and counterclaims manifest that many members of the Diet disputed the commission's role in the war effort, and that it was important for the commission's members and their allies to defend their record and their ability to seek the common good. Concurrently, a parliamentary committee consisting of many critics of the war, such as the noblemen Carl Fredrik Piper and Jonas Wulfwenstierna, and the vicar Jacob Serenius, was set up to audit the activities of the commission.[19] They focused on how the commission had utilised the allocated resources and if they could account for all the spending rather than investigating the contracts between the merchants and the state. Thus, they did not look into the prices the commission had paid, or if merchants had misused their market position to the detriment of the state. One reason for the limited audit was the fact that the commission's accountant had not been able to finish the account books due to other more pressing matters. It was therefore difficult for the members of the parliamentary committee to provide the Diet with a complete report on the commission's activities. Consequently, the audit did not lead to anything substantial, which irritated Serenius in particular.[20] Instead it was decided that a new commission should be formed consisting of only noble civil servants who would administer the available resources and who would eventually wind down the operations of the commission. The members of the Diet also decided that the regular auditors within the civil administration would go through the commission's account books when they were completed.[21] These moves clearly depoliticised the issue and amounted to a return to the administrative system that had existed prior to 1741.

Instead of targeting the commission, the Diet blamed the generals Henrik Magnus von Buddenbrock and Charles Emile Lewenhaupt, who had been in command of the army. The authorities arrested

[19]Sekreta utskottets protokoll 1742/43, vol. R2810, 14 December 1742, SNA. On the political activities of Piper, Serenius and Wulfwenstierna, see Carlsson (1981: 278, 287, 292–293).

[20]Sekreta utskottets handlingar 1742/43, vol. R2815, Memorial no. 115; Sekreta utskottets protokoll 1742/43, vol. R2810, 18 February 1743; vol. R2811, 10 September 1743, SNA.

[21]Sekreta utskottets handlingar 1742/43, vol. R2815, Memorial no. 115; Sekreta utskottets protokoll 1742/43, vol. R2811, 20 April, 10 September 1743, SNA. See also Åmark (1961: 833).

and later executed the generals for the retreat of the army and subsequent surrender to the Russians. A march of thousands of peasants to Stockholm in 1743 partly influenced this decision. The protesting peasants, who wanted to put pressure on the Diet, demanded peace and that the commanding generals should be held responsible for their actions, but also that the monarchy should be strengthened by the election of a Danish prince as Crown Prince. However, the Diet and the Council of the Realm could not accept an alternative authority in the streets of the capital, so army units met the protestors with military force. Later, the authorities executed six of the peasants' leaders. Around the same time, the government signed a peace treaty with Russia, which resulted in a loss of Finnish territory to the Russian Empire. The Russians also influenced the selection of the new Crown Prince: the Diet picked an obscure German prince named Adolphus Frederick following Russian pressure. The Russians saw this selection as a way to maintain the *status quo* in Sweden (Roberts 1986: 37–38; Sennefelt 2004: 202–203).

The meetings of the Diet in 1740–1741 and 1742–1743 showed the divisions within the political elite concerning the timing and the necessity of mobilising the troops in Finland, and the handling of the poor performance of the army. Raised questions of accountability, especially for merchants taking part in the resource mobilisation process, made it necessary for the merchants to defend their morality and ability to look beyond their own self-interest. However, there was no serious questioning of the war's finances or administration, and there were no interest on the part of disgruntled members of the elite to join forces with the protesting peasants. Instead, the elite defended their joint interests, and the army put down the protests with military means and the state kept its fiscal system intact. Subsequently, the French government soon paid more subsidies to the Swedish state, and the Bank of Sweden continued to expand credit after the war.

3 The Seven Years' War and the Restructuring of the State-Merchant Link

The next war started in 1757 when Austria and France demanded that Sweden took military action against Prussia following Prussia's aggression against Saxony in 1756. Again, France promised to pay large subsidies if Sweden shipped troops to Swedish Pomerania and initiated military operations (Szabo 2008: 36–51). The Council of the Realm decided to agree to the proposals without summoning the Diet since the councillors argued that it was not a formal declaration of war. Instead, it was just a question of fulfilling terms set in the peace of Westphalia 1648, which Sweden had committed to guarantee. According to the constitution, the king and the council could negotiate treaties and fulfil previous treaty conventions, but committing a large troop contingent without first getting the approval from the Diet risked creating discussions about the council's willingness to follow the Diet's instructions. Part of the reason why the council chose to disregard the political risks was the belief that it would be a swift campaign since Prussia was facing a formidable coalition. Thus, a protracted domestic political process could mean that Sweden missed the opportunity to gain a reward at a future peace conference. The councillors thought that Sweden could regain control of what had been lost to Prussia in the peace of 1720, but also that Sweden could receive a colony in the Caribbean. The councillors especially mentioned the island of Tobago as a potential prize. However, there was no unanimity among the councillors. They did agree that the army should be prepared for war and that troops should be sent to Swedish Pomerania, but there were disagreements about the size of the troop contingent, when the troops should be sent, what they should do once they arrived, and how big the subsidy payments should be. The arguments bore many similarities with the ones expressed in 1741: the advocates for action stressed that committing troops was necessary to protect the country's status as a reliable and reputable power in Europe, while the sceptics pointed out practical issues that had not been resolved, such as the availability of resources and the unclear war aims (Trulsson 1947: 202–212; 242–249; Winton 2012b: 12–15).

The final vote in the council was held on 8 June 1757 and on 28 June, the council decided to set up a procurement commission to organise the transport of 13,000 infantrymen and 4000 cavalrymen to Swedish Pomerania and their subsequent support in the province. Just as had been the case in 1741, the main argument for setting up the commission was the need to reduce administrative hurdles and to expedite shipments of army units and supplies as quickly as possible. The commission consisted of eight men: two councillors of the realm, four top-ranking civil servants, one general and one merchant. One of the councillors, Gustaf Fredrik von Rosen, had been a prominent member of the commission in 1741, which meant that he was well acquainted with the tasks ahead. Other members, such as the general Lars Åkerhielm and the merchant

Gustaf Kierman, had also been active participants in the political discussions during the 1740s. They therefore knew the different aspects of the commission's work. The fact that Kierman was also one of the directors of the Bank of Sweden facilitated contacts between the commission and the bank. Additionally, he was a member of the Exchange Office, which consisted of leading merchants who were purchasing Swedish bills of exchange on the international capital markets at pre-determined exchange rates in order to stabilize the Swedish currency. Since the merchants utilised the incoming French subsidies for the bill operations, Kierman could provide detailed information about the workings of the foreign exchange markets. The other members of the procurement commission, such as the noblemen Carl Ridderstolpe and Johan von Wallwik, were all knowledgeable about the finances of the state and the workings of the state's bureaucracy.[22]

In many ways, the practice of the new commission followed the same patterns established by the previous procurement commission. Thus, instead of negotiating broad long-term contracts with a few merchants, the commission relied on many traders to provide the necessary supplies. Some merchants provided large quantities of foodstuffs, while others delivered amounts that were more limited. Johan Albert Kantzou, for instance, sold victuals to the army for a total sum of almost 1.8 million silver dalers, and Isaac Clason and Hans Wittfoth, sold supplies for over 700,000 silver dalers. Concurrently, the wine merchant Johan Georg Yhlén sold wine for only 4900 silver dalers. Likewise, the procurement commission purchased transport capacity from many sea captains and merchants. For example, the skipper Johan Liedbeck provided services for 1500 silver dalers, while the merchants Isaac Clason and Christian Hebbe sold cargo capacity for around 160,000 silver dalers.[23]

From a victualling perspective, Western Pomerania was a better arena for military campaigns than Finland. Grain and peas for example were available locally, and the commission could easily purchase further supplies on other markets in northern Germany, which reduced the need to transport foodstuffs long distances. However, Prussian army units located their winter quarters in Swedish Pomerania in 1757–1758 and 1758–1759 following the Swedish army's retreat to the town of

[22] Utredningskommissionen 1757, Protokoll 1757, 1 July, SMA. On the activities of Kierman and the Exchange Office, see (Müller 2002).

[23] Utredningskommissionen 1757, Huvudbok 1757–1764, SMA.

Table 2 Sources of revenue for the procurement commission, 1757–1764

Source	*Sums in silver dalers*	*Percentage*
Loans from the Bank of Sweden	24,280,834	44.1
French subsidies	11,186,215	20.3
Royal lottery	5,833,333	10.6
Domestic loans	4,290,319	7.8
Loans from the Debt Office	3,050,000	5.5
Loans and fees from the new East India Company	3,000,000	5.5
External loans	2,403,381	4.4
Various other incomes	991,623	1.8
Total	55,035,705	100.0

Source Swedish Military Archives, Stockholm, Utredningskommissionen 1757, Huvudbok 1757–1764

Stralsund and the Rügen peninsula. This situation made it more difficult for the procurement commission to provide the army with mostly local resources. Instead, it had to transport food and other supplies largely from Sweden, which was more costly. Costs also increased when the army spent so much of its time in Swedish Pomerania rather than on enemy territory.[24]

The revenue that the commission had at its disposal was similar to the revenue in the 1740s. Thus, as can be seen in Table 2, a large share of the resources came from loans provided by the Bank of Sweden. Just as in the 1741–1743 campaign, the loans, in the form of bank notes, increased the number of notes in circulation from 13.8 million silver dalers in 1755 to 44 million in 1763. Such increases in volume resulted in price surges on many goods, and in a deterioration of the value of the Swedish currency on international capital markets. The cost of purchasing 100 marks Hamburg banco increased from around 107 silver dalers on average in 1755 to around 235 silver dalers on average in 1762. The Exchange Office, which was supposed to offset such price movements, could not cope with the severe market conditions and the Diet therefore disbanded it in 1761 (Denzel 2010: 344; Winton 2012: 23). Another source of revenue for the commission was the payment of subsidies from the French government, which constituted around 20% of the revenue or around the same percentage as during the 1741–1743 campaign. A new form of revenue was the introduction of a royal lottery. This scheme,

[24] Utredningskommissionen 1757, Huvudbok 1757–1764, SMA; Winton (2012: 18–19).

which entailed the issuing of over 150,000 lottery tickets, was a reply to the problem of not having access to any extraordinary taxes. Since the Diet did not meet, it was not possible for the King or the council index Council of the Realm to issue new taxes. Instead, the procurement commission had to rely mainly on subsidies, loans from the Bank of Sweden and the royal lottery.

When the Diet convened in 1760, it was clear that the military situation in Western Pomerania and the economic and political effects of the military campaign were at the forefront of the discussions. Many members from all estates were critical of the council's decision to join the anti-Prussian alliance. One of the most vocal critics was the noble colonel Carl Fredrik Pechlin, who had served in Pomerania but who had come home to attend the meeting of the Diet. According to him, the councillors had committed a criminal act when they decided to participate in the war without summoning the Diet first. Many argued that all wars, no matter the circumstances, were adventurous and impossible to predict in advance. When the army and navy were engaged in military activities, the estates should therefore always meet. Many also pointed to the fact that the council, through its decision, had increased the government's debt without consulting the Diet.[25] Thus, the critics focused their criticism on the actions of the councillors rather than the commanding generals or the members of the procurement commission who had implemented the council's decisions.

The councillors had supporters who stressed that the limits of the council's maneuverability in relation to foreign powers were unclear in the constitution and that the councillors had good intentions to promote the realm's honour and improvement. In other words, the councillors had only sought the country's best interest and they had not had any intent to redefine or alter the constitution. The Diet should therefore not punish them. Despite these objections, a majority of members decided to dismiss two councillors from their position because of their active promotion of the war.[26]

[25] Mindre sekreta deputationens protokoll 1760/62, vol. R3169, 30 and 31 January 1761; Sekreta utskottets protokoll 1760/62, vol. R3143, 4 and 5 February 1761, SNA.

[26] Mindre sekreta deputationens protokoll 1760/62, vol. R3169, 30 and 31 January 1761; Sekreta utskottets protokoll 1760/62, vol. R3143, 4 and 5 February 1761, SNA.

At the same time as the Diet discussed the responsibility for the war, the members of the Diet also concentrated on providing more resources to the army in Pomerania, and on different solutions to the problems of inflation and a falling exchange rate. Not only the members of the elite, but also many ordinary citizens, debated the fiscal and monetary issues. A growth of printed newspapers and pamphlets, in which many authors commented on the economic situation, fuelled this surge in political interest. In the discussions, many observers expressed the opinion that the ruling oligarchy and its practices were corrupt (Winton 2012: 27–28). Although no one explicitly criticised the procurement commission and its activities, many questioned the role of the merchants in the resource mobilisation process. Thus, many actors challenged the merchants' capacity to serve the common good in a way that the noble civil servants in the commission did not face. Many commentators also argued that it was necessary to reduce liquidity by curtailing the number of loans issued by the Bank of Sweden. Instead of relying on loans from the bank, there was an attempt to increase domestic bond sales, and to start borrowing on international capital markets. The Diet also decided to increase extraordinary taxation in order to address the deficits created by the war (Winton 2015: 61–68).

The vocal criticism of the leading merchants and their close ties with the state continued after the war against Prussia had ended and after the meeting of the Diet had concluded in 1762. Undoubtedly, the continuation of the economic problems and the subsequent rise of public discussions in printed newspapers and pamphlets about how to interpret the situation and what measures the government should implement to address the economic woes drove the criticism. Especially the author Anders Nordencrantz's pamphlets, in which he questioned the motives and morality of the leading merchants, influenced opinions not just in Stockholm but also all over the realm. Nordencrantz targeted in particular the merchants in charge of the Exchange Office, whom he claimed only served their own interest to the determinant of the state (Nordencrantz 1761a, b). Other authors, such as the chaplain Anders Chydenius from the province of Ostrobothnia, continued on the same theme when he stressed that the realm's powerlessness was caused by wealth being accumulated in the hands of a few. In order to address these problems it was necessary to promote the involvement of everyone in the cultivation of the realm, to remove special economic privileges that protected powerful interest groups, and to increase transparency in political life (Chydenius 1765a, b).

The negative views on the role of merchants also spread among burghers, especially those who lived in smaller towns and who did not belong to the patrician elite in Stockholm and Gothenburg. These lower ranking burghers demanded an end to the privileged position of the leading merchants and the promotion of more equal economic opportunities for all towns and burghers (Brolin 1953: 403–408). Consequently, there were very few, even among the burgher estate, who tried to defend the role of the leading traders in society. This lack of support became clear during the meeting of the Diet in 1765, when political actors from all estates accused the members of the former Exchange Office of embezzlement of state funds. Subsequently, the Secret Committee summoned the merchants Johan Abraham Grill, Gustaf Kierman, Johan Henrik Lefebvre and Herman Petersen to answer questions about their transactions with the state and with the Bank of Sweden. Many members of the committee were not satisfied with the merchants' replies and demanded that the authorities kept especially Kierman and Lefebure under surveillance and that the Diet should oversee their business activities. The purpose of this was, according to the lieutenant colonel Fredrik Gyllensvaan, to protect the interests of the population against those that had caused a bread shortage among the realm's inhabitants.[27]

Although a large majority of the members of the Secret Committee defined the merchants as immoral and unable to seek the common good, two noblemen and a bishop tried to protect them. According to these actors, the merchants had legally received the resources, and the government had approved the transactions. Moreover, it equaled tyranny to arrest the merchants before the authorities had properly investigated the issues and the accused had an opportunity to reply to the allegations. Thus, it was wrong to define the merchants as criminals before a court had declared them guilty.[28]

The attempts to protect Kierman and Lefebvre were futile since most members of the Diet saw them as culpable villains who should pay large

[27] Sekreta utskottets protokoll 1765/66, vol. R3272, 20 March and 21 March 1765, SNA.

[28] Sekreta utskottets protokoll 1765/66, vol. R3272, 21 March 1765, SNA.

financial reparations to the state for their involvement in the Exchange Office. The Diet also imprisoned Gustaf Kierman at the fortress Marstrand where he died less than a year later. This fall from grace was remarkable for a man who had been active in politics since the 1730s and who had served as the speaker of the burgher estate during the meeting of the Diet in 1760/1762 (Müller 2002: 144). The actions were clearly a sign that the close relationship between a number of leading merchants and the state had ended. The Diet also took several steps to remove the secrecy that had surrounded many of the transactions between the state and the merchants when the estates implemented a Freedom of the Press Act in 1766. The act abolished pre-publication control of secular publications, as well as introduced the principle of open access to government documents. The change in legislation led to a dramatic increase in publications, which discussed previously secret arrangements, such as foreign policy considerations, subsidy payments and key fiscal decisions (Skuncke 2011; Nordin 2012: 111–117; Bodensten 2018).

All of these efforts manifest that many members of the political elite as well as many commoners questioned the fiscal system, which had relied on a system of loans from the Bank of Sweden and French subsidies, and the arrangement of power, which had included close cooperation between leading merchants and the state apparatus. Although the war ended without any territorial changes and a majority of the members of the Diet removed several of the responsible councillors from office, it became difficult for the ruling elite to return to the economic and political situation prior to 1757. The fiscal and monetary challenges persisted for several years, which in turn spurred demands from groups outside the elite for greater transparency and influence over government decisions. The war had therefore created a momentum for political change, a momentum that was far greater than in 1743 when the elite joined together to defend the existing system against the peasants' charges. In the 1760s, the number of dissatisfied were greater and their social background was more heterogeneous, which made it more difficult for the elite to re-establish its authority. In other words, the answer to military defeat and economic problems evolved from the 1740s, when the answer was to bring in virtuous nobles who could control the vice of merchants, to the 1760s when the response was the monitoring of government officials through the introduction of transparency.

4 Conclusion

The issue of accountability became a key object of political deliberations after the poor performances of the Swedish army against Russia and Prussia. The men in charge had to give account to the Diet and the Diet assigned blame for the perceived failures. In the 1740s, the commanding generals had to take responsibility for the retreat and surrender of the army, while in the 1760s two of the councillors of the realm had to leave in order to appease the critics. Concurrently, the system of mobilising resources was scrutinised, and it was especially the crucial role of the leading merchants that was tested by members of the Diet by calling into question the merchants' patriotism and ability to set aside their self-interest. In their defence, the merchants argued that they could provide detailed market knowledge, which made the procurement process more efficient and cost-effective. They also argued that they did their best despite facing difficult circumstances.

The structure of the resources the procurement commissions utilised and the subsequent close links between the merchant elite in Stockholm and state institutions contributed to the suspicions that other members of the elite, as well as non-elite groups expressed. The large dependence on French subsidies, which was secret information, and the loans from the Bank of Sweden, which a narrow group of people handled, meant that many, who were not members of the elite, could accuse this small circle of men involved in these transactions of serving only a narrow self-interest rather than the common good. For distrustful members of the Diet, having noble civil servants involved in the transactions was one way to reduce threats of moral hazard. Another strategy, which became crucial in the 1760s, was to increase transparency in the state's financial dealings and to broaden the base of creditors. Thus, the financial challenges during the 1760s led to a restructuring of the fiscal system and to a renegotiation of the relationship between the state and the leading merchants in a way that had not been the case in the 1740s. Unlike the 1740s, when it was mostly the peasants who expressed discontent while the elite closed ranks and defended the political system and the existing fiscal arrangements from rupture, the 1760s saw greater dissatisfaction among broader groups in society and an escalation of tensions between the estates.

Although the role of merchants in the financing of the state became a hot political topic in the 1760s, the Swedish state's reliance on the contacts and the resources of traders to organise warfare followed a general European pattern in the eighteenth century. As Aaron Graham has argued, entrepreneurial networks were able to "tap additional resources", which the state was unable to mobilise (Graham 2014: 108. Torres Sánchez 2014: 281–283). The strength of such networks also continued to be apparent in Sweden after the fall of parliamentary rule in 1772. When the absolute king Gustavus III organised a war against Russia in 1788–1790, he utilised a procurement commission, like the previous regime, to handle purchases of supplies to the army and the navy. In order for the commission to succeed with their task, its members had to seek the support of merchants. The war was unpopular among many members of the elite, who viewed the conflict as a sign of unrestrained royal power (Åmark 1961: 844–852; Mattsson 2010: 178–223). Thus, the demand for military resources required the Swedish Crown as well as other European states to reproduce the ties with the merchants even when it threatened to draw criticism and to escalate the war within.

References

Archives

Linköpings stifts- och landsbibliotek, Linköping.
Swedish Military Archives, Stockholm (SMA).
Swedish National Archives, Stockholm (SNA).

Bibliography

Åmark, K. 1961. *Sveriges statsfinanser 1719–1809*. Stockholm: Norstedt.

Anderson, M.S. 1995. *The War of the Austrian Succession 1740–1748*. London: Longman.

Bodensten, E. 2016. *Politikens drivfjäder. Frihetstidens partiberättelser och den moralpolitiska logiken*. Lund: Studia Historica Lundensia.

Bodensten, E. 2018. Political Knowledge in Public Circulation: The Case of Subsidies in Eighteenth-Century Sweden. In *Circulation of Knowledge: Explorations in the History of Knowledge*, ed. J. Östling, E. Sandmo, D.Larsson Heidenblad, A. Nilsson Hammar, and K. Nordberg, 82–104. Lund: Nordic Academic Press.

Brolin, P.-E. 1953. *Hattar och mössor i borgarståndet 1760–1766*. Uppsala: Lundequistska bokhandeln.

Carlsson, I. 1966. *Olof Dalin och den politiska propagandan inför "illa ofreden" Sagan Om Hästen och Wär-Wisa i samtidspolitisk belysning*. Lund: CWK Gleerup.

Carlsson, I. 1981. *Parti–partiväsen–partipolitiker 1731–43. Kring uppkomsten av våra första politiska partier*. Stockholm: Acta Universitatis Stockholmiensis.

Chydenius, A. 1765a. *Källan til rikets wan-magt*. Stockholm: Lars Salvius.

Chydenius, A. 1765b. *Den nationnale winsten, wördsamast öfwerlemnad til Riksens höglofliga ständer, af en deras ledamot*. Stockholm: Lars Salvius.

Denzel, M.A. 2010. *Handbook of World Exchange Rates, 1590–1914*. Farnham: Ashgate.

Dickson, P.G.M. 1987. *Finance and Government Under Maria Theresia 1740–1780*, vol. II. Oxford: Clarendon.

Fynn-Paul, J. (ed.). 2014. *War, Entrepreneurs, and the State in Europe and the Mediterranean, 1300–1800*. Leiden: Brill.

Glete, J. 2007. The Swedish Fiscal-Military State in Transition and Decline, 1650–1815. In *War, State and Development. Fiscal-Military States in the Eighteenth Century*, ed. R. Torres Sánchez, 87–108. Pamplona: Eunsa.

Graham, A. 2014. Public Service and Private Profit: British Fiscal-Military Entrepreneurship Overseas, 1707–1712. In *War, Entrepreneurs and the State in Europe and the Mediterranean, 1300–1800*, ed. J. Fynn-Paul, 87–110. Leiden: Brill.

Hallendorff, C. 1919. Riksens ständers bank 1719–1766, vol. II, *Sveriges Riksbank 1668–1918*. Stockholm: Norstedt.

Ihalainen, P. 2010. *Agents of the People. Democracy and Popular Sovereignty in British and Swedish Parliamentary and Public Debates, 1734–1800*. Leiden: Brill.

Ihalainen, P., M. Bregnsbo, K. Sennefelt, and P. Winton. 2010. *Scandinavia in the Age of Revolution: Nordic Political Cultures, 1740–1820*. Farnham: Ashgate.

Jägerskiöld, O. 1957. *Den svenska utrikespolitikens historia, II:2, 1721–1792*. Stockholm: Norstedt.

Lennersand, M. 1999. *Rättvisans och allmogens beskyddare. Den absoluta staten, kommissionerna och tjänstemännen, ca 1680–1730*. Uppsala: Acta Universitatis Upsaliensis.

Lindström, P., and S. Norrhem. 2013. *Flattering Alliances: Scandinavia, Diplomacy, and the Austrian-French Balance of Power, 1648–1740*. Lund: Nordic Academic Press.

Mattsson, A. 2010. *Komediant och riksförrädare. Handskriftscirkulerade smädeskrifter mot Gustaf III*. Uppsala: Acta Universitatis Upsaliensia.

Melkersson, M. 1997. *Staten, ordningen och friheten. En studie av den styrande elitens syn på statens roll mellan stormaktstiden och 1800-talet*. Uppsala: Acta Universitatis Upsaliensis.

Metcalf, M. 1977. *Russia, England and Swedish Party Politics 1762–1766. The Interplay Between Great Power Diplomacy and Domestic Politics During Sweden's Age of Liberty*. Stockholm: Almqvist & Wiksell International.

Morell, M. 2013. Swedish Agriculture in the Cosmopolitan Eighteenth Century. In *Sweden in the Eighteenth-Century World: Provincial Cosmopolitans*, ed. G. Rydén, 69–92. Farnham: Ashgate.

Müller, L. 2002. Economic Policy in Eighteenth-Century Sweden and Early Modern Entrepreneurial Behaviour: A Case of the Exchange Office. In *Entrepreneurs and Institutions in Europe and Asia, 1500–2000, 127–147*, ed. F. De Goey and J.W. Veluwenkamp. Amsterdam: Aksant.

Nordencrantz, A. 1761a. *Tankar om den höga wexel-coursen och dyrheten i Swerige*. Stockholm: Nyström & Stolpe.

Nordencrantz, A. 1761b. *Owälduga tankar om Sweriges närwarande tilstånd i anseende til wälmågsa och rikedom*. Stockholm: Nyström & Stolpe.

Nordin, J. 2000. *Ett fattigt men fritt folk. Nationell och politisk självbild i Sverige från sen stormaktstid till slutet av frihetstiden*. Eslöv: Symposion.

Nordin, J. 2011. The Monarchy in the Swedish Age of Liberty (1719–1772). In *Scandinavia in the Age of Revolution: Nordic Political Cultutres, 1740–1820*, ed. P. Ihalainen, M. Brengsbo, K. Sennefelt and P. Winton, 29–40. Farnham: Ashgate.

Nordin, J. 2012. L'esprit de paix ou la naissance d'une opposition contre la guerre en Suède au XVIIIe siècle. *Revue d'Histoire Nordique* 14: 97–130.

Parker, G. 1975. *The Army of Flanders and the Spanish Road, 1567–1659: The Logistics of Spanish Victory and Defeat in the Low Countries' Wars*. Cambridge: Cambridge University Press.

Roberts, M. 1986. *The Age of Liberty: Sweden 1719–1772*. Cambridge: Cambridge University Press.

Ryman, B. 1978. *Eric Benzelius d.y. En frihetstida politiker*. Stockholm: Verbum.

Sennefelt, K. 2004. Marching to Stockholm: Repertoires of Peasant Protest in Eighteenth-Century Sweden. In *Northern Revolts. Medieval and Early Modern Peasant Unrest in the Nordic Countries*, ed. K. Katajala, 188–205. Helsinki: Finnish Literature Society.

Sennefelt, K. 2008a. Citizenship and the political landscape of libeling in eighteenth-century Stockholm. *Social History* 33: 145–163.

Sennefelt, K. 2008b. Social and Political Thresholds in Eighteenth-Century Stockholm. *Urban History* 35: 185–201.

Sennefelt, K. 2010. *Politikens hjärta. Medborgarskap, manlighet och plats i frihetstidens Stockholm*. Stockholm: Stockholmia.

Sjöström, O. 2008. Sekreta bihangen 1741 och deras idépolitiska bakgrund. *Sjuttonhundratal*, 5–24.

Skuncke, M.-C. 2011. Freedom of the Press and Social Equality in Sweden, 1766–1772. In *Scandinavia in the Age of Revolution: Nordic Political Cultures 1740–1820*, ed. Ihalainen et al., 133–144. Farnham: Ashgate.

Szabo, F.A.J. 2008. *The Seven Years War in Europe, 1756–1763*. Harlow: Pearson.

Torres Sánchez, R. 2014. In the Shadow of Power: Monopolist Entrepreneurs, the State and Spanish Victualling in the Eighteenth Century. In *War Entrepreneurs, and the State in Europe and the Mediterranean, 1300–1800*, ed. Fynn-Paul, 260–283. Leiden: Brill.

Torres Sánchez, R. 2016. *Military Entrepreneurs and the Spanish Contractor State in the Eighteenth Century*. Oxford: Oxford University Press.

Trulsson, L. 1947. *Ulrik Scheffer som hattpolitiker. Studier i hatt regimens politiska och diplomatiska historia*. Lund: Gleerup.

Winton, P. 2006. *Frihetstidens politiska praktik. Nätverk och offentlighet 1746–1766*. Uppsala: Acta Universitatis Upsaliensis.

Winton, P. 2010. La hiérarchie contestée. La reconfiguration de l'équilibre des pouvoirs au sein et entre les ordres du Riksdag suédois, 1750–1772. *Revue d'Histoire Nordique* 10: 31–47.

Winton, P. 2012a. Denmark and Sweden in the European Great Power System, 1720–1765. *Revue d'Histoire Nordique* 14: 39–62.

Winton, P. 2012b. Sweden and the Seven Years War, 1757–1762: War, Debt and Politics. *War in History* 19: 5–31.

Winton, P. 2015. Parliamentary Control, Public Discussions and Royal Autonomy: Sweden, 1750–1780. *Histoire & Mesure* 30: 51–78.

CHAPTER 11

For the Good of the Prince: Government and Corruption in Germany During the Eighteenth Century

Robert Bernsee

The administrative structure of early-modern Germany looks very corrupt from a modern perspective. In many states, it was common to sell offices, to farm taxes or to lease royal demesnes. It was also very usual to pay officials via offices and to recruit them not only by payment of money, but heritage or patronage. Moreover, the administration was surrounded by a veil of secrecy, such that information about the government stayed within the administration. In other words, information concerning the internal affairs of the administration did not reach what we might call or 'term' the 'public sphere'. If those states had been monitored by *Transparency International* today, they would have been ranked somewhere at the bottom of the *Corruption Perceptions Index*, maybe even below countries like Afghanistan or Iraq (Transparency International 2018). Moreover, we would nowadays call them 'failed states' due to their endemic venality and nepotism (Helman and Ratner 1992; Ghani and Lockhart 2008).

R. Bernsee (✉)
University of Goettingen, Goettingen, Germany
e-mail: robert.bernsee@wiwi.uni-goettingen.de

J. Félix and A. Dubet (eds.), *The War Within*,
Palgrave Studies in the History of Finance,
https://doi.org/10.1007/978-3-319-98050-8_11

Although historians did not describe the states in early modern Germany as 'failed' states, they identified the aforementioned practices—those that spread across all European monarchies—as endemically corrupt. This observation is true for German historiography, until the late twentieth century, to some extent. In fact, Martin Göhring (1938) declared the sales of offices as a 'poison' of the *Ancien Régime* in France. Jakob van Klaveren (1957) described corruption as a result of 'weak monarchies', whose intermediary powers were able to maximise incomes from their offices, even though he did not subsume sale of offices under 'corruption'. In the eyes of Franz Quarthal (1987), the practices mentioned are seen by their nature as some sort of corruption. Their interpretations resemble those of historians from other countries, who also denounced the old system, be it in Great Britain or the Dutch Republic as endemically corrupt (Rubinstein 1983). These historians all have one thing in common: they judge the administrative practices of the *Ancien Régime* by their contemporary values.

However, it is questionable to compare current values and norms with those of historic societies, especially in early-modern times. This point becomes evident if one considers the extensive research on the cultural history of early-modern Europe since the late 1980s. Historians such as Linda Levy Peck (1990), Sharon Kettering (1986), and Nathalie Zemon Davis (2000) argued convincingly that patronage and gift-giving were essential parts of European political culture. This includes social interactions within the hierarchy of the court and administration, among noble families and between subjects and officials. Patronage, as Hillard von Thiessen (2010) has stated, followed a specific 'ethos': By such practices, the actors involved pursued values and norms, such as loyalty or charity, that reinforced and enhanced their honour and that of their families. The aforementioned authors also showed that the transition from legitimate patronage to illegitimate corruption was quite fluid during the early-modern period: the norms related to patronage contradicted those that served the 'common good'. Actors involved in practices of patronage could therefore be accused of corruption and lose their position or even their lives. However, the definition of corruption remained blurred in many of the historical studies on corruption.

More recently, other historians, such as Jens Ivo Engels (2014), Frédéric Monier (2014), and Toon Kerkhoff et al. (2013), have been focusing on the phenomenon of corruption itself. Rather like the scholars who have examined patronage, they argue that corruption should be seen as a socially constructed phenomenon that is subject to historical change. They make a distinction between the communication about corruption and the practices criticised. These scholars have been able to show that the perception of corruption underwent certain changes. This finding is especially true for the time around 1800, when the Weberian bureaucracy was implemented in many European states. The social constructivist approach can be traced back to Michael Johnston, an American sociologist. He defined corruption as "the abuse, according to the legal or social standards constituting a society's system of public order, a public role or resource for private benefit" (Johnston 1996). Following his definition, the construction of corruption has always depended on public values or, more precisely, what is understood as 'public'. Like corruption itself, those values are essentially contested concepts whose semantics change historically. An important public value is the concept of 'common good' (or public interest) which has always been closely connected to the an imagined political community (Münkler and Bluhm 2001). Regarding the Johnstonian definition again, the boundaries between 'private' and 'public' are determined by the notion of common good. Due to the fact that 'common good' has been a contested phenomenon since the Middle Ages, it is possible to use a definition for early-modern cases even though the definition implies a public–private dichotomy, which itself is largely seen as a modern concept (Kettering 1986; Engels 2014; Grüne and Tölle 2013). However, in this study, the definition will function as a heuristic device rather than as a rigidly applied tool.

Emphasising 'common good' as a contested phenomenon itself seems to be the major difference between the recent research on corruption and the studies on patronage. The semantics of 'common good' were heavily disputed in the German territories during the eighteenth century, especially in debates on corruption whose participants, depending on their social position, argued for different concepts of common good (Bernsee 2015; Tölle 2012). In the late eighteenth century, the concept was changing: from the 1780s onwards, one can observe an abstract concept of common good that featured prominently in both public debates and the political constitution. One of the earlier concepts was the notion that the prince and his family represented the political community. Thus, 'dynastic good' was seen as equal to the common good not just exceptionally, but commonly. This notion resembles the concepts in other

European monarchies: Guy Rowlands (2002) has called pre-revolutionary France a 'dynastic state', since the family interests of the Bourbons were closely related to state interests, be it practically, legally or theoretically (Rowen 1980). Meanwhile, Samuel E. Finer (1989) pointed out that the British government until the 1780s must be seen as the administration of the monarch.

These thoughts lead us to the core of this chapter: I will argue that many of the administrative practices, as aforementioned, are in accordance with a notion of common good oriented towards the welfare of the prince and his family. This notion became prevalent within the German territories before 1800. The 'old practices', thus, enjoyed a wide acceptance throughout the eighteenth century, at least until the 1780s, when this understanding lost its legitimacy. I will exemplify this argument by analysing both political discourse and administrative structure in two German states, Bavaria and Prussia. The argument, to make it absolutely clear, does not follow the simple equation 'different times, different customs' (Lindemann 2012). A notion of corruption nevertheless existed in both states. To take this circumstance into account, the chapter which follows includes some remarks on what had been perceived as corrupt during the eighteenth century. The chapter consists of five sections. First, I will show that the concept of common good previously mentioned can be extrapolated from public debates and the political constitution of that time. The second part concerns the administrative and fiscal structure as well as its impact and design. In the third section, I will focus on the efforts of the princes to prevent practices threatening their fiscal income. The fourth part contains a few words on the last decades of the eighteenth century, when the 'old administrative' practices lost their legitimacy. Finally, I will conclude by evaluating the material presented with regard to the main argument.

1 The Good of the Prince: Its Context and Construction

It is desirable to give a few insights into the spatio-temporal context, before elaborating on the construction of the concept of common good.. Both Bavaria and Prussia were part of the Holy Roman Empire, and their rulers were formally vassals of the Emperor until the dissolution of the Empire in 1806. Bavaria and Prussia, more precisely, should be understood as a synonym for a collection of territories attributed to a noble family in the sense of a *composite monarchy* (Elliott 1992; Reinhard 1999). In both cases, it was a branch of very powerful houses that ruled this conglomeration of lands—the Wittelsbach family in Bavaria and the Hohenzollern family in Brandenburg-Prussia. Their heads held a rank of a prince-elector, one of the highest positions within the imperial realm. Both families increased their power throughout the entire eighteenth century: the House of Wittelsbach gained the imperial crown for a short time period (1742–1745) and unified the greatest number of territories of the family under one ruler in 1777 (Körner 2009). The Hohenzollern family obtained kingship in 1701 and acquired several territories in the course of the eighteenth century, either by inheritance (East Frisia) or by conquest (Silesia) (Clark 2006). Both houses competed with others that expanded outside the imperial realm and even occupied thrones, for instance in Great Britain (Hanover) or, at least temporarily, in Poland (Wettin). The heads of these great houses, mostly princes, could act fairly autonomously from the imperial authorities, although they remained vassals of the Emperor. The Emperor nevertheless possessed some instruments to discipline the princes—and to curb their ambitions. He, was, for instance, closely allied with the ecclesiastical principalities—and with the estates within the territories of the princes, the so-called *Landstände* (Stollberg-Rilinger 2006).

This point leads us to the main subject of the current section, the construction of a notion of common good that focused on the welfare of the prince and his family. One can observe the constitution of this idea on two levels: public discourse and the political constitution. The political debates were characterised by collaboration and conflicts between the two main political actors, the prince and the estates (*Landstände*) (Bahlcke 2010). The constitution of the *Landstände* could differ from one territory to another, but in most cases, the estates consisted of the landed nobility, the clergy and the cities. In the public debates, both sides—prince and estates—claimed to be the true representative of the political community (Stollberg-Rilinger 1999; Seresse 2005). Thus, they perceived the common good as equating either to the good of the estates or the good of the prince and his dynasty. For that reason, both sides attempted to expand their access to resources at the expense of the other, while publicly arguing for the benefits of the common good. The estates were supported by the Holy Roman Emperor—the 'natural' opponent of the German princes—and by other imperial institutions, such as the

Imperial Chamber Court (*Reichskammergericht*) in Wetzlar. Apart from these institutions, the published work whose authors mainly argued for the position of the *Landstände*, also played an important role. In particular, these texts, mostly written by academics, circulated throughout the Empire (*Reichspublizistik*) and were important for the formation of a 'public' opinion throughout the eighteenth century (Stolleis 2012; Arndt 2013). The position of the prince, conversely, was supported by a new group of experts, the so-called cameralists, that had gained increasing importance since the early-eighteenth century. These men, mostly employed either at universities or princely governments, challenged the claims of the estates and emphasised that the common good would only be improved by the rise of the ruling dynasty. Therefore, they argued for increasing the income of the central power through fiscal expansion. Johann Heinrich Gottlob Justi is a good example of this phenomenon. The Prussian cameralist argued in his book *System des Finanzwesens...* (1766) that 'the happiness of the ruler cannot be separated from that of his subjects'—and vice versa. Extracting money would not adversely impact the 'welfare of the people', as Justi stated, if this process was executed 'without prejudicing the substance of the country and without complaints from the subjects'. In another book, Justi (1758) named the most important fields that should be funded by expenditures of the state, thus benefiting the common good, stating, 'There is no doubt that the expenditures for the person and the family of the ruler [...] are not first ranked among all government expenses, once domestic and external security has been ensured through provision of sufficient military forces'. In other words, the army and court were the predominant instruments to enhance a 'happiness' that was focused on the ruler. Generally speaking, the notion that the good of the prince and his family is tantamount to the common good became an important component of public discourse and reinforced the legitimacy of the ruling family.

Therefore, it can be hardly be considered surprising that this notion was implemented in the political constitution of the German monarchies. This fact is observable for 'house' laws and other regulations with constitutional status. 'House' laws comprised a set of rules that regulated issues of inheritance, family matters and property for the royal dynasty. These rules included norms concerning wardships and succession as well as financial provisions and rights of family members (Weitzel 1982; Mohnhaupt 2000). For the purposes of this article, it is important to note that house laws also contained the structure and content of the fee tail, the *Fideikommiss*. The fee tail, a very common institution of the European nobility, defined the dynastical property and separated it from the personal property of each family member (Eckert 1992). In this way, it also incorporated the resources of the realm in case of royal houses—not only in Germany, but even in France (Rowlands 2002). The Prussian fee tail—or more precisely the fee tail of its ruling family—was established by changes in the house law in 1710 and 1713 (Pečar 2011). King Frederick William I decided to forbid any alienation of the dynastical property and demanded that his successors should acquire new lands and other assets. Interestingly, he invited his servants to police? this interdiction. The king's aim was to increase the financial income of his dynasty and, therefore, improve the common good of the Prussian monarchy. His successor, King Frederick II, not only followed these rules, hee also implemented them in his famous law code, *General State Laws for the Prussian States* (in German: *Allgemeines Landrecht der preußischen Staaten*), which was enacted in 1794, shortly after his death. The great king, who is commonly known as the 'first servant of the state', used the word 'state' in this law code, but the latter contained some hints that he actually meant dynasty. This circumstance, ignored even by historians such as Reinhart Koselleck (2006), becomes evident if one takes a look at two passages of the code: First, it allowed the king as 'head of state' to use the resources of the 'state property' exclusively—or, in other words, the code provided the usufruct that is an essential part of the fee tail as well. Second, defamation of the 'state' did not only include the king, but also his whole family. Thus, there is some evidence to interpret 'head of the state' as head of the dynasty. One can find other hints in the writings of Frederick II himself. For example, he wrote the first history of the Hohenzollern dynasty and used the book to aggrandise himself as a dynastic head of great splendour (Pečar 2016). In both house laws and general law code, we can easily see that there was no distinction between the state and dynasty as political institutions. Moreover, common good was equated to the good of the dynasty and its ruling member, in this case the Prussian king.

In a nutshell, the prevailing thought in both public debates and the political system was to understand common good as a concept that was wholly identified with the welfare of the prince and his dynasty. This understanding played a major role while legitimising fiscal instruments. The prince was not only prince, but also the head of a dynasty. Thus, he had to act to preserve his reputation and that of his family.

This reputation could be improved by acquiring thrones or manors, by prestigious construction projects, by the number of the prince's/royal clients—and by military success. However, all these actions needed fiscal resources and, therefore, an effective administration.

2 Serving the Prince: The Administration and Its Instruments

The administrative structure of German principalities had some general characteristics that must be sketched, before a detailed analysis of the practices can follow. The structure mirrored the political situation and was a binary one in that both political actors—prince and estates—controlled their own authorities (Brakensiek 2014; Neu 2011). The allocation of 'competences' and the degree of collaboration varied from one territory to another, like the constitution of the *Landstände* themselves. 'Competences', however, does not mean that the authorities were organised functionally. In fact, administrative units often dealt with a broad range of executive and juridical issues in both Bavaria and Prussia, especially on the local level. A separation of powers in a modern sense did not exist. If one focuses on the princely or royal administration, it must be noted that its structure was highly changeable during the eighteenth century. The personal relation between prince and servant determined the administrative body, particularly the range of specific offices. This meant that if the relationship went well, the servant could acquire more power, otherwise, it would be the other way around. The relationship between prince and servant must, first and foremost, be seen as personal one: It ended in most cases with the death of the servant, because retirement was unusual and so were pensions. Contemporaries used to characterise this relationship as similar to a lord–vassal relationship, for instance, in comments on the Bavarian civil code written by the Bavarian minister Kreittmayr (1768), even as a 'political wedlock' as in a book on the relationship between master and servant published by Carl Friedrich Moser (1761). Furthermore, having an arcane policy, in which actions within the administration remained invisible to outsiders, was an important attribute of princely government. Administrative records did not even circulate within the government, and only the prince had insight an overview into the general data of the administration, at least theoretically. In practice, he had very insufficient information about what was occurring inside the administration until the end of the eighteenth century, although the tendency to collect data improved (Behrisch 2016). The *Arcanum* reflected the notion that the administration belonged to the prince: it was his 'private affair' and, thus, none of anyone's business but his own or his family. We will see that the same is true for other practices that seem to be as corrupt as the *Arcanum* from a modern perspective.

The princely governments in both Bavaria and Prussia featured several practices that were typical fiscal instruments in many parts of early modern Europe. First to be analysed here is the sale of offices. This practice, broadly defined, expanded considerably in both Bavaria and Prussia during the eighteenth century (Reinhard 1979; Doyle 1996). Entitlements to administrative posts were often sold throughout the whole century, especially in Bavaria. This observation is true for positions at the local level of the administration, the so-called *Pflegen* (Press 1983). The case of a man named Sedlmayr illustrates this situation (Bayerisches Hauptstaatsarchiv 1792). According to records, he asked the prince-elector to sell him an entitlement for a court clerk or commissioner of a *Pflege*. Sedlmayr needed it as dowry for his daughter to increase her chances in the marriage market. As a result, he paid 33,500 guilders to the *Churfürstliche Deutsche Schulfonds* in exchange for this legal title.

Another, more hidden way of selling offices was a security deposit called *Amtsbürgschaft*. At that time, paying a fixed sum to the prince or the incumbent of an office, upon entering the royal service, was a common practice (Reinhard 1979). This institution was very useful for the Bavarian Prince: he could use the money for his own purposes as long as the office existed. Proponents argued that *Amtsbürgschaften* functioned as a kind of loan at reduced rates of interest (Bayerisches Hauptstaatsarchiv 1790). In the light of this finding, it is scarcely surprising that the Prussian kings used this institution as well. selling offices in its more ordinary form had been widely used until the 1750s. Frederick William I, especially. financed his expenditure by selling posts on the local level and by selling simple honorific titles to which no rights were attached (Möller 1980). These practices apparently decreased afterwards, under the reign of Frederick II. However, this evidence does not mean that the latter condemned or even abolished the 'old practices'. The crude selling offices had been of relatively little importance to the Prussian kings in funding or as a means of funding their expenditure during the eighteenth century. Another fiscal instrument, the royal lease-holding, was much more important, especially in Prussia, wherein the king was by far the largest landowner in his territories. Since the 1710s, he had leased his demesnes including all land and people to non-noble men who became the so-called *Domänenpächter* (Müller 1965). Those men had to pay a one-off security deposit and an annual rent that was calculated based on the annual revenue of the domain. Although the contract was officially limited to six years, many tenants remained in office much longer. The domain they leased stayed within families for generations in some cases. One could say that a new social class originated from this practice. However, one would ask, why did the king leave the demesnes to specific tenants for such a long time? On the one hand, those non-noble tenants were skilled people, whose ability to cultivate the land were even enhanced over time and who were useful for the king. On the other hand, the king tried to avoid reimbursements that would be necessary to compensate the investments of the leaseholder if the tenant changed. The royal lease-holding can generally be seen as a variety of sale of offices, because the tenant was the representative of the king and held jurisdiction over the subjects of the demesne, at least until the 1770s (Müller 1965; Wienfort 2001). Cameralists such as Justi praised this kind of resource as the best opportunity to raise princely revenues (Justi 1766). This instrument, in fact, provided one-third to half of the Prussian tax income during the eighteenth century (Ullmann 2005).

Two other sources were significant for income: tax-farming and monopolies. Tax-farming gained rising importance for Prussia, particularly after the Seven Years' War. King Frederick II invited French financial experts to establish and manage a Prussian version of the French *Ferme générale* in the early 1760s. With the help of these people, he founded a special authority: the *Administration générale des accises et des péages*, or the *Regie*. This administrative unit was allowed to collect indirect taxes, especially the excise, and customs in the name of the crown. It had to pay a fixed sum to the king that was based on the revenues of 1765/1766 (Kiser and Schneider 1994). The *regisseurs généraux* who were of French origin benefited enormously and exclusively from the profits, as did the Prussian King. In fact, the *Regie* provided 24 million thalers altogether until its dissolution in 1786 (Klein 1974). One-third of the fiscal income was earned from tax-farming between 1766 and 1786. While monopolies were of less importance in Prussia, this fiscal instrument had a substantial significance in Bavaria. Specifically, monopolies on salt and beer constituted circa one quarter of the fiscal income in the 1760s and probably afterwards as well (Klein 1974).

Consequently, the fiscal instruments mentioned—sale of offices, royal lease-holding, tax-farming and monopolies—were in accordance with the good of the prince: These instruments financed the growing expenditure, particularly for military purposes and the court: It is to be noted that the Prussian army had grown from 30,000 soldiers in 1713 to 194,000 in 1786 (Kiser and Schneider 1994). The costs for the Bavarian court had risen from 1.4 to 2.5 million guilders between 1701 and 1799 (Klein 1974). The military did not only enhance the power of the Prussian monarchy, and court expenses were not just a simple waste of money. Rather, both had positive effects on the reputation of the prince and his family, especially among the high nobility in Europe (Friedrich 2012). Reputation, indeed, was a driving force behind the actions of noble families in general (Asch 2008). It did not matter that those instruments, especially tax-farming, probably hit the population severely. This effect was not part of the 'welfare equation' and, thus, did not hurt the common good as it was perceived at the time.

This issue becomes obvious when looking at the payments within the administration. In both states, the personnel were not usually paid by means of fixed salaries. Rather, they received the money directly from the subjects as fees or charges. These emoluments, called *Sporteln*, were the main income of many servants in several cases. In Prussia, for instance, *Sporteln* or other fees could amount from 25 to 50% of the salary (Straubel 1998). This salary structure was not irrational, but quite beneficial for the prince, because in this way, he was freed from paying high salaries, especially in times of insecure income caused by famines or wars. Thus, he did not need an administrative structure that made it possible to transfer financial resources between the different departments or to monitor the behaviour of his servants extensively (Kiser and Schneider 1994; Swart 2009). This argument is also true for the fiscal instruments mentioned, which provided a predictable amount of income because they mostly consisted of lump sums. Hence, the prince became independent of economic disruption.

The princes, nevertheless, had to observe restrictions while extracting fiscal resources via several ways: First, they could not extort contributions from the subjects indefinitely, if they did not want to provoke riots among them. Second, the princes could not antagonise the *Landstände* too much while interfering in their prerogatives through financial exactions. This is because the estates had, until the end of the eighteenth century, several instruments to defend themselves from such attacks. They could appeal to the imperial institutions, as happened in Prussia (Asch 2008), refuse to pay levies to the prince (Seitz 1999) or accuse the prince of damaging the common good publicly (Bernsee 2017). In this regard, it should be added that issuing bonds or taking loans was rarely an option to finance expenditure. One reason for that was the poorly developed financial market, especially in Germany. In particular, when Prussia tried to fund the war against France after 1795 through loans, it was hardly possible to mobilise a sufficient amount of money from German banks (Real 1991). The other reason related to the rights of the *Landstände*: the prince could ask them for loans, but he had to reckon with the *Landstände* possibly demanding an extension of their prerogatives in return. Bavaria, for instance, had been heavily in debt since the 1720s (Klein 1974). For these reasons, the estates functioned as creditor and could maintain a strong stance against the prince.

A modern perspective on corruption involving a strict separation between the public and the private sphere, administrative practices, such as emoluments and sale of offices in its several varieties, may be seen as abusive, due to the fact that office holders benefited personally from them. However, these practices corresponded with the notion of common good that was equated to the welfare of the prince and his family. Or in this sense of the term of this definition of 'common good', they can hardly be described as 'corrupt'.

3 Harming the Prince: Corruption and Its Prevention

Having said that these practices could not be understood as abusive ones, one might wonder what constituted corruption back then. However, all of the named practices could be exploited if the tenants, tax-farmers or royal servants extracted too many resources from the subjects. Riots could be a consequence of such actions and it could eventually disturb the political order. Such practices could jeopardise the income of the prince and, thus were seen as abusive by contemporaries. Other forms of corruption were the misappropriation of royal money and unacceptable payments from parties outside the administration. Both challenged the personal loyalty of the servant that was solely directed towards the prince and his family.

The princes implemented some mechanisms to prevent those abuses: First, the emoluments were strictly specified in court or charge regulations. Specifically, the so-called *Hof- und Taxordnungen* or *Sportelordnungen* contained tables that included a specific amount of the fee for every transaction of a servant (Vogel 1960). If the servant took more money from the subject than allowed, he could be impeached and eventually punished by the prince. This kind of behaviour, nevertheless, was not labelled as corruption in contemporary penal codes. For instance, it remained unnamed in the *Codex Juris Bavarici Criminalis* of 1751. Second, the aforementioned security deposits, *Amtsbürgschaften*, comprised a variety of sale of offices, but they obviously had a safety function for the prince. This is because he could substitute the loss with the deposited funds, if irregularities occurred in the accounts However, it should be noted that these deposits were often considerably less than the money in the coffers, as Bavarian officials stated (Bayerisches Hauptstaatsarchiv 1790). A mechanism for the checking of the coffers also was lacking.

This point leads to consideration of instruments used by princes to monitor their servants, which meant that decisions within the administration were made collegially. Members of collegial boards decided on administrative affairs jointly and unanimously. King Frederick William I once stated that he preferred collegiality because of its ability to prevent favouritism among the highest officials (Hubatsch 1983). Preventing the occurrence of 'corruption' represents only one function of collegiality. The other, probably more important one was to preserve the social hierarchy within the administration. Another instrument to reduce corruption could be a visitation of the administrative units, either by high officials or the prince himself: The Prussian kings, especially Frederick II, usually travelled around their territories to ascertain whether everything was going as it should. Although this travelling should also be understood as part of Frederick's self-dramatisation as a caring ruler, it might have had some influence on the discipline of the royal servants. In the Bavarian government, specific royal servants monitored the local office holders. These men acted as heads of *Rentämter*, the regional administrative units. Their task was two-fold: They should check the princely chests coffers on the one hand and track complaints made by the subjects on the other (Rauh 1988; Näther 2018). In actual practice things were different, especially given that the regular visitation, the *Rentmeisterumritt*, did not take place for ten, twenty or even 40 years in many administrative units (Rankl 1997).

It has anyway, been disputed in the literature how rigidly the princes and his authorities applied these rules and used these instruments. One can find little evidence that the enforcement of the named mechanisms had been undertaken on a high level even up until the late eighteenth century. Deviant actions did not seem to be persecuted in most cases (Rankl 1997). This is also true for the emoluments, the *Sporteln*. 'Overcharging' by officials obviously remained a practice until the end of the eighteenth century, as contemporaries, like Simon Rottmanner (1783) stated. A reason for this being the case could be the role that honour played as a mechanism of trust within the administration, especially because control mechanisms that were strongly institutionalised and enforced could damage the perceived honesty of officials and, therefore, the reputation of the prince himself and of his family (Reinhard 1999). It must be kept in mind that, like the prince, servants, especially noble ones at the top of the administration, acted for the interests of their family. For the prince, it was much more important that his servants provide personal loyalty to him than that they followed the rules in detail.

Nevertheless, this personal loyalty could turn into personal disloyalty, if the servant went beyond acceptable limits, particularly if his behaviour caused a great stir in public. Such a 'public' reaction could happen because many of the subjects simply lacked the ability to read the *Tax*- and *Sportelordnungen* that designated the limits for emoluments the royal servants were allowed to charge. An example of how the princes dealt with servants who went beyond acceptable limits is the case of the Prussian minister Friedrich Christoph von Görne during the reign of Frederick II in the early 1780s. Görne was the head of the *Seehandlung* which was a trading company located in Konigsberg that was mostly owned by the king. He had speculated in Polish real estate—on his own account, using royal money that he had eventually lost (Sieg 2003). Owing to these actions, he was accused of misappropriation and finally imprisoned by a royal court. The court emphasised specifically that Görne had forgotten to act in accordance with his status, in other words, to be like a person of 'excellent fidelity bound by status, dignity and oath' (Anonymous 1784). He obviously had acted dishonestly and broken his personal oath to the king. His case shows that princely servants had to consider the limits of their actions in ways that often remained implicit. This case also reflects another point: in his bill of indictment, reference was invariably made to the 'good of his majesty the Prussian king' instead of the 'good of the Prussian people' or something similar. Thus, this case demonstrated once again that the common good was predicated on the good of the prince.

This section confirms that a simple explanation of corruption along the motto 'different time, different customs' fails. There was a specific notion of corruption and certain instruments to prevent it, even in a system that looks corrupt from a modern perspective. Its foundations were different, however: along with honour, it was the personal relationship between prince and servant that determined what was to be considered as corrupt.

4 Changing Common Good: Different Concepts and Administrative Reforms

The Görne case leads to the fourth part of this article: from the 1780s, the old administrative practices had begun to become completely illegitimate and were confronted with a new notion of common good, especially among the public. Critique of the prevailing fiscal practices had already appeared before the 1780s. Moreover, it formed part of the political conflict between the prince and the territorial estates. The latter especially—the *Landstände*—had criticised the sale of offices, tax-farming and princely patronage as endemic abuses. One case, albeit from 1786, illustrates this situation. At that time, the Bavarian *Landstände* criticised the administration of prince-elector Carl Theodor publicly. They particularly denounced the sale of both offices and monopolies as endemically corrupt. Both would lead to the demise of Bavaria in their opinion (Anonymous 1787). Their solution was simple and insightful: they mentioned the prince to consider members of the *Landstände* for such posts in future. Obviously, their critique was grounded on personal interests of their members, since pecuniary requirements to gain access to the administration simply thwarted their privileges, particularly the inheritance of offices. The extensive use of selling offices and monopolies would furthermore have jeopardised the scope of the estates-based branch of the administration where most office holders had inherited their posts from their ancestors. Corruption charges, thus, were an opportunity to claim resources for the members of the *Landstände*. The prince—or, more precisely, his proponents—struck back by accusing the estates of corruption. In their opinion, the *Landstände* only pretended to support the 'common good' but actually pursued their personal interests at the expense of the 'real' common good that was represented by the prince and his family. Moreover, they praised the 'so called sale of offices' as an opportunity to 'restore the natural and rational equality among the members of the state', since it removes 'all family relations, the useless merits and empty claims of noble birth' (Anonymous 1786). In other words, they argued that the inheritance of offices, rather than the sale of offices, was corrupt. Apart from these different views on recruitment practices, however, both parties shared patrimonial concepts of common good, although in different forms: while the proponents of the princely administration argued for a concept that highlighted the prince and his family, their opponents imagined a 'common good' that was based on the noble families constituting the *Landstände*.

A new critique appeared in public, distinct from this conflict, in the 1780s. Its advocates drew on previous arguments and added some more: emoluments became a sort of bribery, the *Arcanum* lost its acceptance, and so did the administrative division into a princely and an estates-based branch. Moreover, the new critique was founded on a new concept of common good. It was neither the prince nor the estates, but rather the whole population that represented the political community and, thus, determined the common good. A new generation of princely servants, influenced by authors like Jean-Jacques Rousseau, Adam Smith or Immanuel Kant, supported the new concept and used corruption to delegitimise the existing administrative practices (Bernsee 2015).

In Bavaria during the early 1780s, these princely servants organised themselves into secret societies, particularly the *Order of the Illuminati*, and published, mostly anonymously, pamphlets that included a fundamental criticism of the administrative structures, identifying them as fundamentally corrupt (Bernsee 2013). Members of the *Illuminati* especially sought to improve the morality within the government while reforming the existing system. To further reinforce these aims, these young men tried to acquire administrative posts by themselves or to enhance the influence of their respective factions within the administration. However, they saw themselves as the moral and intellectual elite of Bavaria, dedicated to secure and promote the 'common good'. However, here this young generation of princely servants failed to achieve its goals. Rival factions within the administration ensured that the members of the secret society were prosecuted by the prince and the *Illuminati* eventually dissolved. After the French Revolution in 1789 similar processes occurred in Prussia. It was especially the works written by the French revolutionary Comte de Mirabeau (1788, 1789) on the Prussian court and Frederick II's administration that triggered the debate within the North-eastern German monarchy. Mirabeau particularly focused on the degeneracy of the court and on the 'negative consequences' of tax-farming. While targeting Prussian institutions, he arguably was aiming at its French counterparts which eventually became a symbol of the corrupt Ancien Régime in Revolutionary France. However, apart from his negative image of Frederick II's government, his interpretations were used by a younger generation of royal servants publicly and within the government. Like in Bavaria, these Prussian servants, certain of their moral and intellectual superiority, produced publications and founded secret societies to fight abuses within the administration, but were both prosecuted and convicted by the Prussian government (Bernsee 2013).

The new notion of common good, nevertheless, had acquired the status of the prevailing concept around 1800, after reforming officials that were often part of the previous 'anti-corruption movement' had grown in importance within the administration of both monarchies. In 1799, after the death of the former prince-elector, the new Bavarian government initiated a reform policy to abandon the old system that was perceived as endemically corrupt by its influential members, such as Maximilian de Montgelas (Weis 1970). In Prussia, critics attributed the Prussian defeat by Napoleonic France in 1807 to the abusive fiscal administration (Buchholz 1808a, b). Like in Bavaria, royal servants like Karl August von Hardenberg used such kind of corruption charges to delegitimise the old system and to push bureaucratic reforms forward (Hardenberg 1931). This process took place at a time when the political environment changed dramatically: the Holy Roman Empire was gone in 1806 and so were its institutions. The *Landstände* thus, lost their backbone and dissolved in many German states. Many of the latter changed their political constitutions significantly in order to face the Napoleonic challenge.

Both Bavaria and Prussia survived as kingdoms at the dawn of the nineteenth century. The reformers implemented new administrative structures, such as bureaucratic hierarchies, a division of work based on function, fixed salaries or recruitment by merit. The monarchy itself did not lose its legitimacy due to the fact that the reformers ascribed the corruption of the old regime to the previous princes, Carl Theodor and Frederick William II, while characterising the reign of Frederick II as an exemplary one. The governance of the latter, although it did not deviate from the others, was re-interpreted by the reformers as a desirable one. The princely administration, however, became the a superseded and corrupt one in the eyes of contemporaries. Dynastic and state property were strictly separated from each other, as had already happened in France, as were the notions of common good and the good of the prince and his family.

5 Conclusion

In this chapter, I argued that administrative practices, such as sales of offices, tax-farming, payment by fees or royal lease–holding, enjoyed acceptance in the German states until the late eighteenth century. These practices were supported by a notion of common good that focused on the welfare of the prince and his family. Thus, it was for the 'general welfare' that the instruments helped to increase the amount of fiscal income and allowed the financing of larger armies or other assets that improved the prestige of the ruling dynasty. However, this does not mean that everything which is understood as corruption today was allowed: rather, the authorities strictly regulated emoluments, especially to prevent riots. The royal servants had to be personally loyal to the prince; if they acted disloyally, for instance through misappropriation, the servants could be punished and imprisoned at his orders. Nevertheless, it was not before the 1780s, when a new notion of common good appeared in public debates, together with a new concept of government. This ultimately became the main interpretative framework twenty years later, when reform-minded officials gained in importance in both Bavaria and Prussia.

In other words, one should understand the expansion of tax-farming or royal lease-holding during the eighteenth century as a process legitimised by a contemporary concept of the common good. These fiscal instruments were quite effective, especially in Prussia. Throughout the century, one can observe an extraordinary growth of tax income, driven by revenues from these sources. This development made it possible to maintain a huge military. In Bavaria, the fiscal income more or less stagnated throughout the century: the ruling dynasty opposed strong estates and only controlled a few demesnes. Moreover, the rulers could not develop such an effective system of revenue extraction as the Prussians did. The administrative practices discussed, however, had their limits in successfully extracting resources, compared with a modern bureaucracy. This comparison obviously is anachronistic. First, contemporaries simply did not have any knowledge the advantages of the Weberian bureaucracy; they had to discover it. Second, a modern bureaucracy is based on a concept of common good that is focused on an abstract entity such as a 'nation'. It is important to bear in mind that this concept is different from the notion that dominated public debates until the end of the eighteenth century.

The findings of this chapter refer to two political entities of the Holy Roman Empire: Bavaria and Brandenburg-Prussia. Although both represent very important territorial conglomerates in terms of power, population or territory, they are very specific examples with a restricted applicability to other territories (of the Holy Roman Empire). The empire did not only consist of major hereditary principalities, but also included free imperial cities, ecclesiastical principalities and numerous minor states with hereditary succession Analysing any of those entities might provide different results—or, at least, a broader view on the legitimacy? of the old practices. This point is especially true when it comes to the Habsburg lands, due to the fact that the Emperor, the defender of the *Landstände*, was also in need of fiscal resources and confronted the estates in his own territories. More research on this topic is requested in the future to gain a better understanding of 'the war within' the administrations in German states.

References

Anonymous author. 1784. Criminal-Urtheil in Sachen des gewesenen K. Preußis. geheimen Etats-Ministers, Friedrich Christoph von Görne, Berlin, den 25. April 1782. Aus beglaubigter Handschrift. *Patriotisches Archiv für Deutschland* 1: 409–489.

Anonymous author. 1786. *Unvorgreifliche Anmerkungen zu der berüchtigten Broschüre: Ueber den Diensthandel deutscher Fürsten*. S. l.

Anonymous author. 1787. Vorstellung der bayerischen Landschaft an Se. Churfürstl. Durchlaucht von Pfalz. *Neueste Weltbegebenheiten des Jahrs 1787. Erzählt von einem Weltbürger* 4 (1): 65–69, 73–76, 81–84, 89–92, 97–100, 105–108.

Arndt, Johannes. 2013. *Herrschaftskontrolle durch Öffentlichkeit. Die publizistische Darstellung politischer Konflikte im Heiligen Römischen Reich 1648–1750*. Göttingen: Vandenhoeck & Ruprecht.

Asch, Ronald G. 2008. *Europäischer Adel in der frühen Neuzeit: Eine Einführung*. Cologne: Böhlau.

Bahlcke, Joachim. 2010. *Landesherrschaft, Territorien und Staat in der Frühen Neuzeit*. Munich: Oldenbourg.

Bayerisches Hauptstaatsarchiv. 1790. GR, fasc. 127/59.

Bayerisches Hauptstaatsarchiv. 1792. GR, fasc. 130/67.

Behrisch, Lars. 2016. *Die Berechnung der Glückseligkeit: Statistik und Politik in Deutschland und Frankreich im späten Ancien Régime*. Ostfildern: Thorbecke.

Bernsee, Robert. 2013. Corruption in German Political Discourse Between 1780 and 1820: A Categorisation. *Journal of Modern European History* 11 (1): 52–71.

Bernsee, Robert. 2015. Delegitimation Through Corruption: Legal and Administrative Changes During the Napoleonic Era (1800–1820). *Střed / Centre. Journal for Interdisciplinary Studies of Central Europe in the 19th and 20th Centuries* 7 (1): 9–33.

Bernsee, Robert. 2017. *Moralische Erneuerung: Korruption und bürokratische Reformen in Bayern und Preußen, 1780–1820*. Göttingen: Vandenhoeck & Ruprecht.

Brakensiek, Stefan. 2014. Einleitung: Herrschaft und Verwaltung in der Frühen Neuzeit. In *Herrschaft und Verwaltung in der Frühen Neuzeit*, ed. Stefan Brakensiek et al., 9–14. Berlin: Duncker & Humblot.

Buchholz, Friedrich. 1808a. *Gemählde des gesellschaftlichen Zustandes im Königreiche Preussen, bis zum 14ten Oktober des Jahres 1806. Vom Verfasser des neuen Leviathan. Erster Theil.* Berlin and Leipzig: n.n.

Buchholz, Friedrich. 1808b. *Gallerie Preussischer Charaktere. Aus der französischen Handschrift übersetzt.* Germanien: n.n.

Clark, Christopher. 2006. *The Iron Kingdom: The Rise and Downfall of Prussia, 1600–1947.* London: Allen Lane.

Davis, Nathalie Zemon. 2000. *The Gift in Sixteenth-Century France.* Oxford: Oxford University Press.

Doyle, William. 1996. *Venality. The Sale of Offices in Eighteenth Century France.* Oxford: Clarendon Press.

Eckert, Jörn. 1992. *Der Kampf um die Familienfideikommisse in Deutschland. Studien zum Absterben eines Rechtsinstituts.* Frankfurt am Main: Lang.

Elliott, John H. 1992. A Europe of Composite Monarchies. *Past & Present* 137 (November): 48–71.

Engels, Jens Ivo. 2014. *Die Geschichte der Korruption: Von der Frühen Neuzeit bis ins 20. Jahrhundert.* Frankfurt am Main: Fischer.

Finer, Samuel E. 1989. Patronage and the Public Service in Britain and America. In *Political Corruption. A Handbook*, ed. Arnold J. Heidenheimer et al., 102–106. New Brunswick, NJ: Transaction.

Friedrich, Karin. 2012. *Brandenburg-Prussia, 1466–1806: The Rise of a Composite State.* Basingstoke: Palgrave Macmillan.

Ghani, Ashraf, and Clare Lockhart. 2008. *Fixing Failed States: A Framework for Rebuilding a Fractured World*. Oxford: Oxford University Press.

Göhring, Martin. 1938. *Die Ämterkäuflichkeit im Ancien régime*. Berlin: Ebering.

Grüne, Niels, and Tom Tölle. 2013. Corruption in the Ancien Régime: Systems-Theoretical Considerations on Normative Plurality. *Journal of Modern European History* 11 (1): 31–51.

Hardenberg, Karl August von. 1931. Über die Reorganisation des Preußischen Staats, verfasst auf höchsten Befehl Sr. Majestät des Königs vom 12.09.1807 (Rigaer Denkschrift). In *Die Reorganisation des preussischen Staates unter Stein und Hardenberg. Part 1. Allgemeine Verwaltungs- und Behördenreform, Vol. 1: Vom Beginn des Kampfes gegen die Kabinettsregierung bis zum Wiedereintritt des Ministers vom Stein*, ed. Georg Winter, 302–363. Leipzig: Hirzel.

Helman, Gerald B., and Steven R. Ratner. 1992. Saving Failed States. *Foreign Policy* 89: 3–20.

Hubatsch, Walther. 1983. Brandenburg-Preußen. Verwaltungsentwicklung von 1713–1803. In *Deutsche Verwaltungsgeschichte, vol. 1: Vom Spätmittelalter bis zum Ende des Reiches*, ed. Kurt G. A. Jeserich et al., 892–941. Stuttgart: DVA.

Johnston, Michael. 1996. The Search for Definitions: The Vitality of Politics and the Issue of Corruption. *International Social Science Journal* 48: 321–335.

Justi, Johann Heinrich Gottlob. 1758. *Staatswirthschaft oder Systematische Abhandlung aller Oekonomischen und Cameral-Wissenschaften, die zur Regierung eines Landes erfodert werden. Zweyter Theil, Welcher die Lehre von dem vernünftigen Gebrauche des Vermögens des Staats, und mithin die eigentliche Cameral- oder Finanz-Wissenschaft in sich begreift. Nebst einem vollständigen Register über beyde Theile*, 2nd ed. Leipzig: Breitkopf.

Justi, Johann Heinrich Gottlob. 1766. *System des Finanzwesens, nach vernünftigen aus dem Endzweck der bürgerlichen Gesellschaften und aus der Natur und aller Quellen der Einkünfte des Staats hergeleiteten Grundsätzen und Regeln ausführlich abgehandelt*. Halle: Renger.

Kerkhoff, Toon, Ronald Kroeze, and Pieter Wagenaar. 2013. Corruption and the Rise of Modern Politics in Europe in the Eighteenth and Nineteenth Century: A Comparison Between France, The Netherlands, Germany and England—Introduction. *Journal of Modern European History* 11 (1): 19–30.

Kettering, Sharon. 1986. *Patrons, Brokers, and Clients in Seventeenth-Century France*. New York et al.: Oxford University Press.

Kiser, Edgar, and Joachim Schneider. 1994. Bureaucracy and Efficiency: An Analysis of Taxation in Early Modern Prussia. *American Sociological Review* 59 (2): 187–204.

Klein, Ernst. 1974. *Geschichte der öffentlichen Finanzen in Deutschland (1500–1870)*. Wiesbaden: Steiner.

Körner, Hans-Michael. 2009. *Die Wittelsbacher. Vom Mittelalter bis zur Gegenwart*. Beck: Munich.

Koselleck, Reinhart. 2006. *Begriffsgeschichten. Studien zur Semantik und Pragmatik der politischen und sozialen Sprache*. Frankfurt am Main: Suhrkamp.
Kreittmayr, Wiguläus Xaver Aloys von. 1768. *Anmerkungen über den Codicem Maximilianeum Bavaricum Civilem*, vol. V. Munich: Vötter.
Lindemann, Mary. 2012. Dirty Politics or 'Harmonie'? Defining Corruption in Early Modern Amsterdam and Hamburg. *Journal of Social History* 45 (3): 582–604.
Mirabeau, Honoré-Gabriel Riquetti. 1788. *De la monarchie prussienne sous Frédéric le Grand*. London: n.n.
Mirabeau, Honoré-Gabriel Riquetti. 1789. *Histoire secrete de la cour de Berlin. Ou Correspondance D'un voyager françois, depuis le 5 Juillet 1786 jusqu'au 19 Janvier 1787. Ouvrage posthume*, 2 vol. S. l.
Mohnhaupt, Heinz. 2000. Die Lehre von der 'Lex Fundamentalis' und die Hausgesetzgebung europäischer Dynastien. In *Historische Vergleichung im Bereich von Staat und Recht. Gesammelte Aufsätze*, ed. Heinz Mohnhaupt, 1–33. Frankfurt on the Main: Klostermann.
Möller, Horst. 1980. Ämterkäuflichkeit in Brandenburg-Preußen im 17. und 18. Jahrhundert. In *Ämterkäuflichkeit. Aspekte sozialer Mobilität im europäischen Vergleich (17. und 18. Jahrhundert)*, ed. Klaus Malettke, 156–176. Berlin: Colloquium.
Monier, Frédéric. 2014. 'Mais la veritable corruption n'existe plus'. Les patronages à l'ère de la critique. In *Les coulisses du politique dans l'Europe contemporaine, Vol. II: Patronage et corruption politiques dans l'Europe contemporaine*, ed. Frédéric Monier et al., 13–32. Paris: Armand Colin.
Moser, Friedrich Carl. 1761. *Der Herr und der Diener, geschildert mit Patriotischer Freyheit*. Frankfurt am Main: Raspe.
Müller, Hans-Heinrich. 1965. Domänen und Domänenpächter in Brandenburg-Preußen im 18. Jahrhundert. *Jahrbuch für Wirtschaftsgeschichte* 6 (4): 152–192.
Münkler, Herfried, and Harald Bluhm. 2001. Einleitung: Gemeinwohl und Gemeinsinn als politisch-soziale Leitbegriffe. In *Gemeinwohl und Gemeinsinn. Historische Semantiken politischer Leitbegriffe*, ed. Herfried Münkler and Harald Bluhm, 15–28. Berlin: Akademie-Verlag.
Näther, Birgit. 2018. *Die Normativität des Praktischen: Strukturen und Prozesse vormoderner Verwaltungsarbeit: Das Beispiel der landesherrlichen Visitation in Bayern*. Münster: Aschendorff.
Neu, Tim. 2011. *Die Erschaffung der landständischen Verfassung: Kreativität, Heuchelei und Repräsentation in Hessen (1509–1655)*. Köln et al.: Böhlau.
Pečar, Andreas. 2011. Dynastie. Norm und Wirklichkeit im Hause Hohenzollern. In *Friedrich der Große und die Dynastie der Hohenzollern. Beiträge des fünften Colloquiums in der Reihe 'Friedrich300' vom 30. September / 1. Oktober 2011*, ed. Michael Kaiser and Jürgen Luh. https://www.perspectivia.

net/publikationen/friedrich300-colloquien/friedrich-dynastie/pecar_dynastie, 29 June 2018.

Pečar, Andreas. 2016. *Die Masken des Königs. Friedrich II. von Preußen als Schriftsteller*. Frankfurt on the Main: Campus.

Peck, Linda Levy. 1990. *Court Patronage and Corruption in Early Stuart England*. Boston et al.: Unwin Hyman.

Press, Volker. 1983. Die wittelsbachischen Territorien. Die pfälzischen Lande und Bayern. In *Deutsche Verwaltungsgeschichte, vol. 1: Vom Spätmittelalter bis zum Ende des Reiches*, ed. Kurt G. A. Jeserich et al., 552–599. Stuttgart: DVA.

Quarthal, Franz. 1987. Korruption in Gesellschaft und Staat des Ancien Régime. *Sozialwissenschaftliche Informationen* 16 (1): 41–46.

Rankl, Helmut. 1997. Der bayerische Rentmeister in der frühen Neuzeit. Generalkontrolleur der Finanzen und Justiz, Mittler zwischen Fürst und Bevölkerung, Promoter der 'baierischen Libertät'. *Zeitschrift für bayerische Landesgeschichte* 60: 617–648.

Rauh, Manfred. 1988. *Verwaltung, Stände und Finanzen. Studien zu Staatsaufbau und Staatsentwicklung Bayerns unter dem späteren Absolutismus*. Munich: Kommission für Bayerische Landesgeschichte.

Real, Willy. 1991. Die preußischen Staatsfinanzen und die Anbahnung des Sonderfriedens von Basel 1795. *Forschungen zur Brandenburgischen und Preußischen Geschichte—Neue Folge* 1 (1): 53–100.

Reinhard, Wolfgang. 1979. Staatsmacht als Kreditproblem. Zur Struktur und Funktion des frühneuzeitlichen Ämterhandels. *Vierteljahrschrift für Sozial- und Wirtschaftsgeschichte* 61 (3): 289–319.

Reinhard, Wolfgang. 1999. *Geschichte der Staatsgewalt: Eine vergleichende Verfassungsgeschichte Europas von den Anfängen bis zur Gegenwart*. Munich: Beck.

Rottmanner, Simon. 1783. *Unterricht eines alten Beamten an junge Beamte, Kandidaten und Praktikanten*, vol. I. Linz: n.n.

Rowen, Herbert H. 1980. *The King's State: Proprietary Dynasticism in Early Modern France*. New Brunswick, NJ: Rutgers University Press.

Rowlands, Guy. 2002. *The Dynastic State and the Army Under Louis Xiv: Royal Service and Private Interest, 1661–1701*. Cambridge: Cambridge University Press.

Rubinstein, William D. 1983. The End of 'Old Corruption' in Britain, 1780–1860. *Past & Present* 101 (1): 55–86.

Seitz, Jutta. 1999. *Die landständische Verordnung in Bayern im Übergang von der altständischen Repräsentation zum modernen Staat*. Göttingen: Vandenhoeck & Ruprecht.

Seresse, Volker. 2005. *Politische Normen in Kleve-Mark während des 17. Jahrhunderts. Argumentationsgeschichtliche und herrschaftstheoretische Zugänge zur politischen Kultur der frühen Neuzeit*. Epfendorf: Bibliotheca Academica.

Sieg, Hans Martin. 2003. *Staatsdienst: Staatsdenken und Dienstgesinnung in Brandenburg-Preußen im 18. Jahrhundert (1713–1806)*. Berlin: de Gruyter.

Stollberg-Rilinger, Barbara. 1999. *Vormünder des Volkes? Konzepte landständischer Repräsentation in der Spätphase des Alten Reiches*. Berlin: Duncker & Humblot.

Stollberg-Rilinger, Barbara. 2006. *Das Heilige Römische Reich Deutscher Nation. Vom Ende des Mittelalters bis 1806*, 2nd ed. Munich: Beck.

Stolleis, Michael. 2012. *Geschichte des öffentlichen Rechts in Deutschland. Vol I.: Reichspublizistik und Policeywissenschaft 1600–1800*, 2nd ed. Munich: Beck.

Straubel, Rolf. 1998. *Beamte und Personalpolitik im altpreußischen Staat. Soziale Rekrutierung, Karriereverläufe, Entscheidungsprozesse (1763/86-1806)*. Potsdam: Verlag für Berlin-Brandenburg.

Swart, Koenraad W. 2009. The Sale of Public Offices. In *Political Corruption: A Handbook*, ed. Arnold J. Heidenheimer and Michael Johnston, 3rd ed., 95–106. New Brunswick, NJ: Transaction Publishing.

Tölle, Tom. 2012. Der Fürst, die Finanzen und die Familien. Korruptionskommunikation im Umfeld Joseph' Süß Oppenheimers. *Zeitschrift für Württembergische Landesgeschichte* 71: 255–287.

Transparency International. 2018. Corruption Perceptions Index 2017. https://www.transparency.org/news/feature/corruption_perceptions_index_2017. 28 June 2018.

Ullmann, Hans-Peter. 2005. *Der deutsche Steuerstaat. Geschichte der öffentlichen Finanzen vom 18. Jahrhundert bis heute*. Munich: Beck.

van Klaveren, Jacob. 1957. Die historische Erscheinung der Korruption, in ihrem Zusammenhang mit der Staats- und Gesellschaftsstruktur betrachtet. *Vierteljahrschrift für Sozial- und Wirtschaftsgeschichte* 44: 289–324.

von Thiessen, Hillard. 2010. *Diplomatie und Patronage: Die spanisch-römischen Beziehungen 1605–1621 in akteurszentrierter Perspektive*. Epfendorf: Bibliotheca Academica.

Vogel, Hartmut. 1960. *Sporteln und Sporteldelikte. Eine Untersuchung über die historische Entwicklung und gegenwärtige Bedeutung der Sporteldelikte, verbunden mit einem Abriss der Geschichte des Sportelwesens*. PhD diss., University of Göttingen.

Weis, Eberhard. 1970. Montgelas' innenpolitisches Reformprogramm. Das Ansbacher Mémoire für den Herzog vom 30.9.1796. *Zeitschrift für bayerische Landesgeschichte* 33: 219–236.

Weitzel, Jürgen. 1982. Die Hausnormen deutscher Dynastien im Rahmen der Entwicklungen von Recht und Gesetz. In *Der dynastische Fürstenstaat. Zur Bedeutung von Sukzessionsordnungen für die Entstehung des frühmodernen Staates*, ed. Johannes Kunisch, 35–48. Berlin: Duncker & Humblot.

Wienfort, Monika. 2001. *Patrimonialgerichte in Preußen. Ländliche Gesellschaft und bürgerliches Recht 1770–1848/49*. Göttingen: Vandenhoeck & Ruprecht.

Author Index

J. Félix and A. Dubet (eds.), *The War Within*, Palgrave Studies in the History of Finance,
https://doi.org/10.1007/978-3-319-98050-8

L

M

N

Lak Index

J. Félix and A. Dubet (eds.), *The War Within*,
Palgrave Studies in the History of Finance,
https://doi.org/10.1007/978-3-319-98050-8

Subject Index

J. Félix and A. Dubet (eds.), *The War Within*, Palgrave Studies in the History of Finance, https://doi.org/10.1007/978-3-319-98050-8

The manufacturer's authorised representative in the EU is Springer Nature Customer Service Centre GmbH, Europaplatz 3, 69115 Heidelberg, Germany. If you have any concerns regarding our products, please contact ProductSafety@springernature.com

Printed and bound by CPI Group (UK) Ltd, Croydon, CR0 4YY

30/09/2026

02225597-0004